Peasants and Monks
in British India

Peasants and Monks
in British India

William R. Pinch

UNIVERSITY OF CALIFORNIA PRESS

Berkeley / Los Angeles / London

University of California Press
Berkeley and Los Angeles, California

University of California Press, Ltd.
London, England

© 1996 by
The Regents of the University of California

Library of Congress Cataloging-in-Publication Data

Pinch, William R., 1960–
    Peasants and monks in British India / William R. Pinch.
      p. cm.
    Includes bibliographic references and index
    ISBN 0-520-20060-8 (alk. paper). —ISBN 0-520-20061-6
(pbk. : alk. paper)
    1. Rāmānandīs. 2. Vaishnavism—social aspects.
BL1287.542.P56 1996
305.5 633 0954—dc20   95-18661

Printed in the United States of America
9 8 7 6 5 4 3 2 1

Contents

A Note on Translation
and Transliteration

Unless otherwise noted, all translations are my own. I have endeavored to transliterate Hindi terms as they sound, without the use of diacritical marks. The main difference readers may notice is that the final 'a' employed in the transliteration of Sanskrit (which is silent in Hindi) is often dropped. The general exception to this rule is with words that are familiar in English usage, such as *karma, dharma, varna, Vaishnava, Shaiva,* etc.

Acknowledgments

The research and writing of this work has occurred on three continents and in eight cities, beginning in 1986 and ending in 1995. Along the way I piled up many professional debts, but none more substantial than that owed to Walter Hauser, save for whose selfless guidance over the course of the 1980s I would not have had the great good fortune to become a historian of India.

The book itself benefited from the discerning eyes of teachers, colleagues, editors, and others. In addition to Walter Hauser, these include Richard B. Barnett, William B. Taylor, R. S. Khare, Tessa Bartholomeusz, Christopher V. Hill, Rosemary Hauser, Philip Lutgendorf, Romila Thapar, Lynne Withey, Barbara Howell, Bruce Masters, Ann Wightman, Richard Elphick, Jennifer Saines, two anonymous readers for the University of California Press, and Mark Pentecost, copy editor for the Press. I am grateful for their many contributions, textual and otherwise, whether in the doctoral thesis stage, while transforming the thesis into a book, or while preparing the manuscript for publication. Portions of chapters were presented at public lectures and seminars. These occurred at the University of Virginia, the University of California at Berkeley, North Carolina State University, Wesleyan University, the School of Oriental and African Studies at the University of London, and the University of Pennsylvania; related papers were also presented at regional and national meetings of the Association for Asian Studies. My thanks to those who made these occasions possible and to those who attended and offered their reactions.

For their help during the research and writing, I wish to acknowledge the following: Shaibal Gupta and the A. N. Sinha Institute for Social Studies in Patna, for providing the necessary institutional affiliation; Surendra Gopal and Hetukar Jha of Patna University for their kind hospitality, and the latter in particular for allowing me to consult his collection of the Patna District Village Notes during the untimely closure of the local record room; my research assistants, S. K. Pathak, Ram Prasad Shrivastav, and Ejaz Hussain; Dr. A. P. and Mrs. S. P. Bakshi, for welcoming us to Patna; Mira and Suresh Prasad Shrivastava, our hosts in Arrah; Sukirti Sahay, for assisting in the translation of Bihari passages; K. S. Chalapati Rao and Bhupesh Garg of the Institute for the Study of Industrial Development, New Delhi, for introducing me to the Institute's digital map-making technology and allowing me to construct a base map for the present work; Philip McEldowney of Virginia's Alderman Library and Stephen Lebergott of Wesleyan's Olin Library, for providing books and references at short notice; the U.S. Library of Congress foreign book acquisitions project, and of course the American taxpayers who fund it and, on occasion, me. I am particularly indebted to Kailash Chandra Jha, formerly of the U.S. Library of Congress in New Delhi, now with the American Embassy, for his invaluable help over the past thirteen years.

The research was funded by a grant from the U.S. Department of Education, with additional research and writing support from the Social Science Research Council and the American Council of Learned Societies, for all of which I am grateful. Thanks are owed as well to Dr. Uma Das Gupta, regional director of the U.S. Educational Foundation in India, who did so much to make our stay in Calcutta both comfortable and enjoyable, and to Dr. Pradeep Mehendiratta of the American Institute of Indian Studies for facilitating the complex logistics of research approval from the Government of India. I wish to acknowledge the support received from the directors and staff of the Bihar District Record Rooms (in Gaya, Patna, and Arrah), the Bihar State Archives in Patna, the National Archives in New Delhi, the National Library in Calcutta, and the Oriental and India Office Collection of the British Library in London. Of course, none of the above-named individuals or institutions are in any way responsible for errors, omissions, or misinterpretations herein.

Finally, family and friends have sustained me over the past decade of research and writing. I can only offer in return my love and gratitude, and pray that Rosemary and Walter, Kailash and Abha and Sona and Rumki, Pete and Gary and Sheila and Sarah, Quatro and Joan and Collin, Helen and George, Jennifer and Pearse, and my parents will forgive my sentimental need to single them out in particular.

Vijay Pinch
London
13 July, 1995

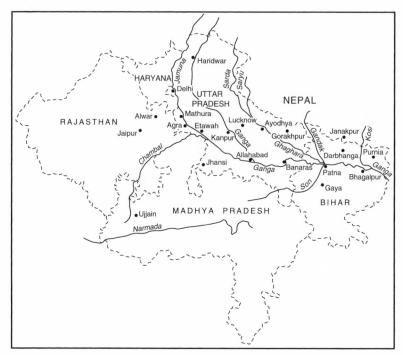

Northern India.

Introduction: Peasants, Monks, and Indian History

According to strict social science definitions, colonial India was a peasant society. By far the vast majority of the population of the subcontinent lived in villages, and well over half the working population was engaged directly in agriculture. These villages were not isolated communities: the urban population was small by comparison but substantial, and urban magnates maintained important social, economic, and political ties to the countryside to secure the steady stream of agricultural goods that sustained city life. The state was organized into territorial provinces that transcended lines of caste and clan and whose complex bureaucratic dimensions reflected the agrarian revenue potential. Clear cultural, social, economic, and political distinctions could be and were made between town and country. Most importantly, the typical unit of production was the family household, which may or may not have owned the land upon which it worked but, regardless, directed its combined labor to the cultivation of crops.[1]

Colonial India also had a history of significant religious variety. Indeed, few visitors to the subcontinent over the last twenty-five centuries—from Alexander to al-Biruni to Attenborough—have failed to make note of this fact.[2] Fewer still have failed to remark upon the vast numbers of holy men who wander the subcontinent, reside in its villages, towns, and cities (often near shrines) and throng its sacred places. These holy men, known generically as *sadhus* (Hindu) and *fakirs* (Muslim), can be described as monks inasmuch as they belong to one of many Indian monastic traditions of social detachment and spiritual discipline. As in the European tradition, however, monasticism in India encompasses a wide variety of religious experience. While frequent pilgrimage, alms, and tests of physical endurance are and have long been important aspects of the lives of many Indian monks, Indian monasticism cannot be reduced to itinerancy, begging, and asceticism.[3] Many monks are and have long been devoted to careful study and spiritual contemplation, conducted entirely within the walls of a sanctuary in an attempt to create a paradise on earth. Still others were expert in the arts and science of warfare.[4] Though the institutionalized forms of charity—such as the creation of hospitals—common to western monasticism have not been nearly so prominent in India, many Indian monks were respected as able healers,[5] and service (*seva*) remains a central ideal of most Indian religious traditions. Indeed, the ritual removal of Indian monks from "worldly" concerns has long presaged (and was preparatory to) their active engagement in the world, whether conducted from a religious center or as part of an itinerant or soldiering lifestyle. Finally, Indian monks come from all sections of society, including the peasantry, though the degree to which monastic orders recruited from the ranks of the lowborn in rural society (whether peasants or artisans) varied. However, at least one major monastic community—the *Ramanandi*s, who look to Ramanand of fourteenth-century Banaras for religious inspiration—has long been dedicated to the recruitment of novices (both male and, to a lesser degree, female) from the entire social spectrum. Understanding how this Ramanandi recruitment philosophy has worked in historical practice, particularly during the colonial era, is one of the aims of this book.

Indian peasants and monks did not live in social and religious isolation, from the world or from each other. Indeed, the lives of peasants and monks in colonial India were (and are) intricately intertwined: monks depended on peasants for agrarian labor, material sustenance, and monastic recruitment; peasants looked to monks for spiritual guidance, religious knowledge, and ideological leadership. Both expressed increasing concern in the colonial era with questions of religious identity and social status, in part because those questions had immediate and long-range political and economic ramifications. Peasants and monks addressed those questions by advocating both attacks on and manipulations of social hierarchy, that is, caste. The story of those attacks and manipulations, and their implications for colonial India, make up a large part of the history described in this book. However, this history also includes significant religious and cultural change, which should not be ignored.[6] Furthermore, the world that peasants and monks lived in, and assisted in creating, came to occupy a central place in the history of colonial and nationalist India.

That world is with us still, nearly a half-century since independence from British rule, and, it can be argued, contributes to the ongoing crisis of religion and the state in north India.

This book, then, is a history of the ways in which religion intersected with dramatic political and social change in colonial India. It will come as no surprise to social historians that religion has been drawn upon to express material complaint in times of rural social, political, and economic stress;[7] a corollary, in modern south Asia at least, is that monks have readily assumed the burdens of peasant advocacy.[8] But, despite the importance of radical monks who led rural rebellions, most of the social history that has described them does not explain the role of religion, or the exceptionally religious, in peasant society; rather, it merely comments upon the fact. This is as true for colonial India as it is for late antique Rome. Peter Brown has observed that social historians of the late Roman empire have "tended to stress the spectacular occasions on which the holy man intervened to lighten the lot of the humble and oppressed: his open-handed charity, his courageous action as the spokesman of popular grievances—these have been held sufficient to explain the role of the holy man." But, Brown adds,

such a view sees too little of the life of the holy man. . . . Dramatic interventions of holy men in the high politics of the Empire were long remembered. But they illustrate the prestige that the holy man had already gained, they do not explain it. They were rather like the cashing of a big cheque on a reputation; and, like all forms of power in late Roman society, this reputation was built up by hard, unobtrusive (and so, for us, partly obscure) work among those who needed constant and unspectacular ministrations.[9]

Certainly there are plenty of cases of peasant grievance expressed in religious language in Indian history; likewise there is no shortage of peasant movements led by holy men. Indeed, some of those grievances and movements find their way into this book. But I would be telling only half the story were I to confine myself to such matters, because the long process of change that allowed monks to lead peasant movements in Gangetic India under colonial rule was as much ideological, cultural, and religious as it was material, economic, and social. The history of peasants and monks in the nineteenth and twentieth centuries in India includes the growth and transformation of a conscious "Hindu" historical discourse, which itself was the result of a prolonged process of religious institutionalization.[10] That history is also the story of the coming of age of the "middle peasant"—the tenant farmer and small proprietor, clinging tenaciously to the margin of property—however one chooses to describe his politics and understand his fate.

A main purpose of this work, consequently, is to explore directly and in depth the religion that aids in defining the world of the Gangetic peasantry in colonial India. This involves broadening the working definitions of religion beyond the personal and private to include much of what is normatively considered political, social, and economic; it also involves understanding peasants in terms not only of what they do—i.e., their labor, behavior, riots, and occasional rebellions—but also of what they believe and think and say and write. I hope that by so doing we gain a better sense of the mental worlds that produced and gave meaning to action in colonial north India, whether that action was violent or gentle, religious, social, economic or political.[11] This recourse to culture and, ultimately, religion should not be seen as an abandonment of social history as such, but as a recognition that while social history has enabled us to ask important questions, it has not provided the tools with which to craft satisfactory answers.

Religion, Politics, and History in India

India has long been represented as a place of timeless peasants and ageless monks, and not just by an intellectual elite that is today labeled "Orientalist."[12] To the British administrator, the peasant represented an India that was noble, honest, and good. The monk, by contrast, represented an Orient that was mysterious, unpredictable, and dangerous. In ideological terms, this was a necessary juxtaposition: the colonial official, steeped in both utilitarian philosophies of rule and romantic notions of benevolent despotism, saw himself as the protector of the common man—the peasant—against the extortions of idle, urban elites and the corruptions of corrosive superstition.[13] Thus the picture of the hardy peasant and his negative imprint manifest in the nefarious monk were central to the strategic—and for the most part unconscious—posturings of British colonial officials on the right side of history.

But the image of India as peasant and monk writ large was not confined to European imaginations: Mohandas K. Gandhi's political technique played on British idealizations of the peasantry and monasticism and of India generally. From the nationalist perspective, the ability of the Indian National Congress to control the peasants and monks of India was of less importance than the British perception that Congress possessed the ability to do so. And Gandhi, who represented both humble peasant and simple monk, seemed to speak for India's masses, whether or not he could control them. The peasant-monk ethos defined Gandhi's very existence: his simple garb, his spare meals, his *ashram* (sanctuary), his celibacy, his daily routine of meditation and constructive work, his nonviolence—all evoked ideals of religious asceticism and rural simplicity. This ethos, and the relentless dedication to truth (*satyagraha*) that sustained it, afforded Gandhi substantial moral influence, for a time, among peasants and monks as *mahatma,* great soul.

Gandhi as mahatma was both more and less than an imagined miracle worker, a figment of rural imaginations run rampant.[14] Because Gandhi seemed able to speak to India's monks, the British were soon convinced that he could speak for India's peasants. This conviction emerges with crystal clarity in the official reaction to the fact that hundreds of monks attended the 1920 Indian National Congress meeting in Nagpur, anxious to see and hear the man who was bringing mass politics to the national level and to involve themselves in his—and in many ways their own—political idiom. An observer dispatched to report on the Nagpur proceedings to the government noted in his account that "an association of the most powerful sadhus called *Nagas* [soldier monks] had been formed at Nagpur" and that "a meeting of over a hundred of these sadhus had been held in the Congress Camp and they had decided to undertake non-cooperation propaganda."[15] Great significance was attached to this act, since it was maintained that these "sadhus visited most of the villages and towns and the masses had a high regard for them, and thought a great deal of their instructions and preachings. When these Nagas took up non-cooperation, the scheme would spread like wild fire among the masses of India and eventually Government would be unable to control 33 crores of people and would have to give Swaraj."[16] The official report also noted that Gandhi personally thanked the sadhus for their support and urged them to "visit the vicinities of cantonments and military stations and explain to the native soldiers the advisability of giving up their employments"—thus recalling the fears of sepoy disloyalty that still resonated after the rebellion of 1857. After the Nagpur Congress, the intelligence branch of government would become increasingly concerned with the activity of "political sadhus."[17]

Colonial and nationalist idealizations of peasants and monks were reductive, one-dimensional, and misleading: most peasants and monks in

British India were not immediately concerned with the national implications of colonial rule, let alone nationalist politics—despite Bankim
Chandra Chattopadhyay's (1838–1894) late nineteenth-century fictional
representations of patriotic sadhus sprung organically from the soil of
Bengal and ranged against oppressive, foreign rule; despite Gandhi's desire to attract the participation of peasants and monks in a mass-based
nationalism; and despite Nehru's efforts to lecture peasants on the meaning of *Bharat Mata*—mother India—in the 1930s.[18] But peasants and
monks were not unconcerned with politics and their place in an Indian
nation. Rather, their politics were locally defined, their concept of nation (as country) deeply embedded in Indian social and cultural history.[19]
Though their brief engagement in the nationalist politics of India drew
them for the first time into the narrow beam of the historian's search-
light, it was not the first time peasants and monks had combined to bring
about social and ideological change.

The peasants and monks who populate the history of Gangetic India
were historiographically complex, because they could think and speak
for themselves; indeed, their thoughts and opinions are the basis of this
study. Peasants and monks in British India acted and spoke in ways that
seemed strangely out of character for people normally (and normatively)
engaged in agricultural labor and the disciplined pursuit of spiritual truth.
Completely independent of nationalism, many peasants of Gangetic India in the late nineteenth and early twentieth centuries began to voice
loud objections to the servile status that society and the state ascribed
to those who worked the soil. It gradually became clear that many of
those peasants thought of themselves not as cosmically created servants
(*shudra*) devoid of any history, but as the descendants of divine warrior
clans (*kshatriya*) firmly rooted in the Indian past. The dimensions of
those assertions, the discourses drawn upon to articulate them, and the
elite reaction to them reveal a wealth of information not only about peasant culture but of popular ideological change during the colonial era.

Monks, likewise, had strong opinions that informed and were informed by the goings-on in Gangetic society. They were willing and able
(indeed expected) to leave behind the secure confines of the monastery,
the contemplation of sacred texts and images, and the cycles of ritual
and worship, to engage themselves in society's all-too-temporal concerns.
Prior to 1800, such engagement included soldiering, trade, banking, protecting pilgrimage sites and religious endowments, and enlisting as mer-
cenaries in the armies of regional states. But it also included living in villages amongst peasants, artisans, and laborers, and ministering to their

daily religious needs. After 1800 and the colonial monopolization of armed force, involvement in society's concerns meant, increasingly, attending to the vexed question of status and hierarchy, which seemed to have gained political urgency under British rule. Many monks in the nineteenth and twentieth centuries, consequently, dedicated themselves to aggressive (and even, at times, egalitarian) social reform, which included the amelioration of the stigma of physical labor and the inculcation of a just moral order. And because monks confronted these issues in society, the issues eventually confronted them inside the confines of the monastery. The question of social status would consume the energies of numerous monks and peasants during much of the twentieth century; the discourses and ideologies brought to bear to deal with that question are the main concerns of this study.

A history of religious and social change runs up against numerous obstacles in India, not the least of which is the historiography produced by "communalism." It has become by now a truism that colonial officials were quick to ascribe religious identity, particularly Hindu and Muslim "communal" identity, as the motivating force behind all precolonial conflict, in part as a way of justifying their own presence as representatives of a stabilizing, secular force.[20] What is less obvious is the extent to which the tentacles of colonial understanding have gripped Indian historical consciousness and the degree to which nationalist (and much postnationalist) historiography bears their circular scars. This wounded historiography contributes in no small way to the recent political impasse over a fully razed mosque and a partly raised temple in north India.[21] Unfortunately, coming to terms with this fact has often meant the historiographical withdrawal from any discussion of religion as a stimulus to historical change, either directly, as belief and ideology, or indirectly, as the discursive and institutional bases of social reform.

Applied to the day-to-day practicalities of imperial rule, the colonial fixation on an India—past and present—allegedly rife with religious violence inspired colonial officials to distrust the very nature and content of Indian monasticism. This distrust was, in part, inspired by the at times vigorous (if unorganized) resistance offered by unruly bands of armed monks as the English East India Company subdued the huge province of Bengal. Nevertheless, the colonial willingness to see evil and corruption in the figure of the Indian monk was remarkable for its longevity and imaginative creativity. An early example of this can be seen in the writings of Colonel William Henry Sleeman (1788–1856), who is generally credited with the suppression of *thagi* (banditry, thought to have been ritually inspired) in the 1830s. Sleeman held that most Indian holy men were merely bandits, criminals, and rogues in disguise:

Three-fourths of these religious mendicants, whether Hindoos or Muhammadans, rob and steal, and a very great portion of them murder their victims before they rob them. . . . There is hardly any species of crime that is not throughout India perpetrated by men in the disguise of these religious mendicants; and almost all such mendicants are really men in disguise; for Hindoos of any caste can become Bairagis and Gosains; and Muhammadans of any grade can become Fakirs.[22]

Sleeman also alleged that monks were guilty of spreading seditious rumors and recommended the compulsory registration of all such individuals according to a strict Vagrant Act.[23]

The colonial distrust of religion in the context of peasants (and soldiers) was also evident in the rumors that circulated throughout the empire over the outbreak of the 1857 rebellion. Two such rumors were of particular interest and were repeated by none other than Benjamin Disraeli in a speech to Parliament: namely, that the bloody events of that year were in part coordinated by religiously symbolic acts such as the mysterious passing of a *chapati* (thin wheat bread cooked over fire) from village to village and, in what was thought to strike an even deeper chord, the circulation of a lotus flower from sepoy to sepoy through entire regimental units.[24] Three decades later, in the 1890s, the often strident efforts of local sadhus to generate popular support in the countryside for a growing movement to prohibit the slaughter of cows in Uttar Pradesh and Bihar aroused great consternation among provincial officials—a consternation not unrelated to the widespread apprehension that the rebellion of 1857 had been sparked by the use of cow (and pig) fat in the cartridges of the new Enfield rifle.[25]

That sadhus generally were seen as a potential source of criminal mischief by officials of the Raj is evident in the publication in 1913 of a police handbook in Urdu that described the various religious orders and, in detailed line-drawings, examples of representative figures—down to the distinctive sandalwood-paste sect marks.[26] Sadhus would soon be considered a fount of outright sedition with the emergence of a newer form of resistance to colonial rule: mass nationalism. The colonial distrust of monks can be perceived not only in the early disdain for the Mahatma's political style, but also in the official attitude toward monks in north India who gravitated toward Gandhi in the early 1920s. Such monks were derided in the police fact sheets as "political sadhus," about whom almost no information was provided about monastic affiliations.[27] Indeed, if a common feature can be discerned in the tone of the police reports on "political sadhus," it is the official attempt to dispute and discredit the religious credentials of the individuals under scrutiny. For example the police report depicted Swami Biswanand, who would become a prominent labor leader in the coal fields of south Bihar, as a person of "very bad moral character," who was "absolutely inconsistent," and whose "word or actions can never be relied on." Another, Pursotam Das, was portrayed as "a man of low character, [who] frequents prostitutes' houses," and was said to have been "turned out of the Chatubhuj *Asthan* [monastery] by the *Mahanth* [head] for misconduct." A third, Raghubar Saran Kuer, was cited for preaching "race hatred in a violent manner" and for abusing "the police in filthy language; his allegedly weak religious loyalties could be seen in his willingness to shed his "sanyasi dress" and don the clothing of "a national volunteer," i.e., Gandhian homespun cotton.

On first glance, then, the typical "political sadhu" of colonial India seems rather an unsavory fellow. However, the official record of the integrity and character of subjects under police scrutiny cannot be relied upon. It was only to be expected that police and intelligence officials would editorialize negatively about the morals, behavior, and sincerity of religious commitment of individuals opposed to colonial rule. Failure to do so would have risked the loss of important ideological ground to the agitators, and even the possibility of appearing politically unsound oneself. Whatever the "true" moral character of sadhus, their political actions were a function of religious and philosophical commitment and not a reflection of any alleged personal failings.[28] It is equally probable that their political behavior informed their religious outlook. As such, the "political sadhu" represented an important example of the ties that bound religious community, or *sampraday,* to society. Colonial administrators may not have appreciated the subtleties and importance of sampraday; they certainly feared, however, the power of sampraday loyalties to challenge even British imperial authority, and they strove therefore to dismiss the sampraday dimension of what they characterized as a political sadhu "problem."

Despite colonial fears of the political sadhu and Gandhi's own efforts to include sadhus in noncooperation as a symbolic challenge to the British, the colonial disdain for monasticism was to a large degree mirrored in nationalist circles. At the level of province and locality, the monastic orders would have been seen as a throwback to a premodern age, the sectarian complexities of which tended to undercut claims to Hindu political solidarity. Such claims were voiced with increasing stridency throughout the north after 1890, and in increasing proximity to Congress, by such organizations as the *Arya Samaj,* the *Sanatana Dharma Sabha,* and the *Hindu Mahasabha.*[29] Those sadhus willing to subordinate their sampraday loyalties to these new religio-political formations or, alternatively, to the philosophical (and nonviolent) dictates of Gandhi, would have remained within the ambit of nationalist politics, whether defined as secular or Hindu. Without question, many would have been driven away—though measuring such patterns of political involvement is difficult in the extreme. However, one revealing case is that of the peasant leader Swami Sahajanand Saraswati, who was drawn into nationalist politics in 1920–1921 by the force of Gandhi's personality, but who would break publicly with Gandhi in the mid-1920s on the basis of his (Sahajanand's) vision of the obligation of the monk to serve the needs of the oppressed peasant.[30] As I argue in chapter 4, Sahajanand Saraswati's commitment to peasant welfare derived in large part from a conscious dedication to Vaishnava ideals of equality and social reform—notwithstanding the fact that he himself emerged out of a long tradition of Shaiva monasticism that competed vigorously with Vaishnava (and particularly Ramanandi) monasticism for the allegiances of peasant society.

In any event, Congress distaste and colonial disdain for sadhus would soon have historiographical consequences, as official documents and nationalist records emerged after Independence as the main sources for writing Indian political history, the only legitimate subjects of which were seen to be Congress, communalism, and colonialism. In that framework, the only significant figure accorded any kind of creative religious status was Gandhi himself; all other manifestations of socially engaged religion would be read backward from the dramatic events of 1946–1947 (and, later, 6 December 1992) as part and parcel of the communalism that would divide the subcontinent along lines Hindu and Muslim.[31] The work of a number of social historians of provincial politics would remedy to some degree the linear understanding of nationalist history by emphasizing the importance of local contingencies in the evolutionary dynamics of political institution-building.[32] However, insofar as those provincial histories were predicated upon understanding the local dynamics of nationalism, the eyes of these historians were still trained upon those individuals and institutions who articulated the new, totalizing religious sentiments.

In the past decade, a group of scholars referred to as the "subaltern collective" has criticized as "elitist" not only historical approaches that adopt colonial and nationalist agendas as thematic points of departure, but the heavy use of colonial and nationalist documentation (and the unconscious adoption of the mentalities therein). This criticism, though grounded in the conviction that the actions of peasants and workers— "subalterns"—should be understood as part of a failed history of national fulfillment, can also be leveled from the perspective of religion.[33] For members of the subaltern collective, the poverty of this "elitist" historiography is

demonstrated beyond doubt by its failure to understand and assess the mass articulation of this nationalism except, negatively, as a law and order problem, and positively, if at all, either as a response to the charisma of certain elite leaders or in the currently more fashionable terms of vertical mobilization by the manipulation of factions. The involvement of the Indian people in vast numbers . . . in nationalist activities and ideas is thus represented as a diversion from a supposedly 'real' political process, that is, the grinding away of the wheels of the state apparatus and of elite institutions geared to it, or it is simply credited, as an act of ideological appropriation, to the influence and initiative of the elite themselves.

This powerful critique has had the potential to galvanize much historical writing by bringing historians closer to the voices and actions of ordinary people as they grappled with the changes overtaking their lives. An excellent case in point is the subaltern consideration of Baba Ramchandra, a man who would have been disparaged as a "political sadhu" by the government but who was in fact the central instigator of peasant dissent in Awadh between 1919 and 1922. In revisiting this important moment of agrarian radicalism, the historian Gyanendra Pandey contrasts the peasant world of Awadh to the conception of the peasant held by Gandhian nationalists and by the colonial state, and demonstrates thereby the conflicting aims of Indian nationalism and peasant rebellion. Baba Ramchandra is introduced as "a Maharashtrian of uncertain antecedents who had been an indentured laborer in Fiji and then a *sadhu* (religious mendicant) propagating the Hindu scriptures in Jaunpur, Sultanpur and Pratapgarh, before he turned to the task of organizing *Kisan Sabha*s [peasant associations]." As a peasant leader, he evoked the moral world of the god-king Ramchandra of epic Ayodhya to combat expropriative landlord tyranny. That moral world was described in Tulsidas' *Ramcharitmanas,* "a favourite religious epic of the Hindus in northern India and especially beloved of people in this region"; its immediacy in the agrarian environment was reflected in the increased currency of such religiously charged phrases as *"Sita Ram," "Jai Ram,"* and *"Jai Shankar"* as both egalitarian forms of address and as rallying calls for peasants gearing up for political action.[34]

Hidden in the shadows of the subaltern consideration of Baba Ramchandra are the social and religious institutions that underpinned the agrarian radicalism of Awadh. Such institutions provided an autonomous peasant and monastic culture organized to work for progressive change, whether in the context of economic crisis, political mobilization, social reform, or spiritual awakening. It was because of their ties to peasant society through important religious communities that Baba Ramchandra and other sadhus (Sahajanand Saraswati for example) could engage in peasant politics so effectively. In the nineteenth and twentieth-century Gangetic north, many sadhus were committed to a powerful critique of hierarchy that came to constitute a major principle behind social and ideological change. The most important, but by no means the only, proponent of such change in Gangetic north India was the Ramanandi sampraday. Ramanandi social commentary gained institutional momentum over the centuries, but was extremely influential by the early 1800s, as peasant society gravitated toward its progressive and assimilative rhetoric. Baba Ramchandra was very much part of that Ramanandi, Vaishnava ethos, a fact that contributed substantially to his immediate and positive reception by landless and land poor peasants in the countryside.[35]

The links between monks and peasants before the twentieth century were best represented by the individuals and establishments that made up the Ramanandi sampraday. By the turn of the twentieth century, new ideological movements began to emerge from within peasant society itself, spearheaded by populist scholars who asserted genealogical descent in the royal *kshatriya* (warrior) lineages of Ram and Krishna, Vishnu's *avatar*s (earthly forms). Baba Ramchandra's recollections of the peasant dissent in Awadh, not to mention his own recruitment into the peasant movement, place great emphasis on the organizational framework of peasant-kshatriya identity campaigns that were already in place.[36] It should be emphasized that without such a framework peasant activism would have been far less successful and may even have failed to attract the attention of Congress leaders and the colonial state, not to mention later generations of historians.

More recently, the work of Sandria Freitag on community and communalism in the Gangetic north has also focused on the trajectories of popular action in the context of the emergent Indian nation but has distinguished itself from subaltern scholarship by closer attention to the autonomy of cultural and religious change, particularly as expressed in collective action and the symbolic language of crowd violence. For Freitag, religion provided the institutional base for "public arena" activities, such as festivals, in which increasingly wide community identities were expressed with greater political urgency as the colonial era drew to a close.[37] Her stress on popular action (and riots in particular) rather than ideas has the effect of deemphasizing religious ideology as a causal factor in a history that seeks to explain something with massive ideological ramifications, namely, Hindu versus Muslim communalism. This effect is both necessary and intended: Freitag notes at the outset that while we have access to the symbolic language expressed through collective action over time, we cannot know the thoughts of individual rioters as they go about their business.[38] Hence it would be fruitless to speculate on the ideologies that motivated rioters or whether something so finite and discernible as ideology was at work. More importantly, the focus on action in the frame of the public arena provides sufficient evidence to argue that communalism (and, ultimately, Partition) was an unintended consequence of shortsighted colonial strategies combined with nationalist political culture, rather than the political fruition of "age-old" animosities expressed in "insensate violence," as the colonial mythology would have it.

Beneath and within the actions of crowds accommodating themselves to the logistical needs of the colonially malformed and increasingly communalized public arena, however, were significant religious ideologies that were neither Hindu nor Muslim in the political sense. Acknowledging this fact affords greater historical and cultural depth to the history examined by Freitag. For example, after 1900 the colonial state became increasingly concerned with the *Ram Lila* festival, which reenacted annually the life of the god-king Ramchandra in towns and villages throughout the Gangetic north. Official consternation derived from politically motivated innovations in the festival, such as the inclusion of famous rebels from 1857 and well-known extremists (e.g., the Rani of Jhansi on horseback with a British soldier transfixed on her spear, and Lala Lajpat Rai, the fiery Arya Samajist Congressman from the Punjab) in the festival tableaux and processions.[39] As the annual occasion for the celebration of the life of Ramchandra, the Ram Lila was central in the ritual calendar of all Ramanandis. In Ramnagar (across the Ganga from Banaras), the feasting of hundreds of Ramanandi sadhus during the festival afforded substantial political legitimacy to the Maharaja of Banaras, who sponsored the annual performance at considerable expense. The Ramnagar Ram Lila would grow into a thirty-one-day affair and would be performed in an elaborate—and permanent—reproduction of Ayodhya housed within the palace grounds.[40] But whether in Ramnagar or in villages and towns throughout the north, the Ram Lila took on an added importance for peasants claiming (after 1900) a lineal descent from the kshatriya house of Ramchandra, because it represented an annual opportunity to imbibe the grandeur and glory of their most famous progenitor. Hence, to fully appreciate the historical significance of the Ram Lila, it must be understood in the context of Ramanandi monasticism and peasant-kshatriya identity. Together they point to a Vaishnava religiosity on the rise in precolonial and colonial India beneath the rubric of Hinduism that would seek to overtake such religiosity in the twentieth century.[41] Like Hinduism, Vaishnavism was grounded in a long process of institutionalization in festival, pilgrimage, temple construction, monasticism, and mythology. What is more, this institutionalization depended on the creative tensions between political power and religious authority in the precolonial period, prior to the nineteenth-century withdrawal of the state from the popular spectacle that became such a crucial public arena.

Given the degree to which religion obtruded into the political process in colonial India, studies of political action predicated on religious institutions can and should be complemented by inquiries into the political meanings of religion. The injection of the cultural into social history has moved us carefully in this direction, but neither the sporadic irruptions of subaltern rebellion nor the long-term patterns of crowd violence, however eloquent, can speak adequately to the full import of religious ideology in social history. Admittedly, this poses a problem for historians of India, because any study of religion as a motive force in political and social change can be misconstrued as an argument for the fundamentally religious basis of Indian politics. It also poses a problem for many social historians of peasant society, who tread softly when it comes to assessing religion in terms of meaning, since religious consciousness tends to cut across the class lines that make social-historical analysis so meaningful. Notwithstanding these risks, this foray into the religious world of the peasant is especially called for, if for no other reason, because the peasant world was, in large part, religious. Were we to obscure that fact in our historical representation of peasant society, we would be depriving peasants—about whom so much has been written as agents of their own history—of the historical voice they know best. And we would be depriving ourselves, as historians, of important insights not only regarding peasant history but into the ways ordinary people came to terms with the decline of colonial rule and the rise of an Indian nation.

Britain, India, and British India

British India was not simply a place but an amalgam of ideas, politics, and people both British and Indian. The extended exchange of meaning that occurred between Britain and India, the most visible result of which may well be the idea of caste, figures prominently in the emergence of peasant-kshatriya identity and also (though perhaps in a more subtle manner) in the history of Ramanandi monasticism. Hence it is appropriate to describe at the outset the political-cultural dimensions of the colonial world and the ways in which that world touched the lives of peasants and monks in Gangetic India.

The cultural and intellectual exchange between Indians and Britons in colonial India was predicated on an imbalance of power; notwithstanding the ugly face of imperialism (and perhaps because of it), this exchange shaped the very dimensions of colonial culture and turned (to borrow the phraseology of the psychologist Ashis Nandy) India and Britain into intimate enemies. The British empire in India depended upon the effective organization, maintenance, and exercise of force, material as well as ideological. For Nandy, however, more important than any military ordnance was the *idea* of imperial power, embodied in colonial India by the notion of martial valor. The central implication of that important idea in the psychology of imperial rule was the rise and eventual dominance of a muscular, hyper-masculine ethos in imperial India. Hence, "many nineteenth-century Indian movements of social, religious and political reform . . . tried to make Kshatriyahood the 'true' interface between the rulers and the ruled as a new, nearly exclusive indicator of authentic Indianness."[42] It has been suggested in response to Nandy that the search for a martial Indianness only occurred in a narrow "zone of contact," a zone restricted to the urban world of bureaucracy, scholarship, and nationalism and peopled with the "self-conscious Indians" who were "the elite, the articulate, the Westernized." Accordingly, we should seek to know more about the other Indian "'out there,' in the villages far from the Western experience, who is not consciously embattled by the West, not torn about his Indianness, who carries on being his Indian 'self' without a sense of the historical problematic in which he is unwittingly situated."[43]

The peasants of British India were the villagers who lived "far from the Western experience." However, the history of kshatriya reform, which spoke directly to the question of status in a distinctly colonial society, suggests that they were in fact not so greatly removed from the "zone of contact." Torn less about their "Indianness" than their British-Indianness, they were at least as concerned with questions of self and identity as their "westernized, intellectual" compatriots, particularly those in the elite nationalist movement. The aggressive articulation of kshatriya identity in the early twentieth century is evidence of the extent of their involvement in the colonial culture; the desire to appropriate a kshatriya ideal extended deep into peasant society, to productive cultivators on the margin of land-control and status in the Gangetic countryside. Further, what people "out there" wrote, discussed, and believed was based on a sense of the past that relied on myth, legend, and lineage, not to mention British examinations and recapitulations of that myth, legend, and lineage. However, the articulation of peasant-kshatriya identity differed in significant ways from the kshatriyahood of the colonial elite in that the latter usually combined martial status with landed power, imperial certification, and brahmanical patronage. Peasant kshatriyahood, by contrast, lacked all these assets, but drew on Vaishnava identities and discourses nurtured in part by institutional connections to Vaishnava—particularly Ramanandi—monasticism. And, though that monasticism existed in religious centers located far (ideologically if not geographically) from the western experience, it too spilled over on occasion into the "zone of contact."

It has been argued that the popular concern with identity and status was part of, and perhaps a response to, processes of ideological change centered on the notion of caste in British-Indian society—particularly in proximity to the census office.[44] Certainly the thoughts, words, and deeds of peasants and monks in the colonial era confirm that caste was a subject of great interest to all, in large part because the ideology of inequality and status (and, by implication, equality and identity) implicit to caste enabled individuals, communities, and the state to facilitate, moderate, or obliterate social change. And certainly the caste we have come to know in the late twentieth century is in part (some would say in large part) the product of a colonial discourse: British imperial anthropology manifest by the late nineteenth century in a pervasive British-Indian census bureaucracy, which inadvertently reified *brahmanical* hierarchy—or an ideology of inequality articulated by brahmans who resided atop that hierarchy—as part of a process of colonization writ cultural.[45]

But while the empire can be held accountable for many evils, one suspects that the full burden of caste injustices cannot be laid squarely on its shoulders. Status and social rank—and the peasant, monastic, and colonial fixation on status and social rank—should be understood as part of a much older, though perhaps more socially restricted, Indic discourse of *varna*. Scholars have disagreed widely on the degree to which varna represents an integrated, all-encompassing model of and for Indian social relations;[46] few, however, contest the precolonial existence of the discrete religious, political, and economic roles of priest (*brahman*), warrior (*kshatriya*), merchant (*vaishya*), and servant (*shudra*) that make up varna. That varna was conceived by brahmans in the distant past as an implicitly hierarchical division of labor is confirmed by the unimpeachable antiquity of the myth of the primordial man, from whose head and mouth sprang brahmans, torso and arms kshatriyas, loins and thighs vaishyas, and legs and feet shudras.[47] These ideas did not require a European colonial state to ensure their ideological longevity; they did require, however, certain enforced inequalities (including gender inequalities) in post-Vedic, precolonial Indian society—a detailed consideration of which is, fortunately, beyond the scope of this study.

While we can presume that, historically, most brahmans and perhaps many kshatriyas and vaishyas subscribed to the hierarchy implicit in varna, we cannot know the extent to which that subscription was shared by shudras. The historiography of ancient and medieval India suggests that shudras did not necessarily care for the servile status ascribed to them.[48] The principle of social hierarchy, and the fundamental human inequalities that it implied, would have been even more repellent to a substantial portion of the population relegated to a social realm beyond and therefore below the four varna and existing by definition on the periphery of society. Members of this group of perennial outsiders, bound in economic, political, and social servitude to varna society in intricate and myriad ways, have been known generally by a variety of names. They have been derided as *dasyu* (barbarian), *dasa* (slave), *paraiyan* (pariah), and untouchable; they have been patronized as *harijan* (as Gandhi's children of god) and *scheduled* (as names on a government list); and they have asserted themselves as untouchable, *achhut* (untouched) and, more recently, *dalit* (oppressed).[49] For historians seeking to understand the history of this underclass prior to the twentieth century, however, its voices are difficult to discern.

Untouchable, shudra, vaishya, kshatriya, and brahman are large, unwieldy categories. Rendering them socially and economically practicable are a plethora of occupational groupings, known generally as *jati*, that developed over time in Indian society and inclusion in which was thought to be predicated on birth. The thousands of extant jati identities are theoretically locatable within the fourfold varna hierarchy or, without, as untouchables.[50] To the extent the Indic social order was value-laden and led to axioms of physical, moral, and intellectual superiority and inferiority, varna (and the untouchability it implies) represents an interesting analogue to the western notion of race. However, varna and race have differed not only according to strict definitions, but insofar as they evolved in distinctly different geographic, material, and human environments. As is well known, those environments suddenly overlapped with the arrival of the Portuguese near the turn of the sixteenth century, the result of which was the hermeneutic of caste. Caste, and the racial hierarchy that it came to evoke for many Indians and Britons alike, is an important hybrid (and historically locatable) idea that permeates much of the colonial past and the people who lived it.

The colonial understanding of India, increasingly centered on caste,[51] relied on a corps of elite officials who sought to understand and compartmentalize the complexity of religious, cultural, and social life and who presented their amassed data in gazetteers, census reports, surveys, and other encyclopedic compendia. Typical north Indian examples of such men are Francis Buchanan (later known as Francis Hamilton, 1762–1829), James Tod (1782–1835), Henry Miers Elliot (1808–1853), W. W. Hunter (1840–1900), William Crooke (1848–1923), H. H. Risley (1851–1911), George Grierson (1851–1941), and L. S. S. O'Malley (1874–1941). They and others like them worked either for the English East India Company or for the Government of British India. Their role was to study, interpret, and report on Indian society; their research was based on translation, linguistic analysis, philological speculation, statistical surveys, textual study, ethnography, anthropometry, and observation; and their understanding was heavily colored by their cultural predispositions, administrative functions, and political roles. The volumes they produced immediately entered the public domain and, as politically vital information, became authoritative ethnographic, cultural, and historical texts for Europeans and Indians alike. In short, Indian meaning—of obvious importance to the successful functioning of government—

was collected, analyzed, and reproduced in standardized form by the ruling power. This bringing of Indian meaning to political authority was not only necessary for administration, but also served to politically revalidate that body of knowledge. It is not entirely surprising, therefore, that peasant ideologues looked to this official literature in the twentieth century to buttress their kshatriya identities.

Insofar as the official literature often drew on elite Indian sources, especially with respect to caste, this process should also be seen as an official certification of a brahmanical discourse of hierarchy. Great caution must be utilized, therefore, when drawing upon this literature in the context of kshatriya reform, to ascertain whether hierarchy was in fact being popularized or whether it was being manipulated and thereby subverted. Another reason to exercise caution with the official literature—inspired in part by the publication of Edward Said's Orientalism—is the fact that the information therein is colored by the colonial predispositions of its British authors.[52] It is true that all interpretation falls victim at some point to cultural and psychological subjectivism; as Nandy points out in his effort to comprehend the salient psycho-cultural dimensions of colonialism, "The West has not merely produced modern colonialism, it informs most interpretations of colonialism. It colours even this interpretation of interpretation."[53] Like Nandy, we should endeavor to focus upon our own interpretive dilemma and put it to good analytical use, thus making our work all the more meaningful.

By identifying the cultural—and, with Nandy, the psychological—subjectivity of British interpretation in the nineteenth and early twentieth centuries, we can speculate about the nature of British-Indian society during the colonial period. A bulwark of colonial power was the colonial elite's conception of Indian society, especially the idea of caste. Caste was the ideological linchpin of colonial authority, a language of race spoken by the powerful and understood by the powerless, and therefore central to the colonial Indian world. But, as the historian Nicholas Dirks has cautioned, "The assumption that the colonial state could manipulate and invent Indian tradition at will, creating a new form of caste and reconstituting the social, and that a study of its own writings and discourse is sufficient to argue such a case, is clearly inadequate and largely wrong."[54] All the arguments of the cultural hegemony of the colonial state notwithstanding, what is presented in British understanding reflected a form of Indian social, cultural, and religious reality. Historians can and should learn not only from the reflected reality, but from the mode of reflection itself. Going one step further, it can be argued that one cannot be utilized to the exclusion of the other. As a reflection of reality, caste and the body of orientalist literature upon which it relied represents one side of an emergent British-Indian dialogue, a dialogue that developed dialectically into a cultural system all its own: partly British, partly Indian, wholly British-Indian. The other side of that dialogue—grounded in a popular discourse that was all-too-infrequently perceived by colonial officials, not to mention postcolonial scholars who rely overly on colonial commentary—is the understanding and reshaping of social relations by peasants and monks in colonial north India.

The way these peasants and monks came to terms with varna, jati, race, and caste thus forms the central problem of this study. Peasants and monks were particularly well poised to examine these concepts in the context of political action and religious identity in the colonial period. The former were regarded as of low status (i.e., shudra), ostensibly because of their engagement in agricultural labor. Yet their position of relative social inferiority was offset by their significant demographic strength, their centrally productive role in society, and the opportunities for economic advancement that confronted them in the nineteenth century. Buoyed by these material strengths, peasants in Gangetic India began to reject the shudra definitions ascribed to them by the social elite. Likewise, monks did not stand aloof from the worldly concerns of status and hierarchy but remained intensely devoted to a commentary and, more often than not, a critique of that world. The many ways peasants and monks conceived of social relations constituted not only important and overlapping arenas of cultural change during the colonial period, but informed the conception of race and caste after independence from British rule in 1947.

What emerges then is that "Hindu" ideas have impinged in important ways on social and political change in Indian history. This should not appear surprising, inasmuch as the term *Hindu* has long communicated social and political meaning. Persians, Greeks, and Arabs first used variations of the term *Hindush* as a geographic designator to describe the territory to the east of the Indus (ancient *Shindu*) River; "Hindu" later came to be used by Turkish, Persian, and finally European (and especially British) observers as a religious signifier describing someone who followed a system of beliefs (today collectively termed "Hinduism") distinct from the then more familiar Islam.[55] In fact, as the etymological development of this term would indicate, Indian religion may have been too complex and discrepant to be described adequately under the single rubric, as a Hindu-ism. A systematic Hinduism did of course emerge in recent centuries, influenced in part by European attempts to understand Indian religion according to European paradigms, in part by a nationalist movement that sought to draw on noncontradictory religious meanings, and in part by religious reformers who sought to reconcile regional religious contradictions so as to participate in the emerging Indian political discourse of nation and race. Underneath the rubric of that emergent, "modern" Hinduism existed a divisible multiplicity of overlapping religious systems. In the Gangetic north this included, by the eighteenth century, expanding monastic institutions of Vaishnava belief centered on *bhakti,* or love for God. Vaishnava bhakti, or the conception of Vishnu and his avatars as deserving of complete devotion, is the religious ground upon which much of the ideological change described in this study takes place. The following pages are an attempt to reinvest those terms with social and political meaning and in the process instill in social and political history a sense of cultural change.

CHAPTER I

*Sadhu*s and *Shudra*s in North India, ca. 1700–1900

This chapter has three related objectives. First, it introduces and situates Shaiva and Vaishnava monasticism and related religious movements in the late eighteenth and early nineteenth-century
Gangetic north, particularly in the context of expanding colonial rule.
Second, it seeks to understand Indian monasticism not as timeless and
static (which is how sadhus often represent the religious worlds to which
they belong), but as historically measurable, comprising competing social institutions organized around distinct religious and ideological principles and responsive to continually changing political circumstances and
economic pressures. Third, and most importantly, I argue in this chapter that north Indian Vaishnava monastic circles contained strong reformist mentalities evident in the relationships between Ramanandi
monks and people of low status, particularly in comparison to the competing religious perspectives in the central Gangetic region of Bihar and
eastern Uttar Pradesh. These reformist mentalities can be seen as well
in traditions relating to both Shaiva and Vaishnava monastic soldiering
in the precolonial era, with which this chapter begins; however, the main
discussion is focused on the nineteenth century and relies primarily, but
not exclusively, on surveys, censuses, and scholarship produced by the
colonial desire to possess greater knowledge about Indian society. The
subject of Vaishnava reformist mentalities as a basis for ideological change
is pursued in the following chapter, which is a more detailed consideration of Ramanandi views on religion, caste, and inequality in the early
twentieth century.

Subaltern *Sadhus*?

Besides affording an intriguing view of popular ideological change, the history of Indian monasticism is an excellent index of the changing political culture of north India during the transition to colonial rule. Prior to 1800, *gosains* and *bairagis* (Shaiva and Vaishnava monks, respectively) exercised broad political and economic influence as merchants, bankers, and, most importantly, soldiers. Powerful *mahants* (abbots) speculated in real estate and engaged in extensive money-lending activities in order to diversify monastic endowments in urban centers throughout the north, thus facilitating links between the increasingly regional political economies of the late Mughal era.[1] Indeed, Christopher Bayly has suggested that gosains in particular "came the nearest of any Indian business community to the emerging bourgeoisie that European theorists from Sleeman to Marx wished to see."[2] Gosains were so well entrenched in Asian commerce that Warren Hastings saw fit to avail the English East India Company of their good offices in what was ultimately a failed bid to acquire trade relations with Tibet and China in the late 1700s.[3]

Gosains and bairagis were able to engage successfully in trade and finance during the eighteenth century because they not only possessed excellent commercial intelligence and political connections but had access to a sufficient degree of independent armed force to back their profit-making ventures. In fact, the unsettled conditions of the middle of the century can be seen in retrospect to have benefited the monastic armies, since in addition to protecting monastic endowments, sectarian shrines, pilgrimage routes, and commercial interests, gosain and bairagi regiments were increasingly incorporated in the armies of the major regional powers. Hence, despite the early commonality of commercial interests between the new English trader-rulers and the well-placed gosain and bairagi merchants, it was inevitable that in the rich province of Bengal armed monks and Company soldiers would come into conflict. When it did occur, that conflict took the form of a prolonged series of skirmishes in Bengal and Bihar over four decades (1760s to 1800), usually referred to as the "sanyasi and fakir rebellion."

At one level, this rebellion seems to have stemmed from purely materialist motives, namely, from the excessive revenue burdens introduced by the Company on monastic and nonmonastic landlords alike and from the tendency of Company officials to side with landlords in disputes with powerful gosain moneylenders.[4] More important, however, was the fact that sadhus were accustomed to bearing arms while on pilgrimage routes through Bengal and in some cases possessed the right to levy contributions from villages along those routes; in addition, many sadhus sought military service with landlords and petty rajas in the region.[5] Company officials, for their part, were increasingly opposed to such practices and sought to discourage the armed bands of sanyasis and fakirs from operating in the province. One early encounter, recorded by the noted Company surveyor James Rennell who at the time (1766) was mapping territory just south of the Himalayan foothill kingdom of Bhutan, bears testimony to the martial potential of armed monks and the resentment of armed sadhus at the new impositions being placed on them by the Company state. Rennell happened upon a skirmish in progress between Company troops and a force of seven hundred such sadhus; the wounds he received included a saber gash that "cut through my right Shoulder Bone, and laid me open for nearly a foot down the Back, cutting through and wounding some of my Ribs, . . . a cut on the left Elbow, which took off the muscular part of the breadth of a Hand, a Stab in the Arm, and a large cut on the head."[6]

The Company prevailed in that particular confrontation, but over three decades would pass before the *akhara*s (monastic armies) would be disarmed in Bengal or, at the very least, driven beyond Company-controlled territories. This prolonged confrontation between Company soldiers and armed sadhus is generally understood in terms of the Company desire to establish itself as militarily supreme in the province of Bengal. Rarely, if ever, are the ideological implications of the conflict examined by social historians, and the term "rebellion," considered a political overstatement given the nature of the conflict, seems now to have been discarded.[7] However, the phenomenon of armed monasticism certainly posed more than simply a "law and order" challenge for newly ascendant Company officials. Armed sadhus were the very antithesis of the world the company-state was endeavoring to create in the eighteenth and nineteenth centuries, namely, a settled peasant society that would render forth vast agrarian revenues on a regular basis with as little resistance as possible. The modern state in India could not countenance recalcitrant sadhus wandering about the countryside armed, dangerous, often naked, and claiming to represent an alternate locus of authority.[8] The Company needed a modern sadhu: a priestly monk unconcerned with worldly power and given over completely to religious contemplation and prayer. Hence Warren Hastings's proclamation of 21

January 1773 banishing "all Biraugies and Sunnasses [bairagis and sanyasis, or armed Vaishnava and Shaiva monks] who are travellers strangers and passengers in this country" from the provinces of Bengal and Bihar, save "such of the cast of Rammanundar and Goraak [Ramanand and Gorakhnath] who have for a long time been settled and receive a maintenance in land money . . . from the Government or the Zemindars of the province, [and] likewise such Sunasses as are allowed charity ground for executing religious offices." In other words, those sadhus who were "neither vagrants nor plunderers but fixed inhabitants," who "quietly employ themselves in their religious function," could, in Hastings's view, be tolerated.[9]

Armed monasticism holds more than just military and political-cultural interest, however. There are indications that the rise of Vaishnava and Shaiva monastic soldiering afforded, or in some way reflected, increased entry of people of low social status, particularly those deemed shudra by the twice-born elite, into the major monastic orders in Gangetic north India. In this sense, the history of the armed akharas is not unlike that of the Sikhs in the Punjab, the arming of whom, according to W. H. McLeod, was occasioned by the prolonged infusion of *Jat* peasants into the *Nanakpanthi* community.[10] By the eighteenth century the profusion of Jat Sikhs cemented in demographic fact the professed egalitarianism that had long been a powerful ideological component of Guru Nanak's teaching. Hence for McLeod, Sikh hagiography (which speaks of a unilateral decision on the part of Guru Govind Singh to militarize the Nanakpanth in 1699) masks slow processes of social and demographic transformation.

Similarly, it is possible to perceive the social dimensions of militarization by looking within Shaiva and Vaishnava monastic traditions regarding the decision to take up arms. For example, a widely accepted Dasnami legend recorded by J. N. Farquhar in the early twentieth century held that Shaiva monks took up arms during the reign (and with the approval) of the Mughal emperor Akbar (r. 1556–1605) to defend brahman sanyasis against the persecutions of Muslim fakirs. While the motivational elements of this tradition can be challenged on the basis of both historical and historiographical evidence, it is perhaps more significant that Farquhar also related his general impression that the arming of Shaivas relied on the heavy recruitment of shudras into the elite ranks of the Dasnami order.[11] Whether shudras were indeed actively recruited as soldier Dasnamis, or whether the assertion of past military recruitment became a convenient way of explaining the increasing number of shudras in the order, the fact remains that today certain segments of orthodox, high-caste Dasnamis avoid commensal relations with warrior monks because of the latter's supposedly low origins.[12]

One can see stronger suggestions of the involvement of shudras (and, indeed, others of low and marginal status such as women and untouchables) in traditions relating to Vaishnava monastic soldiering. One important Vaishnava narrative holds that the arming of bairagis was the product of a conscious decision made in 1713 by leaders of the four main Vaishnava sampraday—often referred to collectively as the *chatuh-sampraday,* namely, the orders organized around the teachings of Vishnuswami, Madhvacharya, Nimbarkacharya, and Ramanujacharya (in which Ramanandis were included).[13] According to this tradition, the major Vaishnava mahants met at Galta, a temple complex and monastic center very near Jaipur, and decided to resort to arms to defend against increasing attacks by Shaiva monks. Significantly, the Galta meeting in 1713 also marked the emergence of Ramanandis (those who look to Swami Ramanand for inspiration) as the dominant force not only among the followers of Ramanujacharya's teachings, but among Vaishnavas in north India generally.[14] The Galta tradition provides an interesting twist, however: it was also decided in 1713 to declare the untouchable, shudra, and female members of Ramanand's original fourteenth-century coterie of disciples as "illegitimate" transmitters of tradition; in other words, untouchables, shudras, and women would continue to be admitted as Ramanandi novitiates, but henceforth they would have to link themselves to the Ramanandi past via one of the original male, twice-born (in this case, either brahman or kshatriya) disciples of Ramanand. While on the one hand this decision may have reflected the rise of caste mores amongst Vaishnavas, I prefer to interpret it as a move by socially conservative Vaishnavas to limit the ideological effects of what may have been a heavy influx of non-twice-born Ramanandis.[15]

According to a related and specifically Ramanandi tradition recorded by the anthropologist Peter van der Veer in Ayodhya in the 1980s, loosely organized bands of armed bairagis wandered about north India long before 1700 and were given formal military hierarchy by one Swami Balanand in the eighteenth century.[16] Today the Balanand *math* (temple-*cum*-monastery) in Jaipur continues to claim credit for the formalization of the armed Vaishnava akharas. Though elements of the Galta and Balanand traditions appear contradictory (the reasons for which become clearer in the following chapter), they both point to the importance of Ramanandis, and particularly Ramanandis in the Jaipur region, in the formation of soldiering orders among Vaishnavas. That a Vaishnava call to arms should have been associated with the increased influence of Ramanandis is not surprising, since the social liberalism that is associated with Ramanand would have facilitated the process of military recruitment by opening monastic ranks to the lowly.[17] This point is underlined in Ayodhya itself, where a banner emblazoned with Swami Ramanand's famous admonition against inequality—"Ask not of caste and the like, if you love God you belong to God"—decorates the entrance to the *Hanuman Garhi,* the main headquarters of Vaishnava soldier monasticism in north India.[18]

Records housed in the *Kapad Dwara* (warehouse of valuables) of the Jaipur state provide independent corroboration of Vaishnava arms and of attempts to limit the entry of the low-born into the Ramanandi sampraday in the Jaipur region after 1700.[19] In the 1720s and until his death in 1743, Maharaja Jai Singh II evinced a strong interest in religious affairs, particularly religious affairs having to do with the Vaishnava institutions in his realm.[20] And, not unlike Warren Hastings a half century later, Jai Singh II apparently looked askance at the phenomenon of armed monasticism and sought to discourage it. To this end, he solicited and received four separate bond agreements containing pledges from prominent Vaishnava mahants, nine of whom identify themselves clearly as "Ramanandi," to give up the practice of keeping arms and to boycott or otherwise punish those who continued to do so.[21] From separate correspondences it is evident that the Maharaja also solicited opinions from Bengali Vaishnavas regarding the rights of shudras and other low classes, and obtained pledges from Ramanandi mahants and other Vaishnavas not only to maintain strict caste rules in commensal relations but to no longer accept shudra and *antyaj* (low-born) disciples.[22] The fact that Jai Singh II's efforts to impose orthodox behavior on Vaishnava monks involved the demilitarization of the armed akharas in tandem with the barring of low-born novitiates suggests that arms and low status were connected not just in the Maharaja's vision of a neo-orthodox Vaishnavism but in the social-historical reality of Ramanandi monasticism.

Hence, though questions and ambiguities remain, both Vaishnava and Shaiva monastic traditions evince links between soldiering and low status. What requires further elucidation are questions regarding functionality and causation: namely, did the need for an armed defense on the part of the monastic orders compel a relaxation of social restrictions in order to spur recruitment? Or, conversely, was the arming of monks the result of the influx of peasants (as with pastoralist-*cum*-peasant Jats in the Sikh case) and others of low or marginal status into monastic communities, and if so why was militarism the result of that influx? (This is a question that needs greater elaboration with respect to Sikhs as well.) A third possibility that must be considered and that, by implication, obscures any functional relationship between militarization and social change is that the history of monastic soldiering has been used in the more recent past by conservative, high-caste elements in the orders to explain (by way of apologizing for) the contemporary presence therein of shudras, untouchables, and women.[23] An important related question concerns the organizational status of the military akharas in the non-military sections of the religious orders with which they were associated. The tenuous relationships that today exist between "orthodox" (and generally high-caste) Vaishnava and Shaiva monks, on the one hand, and their respective military akharas, on the other, suggest that sectarian traditions regarding the sudden mobilization of the latter in defense of the former may well have masked more prolonged—if contentious—processes of social openness within the orders as a whole. Indeed, the fact that the military akharas survived the monopolization of arms by the East India Company in the late eighteenth and early nineteenth centuries and continue to thrive as important sections of both Shaiva and Vaishnava monasticism in the late twentieth century suggests that their significance to the religious life of north India was (and is) more social than military.[24]

Whatever the answers to these questions, more research is necessary to know the exact fate of the monastic armies after the passing of the eighteenth century. Certainly, despite the loss of an explicit military function, the trappings of military culture implicit to armed monasticism remained for the most part intact under British rule. The soldier sadhu would become domesticated as a conventional monastic type (as naga) and would complement other forms of monasticism organized around scholarship, devotion and worship, itinerancy, or some combination thereof.[25] Given the apparent survival of the culture (if not the function) of military monasticism, it seems likely that members of the wealthy akharas were able to fall back on the substantial endowments, mostly in the form of land, acquired during the turbulent eighteenth century when their military and financial services were in demand. It is also possible that the many thousands of soldier monks supported by the frequent warfare of the eighteenth century simply melted back into the peasant countryside after the supremacy of British-Indian arms had been established in the early nineteenth century. Such an eventuality would be difficult to document; nevertheless, this was the argument of W. G. Orr—whose main evidence was the nineteenth-century proverb that "the man who smears his body with ashes [i.e., the naga sadhu] can wash it clean again, but the man who has his ears pierced (that is, becomes a Yogi) is a Yogi all his days."[26]

*Sadhu*s and the Social Order in the Surveys of Francis Buchanan, 1811–1813

As is clear from the foregoing, any detailed discussion of the social and political dimensions of north Indian monasticism prior to the nineteenth century is fraught with historiographic pitfalls stemming from the general lack of strong documentary evidence with which to confirm or refute religious tradition.[27] This situation changes as we enter the nineteenth century: Company officials sought to gain a more sophisticated social, political, and economic understanding of the society over which they had acquired administrative, judicial, and revenue-collecting powers, and consequently they amassed a wealth of detail regarding the religious dimensions of north Indian life. The history of this acquisition of knowledge about India is well known and need not be repeated here, save to note that the knowledge acquired took a variety of forms. On one extreme was scholarship focused on the literary splendor of ancient India, grounded in Sanskrit philology and brahmanical tradition and best symbolized by the translations of classical texts by such luminaries as Sir William Jones and H. T. Colebrooke. On the other extreme were the likes of James Tod and Francis Buchanan, who combined an interest in traditional Indian historiographies (and particularly kshatriya, or royal, genealogies) with a facility for recording in voluminous detail the political, social, religious, and economic life of specific regions.

Buchanan is of particular importance here, because his accounts of Bihar and eastern Uttar Pradesh include frequent and detailed reference to religious belief, popular modes of worship and religious instruction, and the regional structure of monastic organizations.[28] Such descriptions appear in these accounts in three discrete forms: first, Buchanan's "topographical" sections, which describe each subdistrict jurisdiction, include an assessment of the relative strength and appeal of monastic gurus; second, his descriptions of each caste usually contain reference to its religious customs and attitudes; and third, the same section on caste concludes with a general discussion of the "sages and sects" of the district, organized according to monastic perspective.[29] The value of such a three-tiered approach is that it affords a textured and multidimensional picture of the monastic and religious life of the Gangetic core.

Perhaps the most immediately revealing feature of Buchanan's Bihar accounts, from the monastic perspective, is what they omit: armed monks. Buchanan made only one brief reference to military monasticism, and that only to explain its absence. Noting that many Ramanandi nagas continued to find service "in the armies of the Rajas beyond the Yamuna" (beyond direct British control in what is now Rajasthan, southern Uttar Pradesh, and Madhya Pradesh), Buchanan observed that the few who remained in south Bihar "have been obliged to abandon arms and predatory habits, and for some time their bands have not ventured to traverse the country."[30] Buchanan's village-based sages are closer to the normative image of the nonthreatening monk implicit in Warren Hastings's 1773 proclamation barring itinerant, armed sadhus from passing through in the province of Bengal. A similar portrait would be painted by Horace Hayman Wilson, the eminent Sanskritist of the mid-nineteenth century, who observed that "the tenants of these maths, particularly the *Vaishnavas,* are most commonly of a quiet inoffensive character, and the *Mahants* especially are men of talents and respectability, although they possess, occasionally, a little of that self-importance, which the conceit of superior sanctity is apt to inspire."[31]

In retrospect, it can be argued that with the gradual removal of armed monks from territories controlled by the Company in the late eighteenth and nineteenth centuries, north Indian monasticism turned inward, away from worldly martial pursuits and toward more aesthetic, devotional, and literary accomplishments. In the Vaishnava context, this would have meant a greater emphasis on *rasik*-oriented bhakti, or "devotional aestheticism," which had a constituted powerful strand of both Ram and Krishna worship since the sixteenth century. The rasik tradition emphasizes heightened emotion, the careful perception of sensory experience, and in the Ramanandi context, a focus on Sita as a means of access to Ram; consequently, many "rasiks," as the practitioners of this mode of religious devotion were known, adopted the persona of a handmaid to Sita.[32] As we shall see in the next chapter, many of the main players in the politics of the Ramanandi sampraday in Ayodhya and throughout the Gangetic north were associated with the rasik tradition.

Whatever the particular mode of asceticism, the majority of the sadhus in Buchanan's accounts wielded a great deal of popular influence as village *gurus*—a role that combined the duties of teacher, counselor, spiritual guide, and pious exemplar. Hence it would not be inappropriate to understand them as "guideposts for the common person's society and its changing moral character" and the religious arena they inhabited as a "locus for raising social issues and for initiating and influencing change within Indian society."[33] In addition, these village gurus represented the point of contact between rural peasants and the monastic networks that crisscrossed the subcontinent. Buchanan's work took him through much of deltaic and upper Bengal and the Gangetic core, including regions that became known by 1901 as the Bihar districts of Purnea, Bhagalpur, Monghyr, Patna, Gaya, and Shahabad, and the Uttar Pradesh districts of Basti and Gorakhpur. While all his accounts are of immense social-historical value, three of them—Bihar and Patna (1811–1812), Shahabad (1813), and Gorakhpur (1813)—possess enough religious and social detail to afford an intriguing statistical snapshot of the demography of monasticism and its popular appeal in the early nineteenth century.

Each account begins with a "topography" of the district, organized according to administrative precinct, or *thana*. Bihar and Patna (conforming roughly to the 1901 Gaya and Patna Districts, respectively) contained a total of seventeen thanas of widely varying size and population; Shahabad ten; and Gorakhpur twenty-eight (two of which were completely deserted and most of which were relatively sparsely populated). Buchanan's treatment of each begins with a one-paragraph description of the geographical setting and basic demographic and physical dimensions, then turns to a brief mention of the thana's administrative, police, and juridical personnel. This is followed by a much more detailed statement of the institutional strengths and local authority and appeal of each religious perspective in the thana. Rather than percentages, he employed the Indian *anna* standard of sixteenths; occasionally he would utilize eighths, twelfths, twenty-fourths, and thirty-seconds when greater simplicity could be employed or greater accuracy was called for.

The following, rather lengthy excerpt from Shahabad District's "Dumraong" (variant of Dumraon) thana is typical in many ways of Buchanan's descriptive method:

This jurisdiction, although very large and populous, is so compact, and the native officers of police are so centrically [*sic*] situated, that little inconvenience is felt from these circumstances. The police of a small portion adjacent to Vagsar [var. Buxar, Baksar], at the N.-W. corner of the division, is under the inspection of the military officer commanding that fortress. This is the only division in the district which enjoys the advantage of a court for the trial of small debts, without applying in the first instance to the judge. The commissioner for this court is also the hereditary Kazi, who resides at Kazipur 3 miles N. from Dumraong, the residence of the police officers, and near one side of his jurisdiction, both circumstances attended with considerable inconvenience. The Kazi [judge] confines himself entirely to the deciding of causes [cases?], and attestation of deeds, and appoints deputies to perform all religious ceremonies. Here is also a hereditary Mufti, a description of officer, with which I have not previously met. No Pirzada [Sufi shaikh] resides, and those who become Murids [followers], employ vagrants.

Of the Hindus 4/16 are unworthy to the notice of any sage: 4/16 are of the sect of Sakti; 2/16 adhere to Siva. Of these 6/16 five belong to the Brahmans, and one to the Dasanami Sannyasis. Most of the Brahmans reside [i.e., they do not visit periodically from other thanas], and Ritu Raj Misra, a Sakadwipi, who lives at Vagsar, and is the family priest of the Bhojpur Rajas, has very extensive authority and influence. He is a man of considerable learning, and affects very austere manners, to which last circumstance is probably owing much of his authority, although those who receive sacred instruction from his mouth, are mostly if not entirely of the sects of Saiva or Sakti, he is of the sect of Vishnu; and it is alleged, that the form of prayer, which he gives, is addressed to some form of this deity, which is indeed quite the same to his followers, as they do not understand a word of it. Perhaps however this may be a story invented by some of those, who are envious of his success. As the form of prayer is a profound secret, the truth could not easily be discovered. The Dasanamis have 2 maths, and about 20 smaller houses here called Mathiyas. At the 2 maths there reside about 15 men, who have relinquished the world; some of the inferior houses are occupied by persons, who indulge in the pleasures of matrimony.

3/16 of the Hindus adhere to the sect of Nanak. There are 4 meetings, all belonging to Jagdishpur [a town in central Shahabad], and the men, who preside, abstain from wedlock. Two of these places have the title of (Gadis) thrones.

2/16 of the Hindus adhere to Vishnu, and follow chiefly the Ramawats, but some are disciples of Madhava, and some of Nima; no one, however with whom I met, could tell the number of houses, that belonged to each. There is one Akhara at Dumraong and 40 at Vagsar, all occupied by persons entirely dedicated to God. There are also 50 houses occupied by married persons, who instruct the canaille, and are called Vaishnavas. All were originally Sudras.

1/16 of the Hindus follow the new routes to heaven: the Kavir Pangth has 10 Gurus, who occupy Mathiyas, some of them married, some single; while there are 20 persons, that adhere to the doctrine of Siva Narayan.[34]

The remainder of Buchanan's discussion in this particular thana (as with most other thanas) is focused on the quality of the soil, the types of irrigation, the number of houses of various kinds and their manner of con-

struction, local fortifications, the main places of worship, the major festivals, local history and legend, and any interesting archeological or antiquarian remains in the vicinity.

A few points that emerge in the above excerpt merit special emphasis, inasmuch as they relate to broader patterns in Buchanan's accounts.
First, in each thana Buchanan noted the proportion of the population
(usually between one-eighth and one-fourth, but occasionally as high as
one-half) considered by his informants (of whom more later) to be "unworthy" of religious instruction. He nevertheless included in most of
his topographical descriptions the relatively small proportions dedicated
to such reformist sects as the Kabirpanthis and Sivanarayanis, both of
which were aggressively egalitarian and, indeed, anti-brahmanical and
hence tended to attract followers from a wide social spectrum, including untouchables and "unclean" shudras. Taken together, these facts suggest that while Buchanan's religious description did not altogether ignore the religious views and practices of people deemed extremely
low-status, he nevertheless dealt mostly with what may have been considered acceptable and demographically important, if not respectable,
religious points of view; again, this would reflect the middle and upper-
caste views of the people from whom he gleaned his data, not to mention the Bengali pandits who assisted him in his surveys and who in any
case looked askance at much of Bihari culture. In any event, the lengthy
discussions that usually followed Buchanan's religious tabulations include
local village deities whose worship was often conducted by the socially
and culturally marginalized lower classes; these were the kinds of people, and the kind of religious traditions, excluded in the systematic numerical descriptions that began each section.

The second point that requires emphasis is slightly more complex.
Buchanan's description of the sectarian dimensions in Gangetic Bihar
and eastern Uttar Pradesh took two complementary forms. On the one
hand, Buchanan conceived of three main divisions of Hindu religion:
Shaiva-Shakta, Vaishnava, and *panthi* (the more recent "routes to
heaven" espoused by Kabir, Nanak, and the like). On the other hand,
within these large (and often overlapping) divisions were religious communities organized around the institutional ties of gurus, which usually
took monastic form. Dasnami sanyasis represented the main Shaiva
monastic group; Ramanandis (often referred to as *Ramawats*) the main
Vaishnava monastic group. The main panthi community that emerges
in Buchanan's accounts was the Nanakpanth, associated with the teachings of Guru Nanak, which was particularly influential in south Bihar.

Other, much less prominent (at least, in the Gangetic core regions described by Buchanan) religious perspectives that possessed varying degrees of monastic manifestations were represented by the (Shaiva) *Kanphat* yogi community, which looked to the teachings of the fifteenth-century Gorakhnath (on account of which they are frequently referred to as Gorakhnathi and Gorakhpanthi); the (Vaishnava) *Radhaballabhi* sampraday, centered on the worship of Krishna as Radha's lover; the ("reformist") Kabirpanth, and the more recent (also "reformist") Shivanarayani (centered in nearby Ghazipur District in what is now Uttar Pradesh) and Daryadasi communities (centered in Shahabad District).

At the risk of an overly long aside, it should be noted that there is a tendency to be overly schematic when describing the sectarian dimensions of monasticism. Such a tendency should be carefully qualified if not avoided outright. It is best to understand Vaishnava, Shaiva, and Shakta as terms that refer to distinct yet overlapping, and evolving, systems of religious meaning with broad popular appeal that have been drawn upon in varying degrees by thinkers over the past millennium. Two extremely important figures were Shankaracharya and Ramanujacharya, each of whom is remembered to have identified in complex metaphysical and epistemological discourses the most efficacious way of perceiving divine truth(s).[35] They themselves have long been associated with or, perhaps more precisely, been thought of as founders of major monastic communities with distinct sectarian (Shaiva as opposed to Vaishnava) dimensions. However, while Shankaracharya's status as the founder of the Dasnami order has remained unquestioned by Dasnami sanyasis, Ramanujacharya's status as a formative figure in the Ramanandi sampraday has been a matter of major contention, particularly in this century—a contention best symbolized by the very name that has come to be associated (even as early as the eighteenth century) with the monastic community that for many years viewed Ramanujacharya with great reverence. The examination of the history of this contentious moment in the Ramanandi sampraday, and of the socially radical understanding of the life of the fourteenth-century Ramanand that was re-crystallizing at this time, is the central object of the next chapter. What is important to recognize here is the manner in which individual monks were able to endow the doctrinal tenets and social philosophies of their orders with wider Indic meanings.

Another important and more recent figure in the religious history of the subcontinent is, of course, Guru Nanak, whose perception of an ineffable god became the spiritual fount for Sikhism.[36] However, interpretations of Nanak's teachings varied, and as a result the Nanakpanthis observed by Buchanan in early nineteenth-century Bihar should not be confused with the khalsa Sikhs of the Punjab, though the communities were closely related. Buchanan himself noted that the followers of Nanak were divided into two groups: "the Khalesah sect founded by Govinda [i.e., Guru Govind Singh], and confined in great measure to the west of India," and "the Kholesah or original Sikhs who prevail in Behar."[37] In other words, most Nanakpanthis in Bihar remained aloof from the khalsa-fication of the sampraday. Today, the Nanakpanthis described by Buchanan would be referred to as "Udasin" and see themselves as the caretakers of universal truths articulated by Guru Nanak, particularly as mediated through Nanak's eldest son, the exceptionally long-lived Shri Chand (1494–1629). Upon the death of Nanak, the mantle of leadership in the Nanakpanth passed not to Shri Chand but to one of Nanak's favored disciples, who became known as Guru Angad, thus beginning the succession of ten gurus that would end with Govind Singh.[38] According to modern histories based on prevailing khalsa Sikh hagiography, Shri Chand and his followers were expelled in the sixteenth century from the Sikh community.[39] According to Udasin tradition, by contrast, the links between the Shri Chand and his followers, on the one hand, and the Sikh gurus and their adherents, on the other, remained strong well into the seventeenth century. For example, Udasins have long maintained that the sixth guru, Hargovind Singh, placed his son Gurditta under the personal and spiritual care of Shri Chand, who by this time was nearing the end of his long life. Indeed, not only is Gurditta himself remembered as an important Udasin guru, four of his disciples are said to have founded the principal Udasin subsects.[40]

The history of the gradual bifurcation of Nanakpanthis into what Buchanan called the Khalesah versus Kholesah divisions, or what today would be called Sikh versus Udasin, is closely linked to the changing demography of Sikhism in the Punjab and the rise of a khalsa military culture in the seventeenth and eighteenth centuries—in contrast to developments in the Gangetic north, where the rise of a military ethos in religious communities occurred primarily among Vaishnavas and Shaivas. That division was further hardened by the British recruitment of Sikhs into the Indian army, the rise of the Singh Sabha in and beyond the Punjab, and the emergence of Akali politics surrounding the status of Sikh shrines (controlled before 1925 by Udasins) in the nineteenth and twentieth centuries.[41]

Buchanan's tabulations of monastic groupings within either the

Shaiva-Shakta or Vaishnava rubric are further complicated by the fact that he tended to draw a distinction between monastic gurus and brahman gurus. This practice probably reflected the fact that many of his local monastic informants themselves drew such a distinction;[42] it may also have reflected the socioreligious predilections of the Bengali pandits who assisted him in his data gathering. Despite these factors, however, it is likely that in the case of Vaishnavas, brahman gurus such as the influential Pandit Ritu Raj Misra, mentioned in the extract cited above, were affiliated with Ramanandi teachings—though the exact nature of that affiliation remains unclear.[43] The Ramanandi connections of Vaishnava brahmans emerge in a later passage describing monastic establishments in Buxar (which was, Buchanan noted, the main Ramanandi center in Shahabad District). Buchanan observed that in Buxar "the convents of the Brahmans, who have adopted this [the Ramanandi] order, as usual are confounded with those occupied by Sudras, nor have I been able to distinguish the number of each"; in a characteristic aside, he added that "my Bengalese assistants[,] confounding them [Bihari Vaishnavas] with the Vaishnavas of their own country, hold them in the utmost contempt."[44] In contrast to the Vaishnava credentials of most brahman gurus in Shahabad, Buchanan observed that "most of the Pandits, who act as Gurus in [Bihar and Patna] districts, worship Sakti as their favourite, and are Tantriks."[45] As he proceeded northwest from Shahabad into Gorakhpur District and closer to Ayodhya, which by this time was firmly established as a major Ramanandi monastic and pilgrimage center, Buchanan recorded increasing numbers of brahmans serving as Vaishnava gurus.[46]

Buchanan's observations respecting the religious appeal of gurus may be represented in tabular form. Table 1 below shows the population ratios (shown here as percentages) claimed as adherents by the main monastic communities and brahmans out of those persons said to "receive religious instruction" in the three most detailed of Buchanan's accounts—Bihar and Patna (two separate districts), Shahabad, and Gorakhpur. "Guru patronage" figures are shown for Brahmans, Dasnamis, Ramanandis, and Nanakshahis (from considerations of space, the less prominent religious perspectives, such as Kabirpanthi and Radhaballabhi, are not included). The column to the far right under the heading "RRI/Hindus" shows the total percentage of Hindus who, according to Buchanan, "received religious instruction" from gurus; the four columns to the left show percentages of that total number of Hindus who received religious instruction.

Two points should be kept in mind when reading Table 1. First, and most important, higher percentages of brahman gurus in Shahabad and, more especially, Gorakhpur Districts were Vaishnava in their religious outlook, and though it is difficult to quantify, many of them would have had ties to the Ramanandi sampraday, particularly as Buchanan moved closer to Ayodhya on the western edge of Gorakhpur. This means that the percentage of guru patronage for Ramanandis is much higher in those districts than shown in the table. Second, the gradual rise in the strength of Ramanandis (particularly if we understand increasing numbers of brahman gurus to be Ramanandi) as Buchanan traveled west from Patna and Bihar to Shahabad and thence to Gorakhpur was, in all likelihood, directly related to the gradual rise in the percentages of Hindus who "received religious instruction." The reason for this is the liberal social philosophy of the Ramanandi sampraday, which would have attracted many low-status groups into the institutional and ideological ambit of Vaishnava belief.

Indeed, Buchanan's remarks on religious practice in the Gangetic core, together with comments by other observers through the nineteenth century, indicate that Vaishnava gurus (and Ramanandis in particular) pursued a far more aggressive program of social and religious reform in comparison with their Dasnami and Nanakpanthi counterparts. Consequently, Vaishnava bairagis were drawn from the entire varna spectrum and included not only brahmans but many shudras. I have already related Buchanan's observations respecting the profusion of both brahman and shudra Ramanandi gurus in Buxar, the Vaishnava center of Shahabad District. In Patna, Buchanan remarked that while some Vaishnava gurus are brahman, "most are Sudras."[47] And even in Purnea District near the border of Bengal, where most of the Vaishnava gurus tended to follow the teachings of the Bengali saint Chaitanya, Buchanan noted that "the Ramanandi Brahmans and Vairagi Sudras are usually confounded together, and the name Ramayit [var. Ramawat] is given to both."[48]

Equally important was the fact that Ramanandis, according to Buchanan's accounts, encouraged their lay followers to adhere to a rigid moral code and a strict daily regimen. Describing Vaishnavas as "everywhere the most strict," Buchanan noted that "some few of them here [Bihar and Patna] will neither pray nor even show common civility to any god but those of his own sect."[49] The emphasis on a pure life applied as well to daily diet: "All the Hindus, Brahman or Sudra, of the sect of Vishnu [i.e., Ramanandis or their adherents], are remarkably strict

Table 1 *Guru Patronage in the Gangetic Core, 1811–1813 (percent)*

	Brahman	Dasnami	Ramanandi	Nanakshahi	RRI/Hindus
Patna	14	30	8	39	53
Bihar	14	40	9	37	62
Shahabad	37	23	16	20	76
Gorakhpur	64	11	20	1	85

SOURCE: Buchanan, *Bihar and Patna, 1811–1812*, 1:57–262, and 2:723, table 4 (population); *Shahabad, 1812–1813*, 51–151; "An Account of the Northern Part of the District of Gorakhpur, 1812," 139–345. The population figures used to calculate the above percentages for Shahabad and Gorakhpur rely on the tables provided in Martin, *The History, Antiquities, Topography, and Statistics of Eastern India*, vol. 1 (Behar and Shahabad), Shahabad Appendix, 44; and vol. 2 (Bhagalpoor, Goruckpoor, and Dinajpoor), Goruckpoor Appendix, 9, respectively.

in eating, reject altogether rice cleaned by boiling, all parched grains, and animal food"; by contrast, Buchanan observed that "all the Sudras, except those of the sect of Vishnu, drink avowedly."[50] Adherence to rigorous Vaishnava mores under the tutelage of Ramanandis, even for untouchables, thus afforded a substantial aura of self-respect. Again, Buchanan: "men of impure or vile tribes, who wish to be thought better than their neighbors, and who abstain from meat, fish, and spirituous liquors, are called *Bhakats* [devotees] . . . and at the recommendation of the Vairagis [var. bairagi], who are their gurus, have given up an indulgence of their appetites."[51] Not only were Ramanandis eager to attract followers into the sampraday irrespective of status, especially those derided as "vile" and "impure," but they were ready to encourage a pure lifestyle as a way of undermining the caste discrimination that stigmatized low-status populations.

For Buchanan this picture of purposeful, upright Ramanandi behavior stood in stark contrast to the conduct of the Dasnamis and Nanakshahis. Adherents of the former were "so careless or ignorant that they never have taken the trouble to inquire from their instructor whether the secret prayer is addressed to Siva or Sakti, and they do not understand a word of it." He added in a later passage, while Dasnamis "affect a life of mortification, . . . they are accused of being in private very indulgent to their sensual appetites."[52] Further, he mentioned no special dietary restrictions prescribed by Dasnamis that might have enhanced both the self-image and the social respectability of the lower status groups among their followers. Perhaps more revealing was Buchanan's observation that while Dasnami gurus benefited from the patronage of numerous shudras as lay followers, "Sudras are not admitted into the order."[53]

Buchanan recorded similar criticisms with respect to Nanakpanthis. Based on his extensive discussions with Mahant Govinda Das, a leading Nanakpanthi of Bihar, Buchanan observed that "the *Fakirs* [Govinda Das's own term] of the Kholasah sect of Sikhs [i.e., Nanakpanthis or Udasins] admit into their own order only Brahmans, Kshatriyas and Vaisyas; but among their followers they admit all Hindus, who are not vile; and they entirely exclude all *Mlechchhas* [unclean outsiders], such as Muhammedans or Christians." On the level of theological and devotional commitment evinced by Nanakpanthis, he observed:

The assemblies at the *Sanggats* [meetings] are quite irregular, and depend entirely upon the accidental offerings, that are made. Even at Rekabganj [in Patna City], by far the greatest place of [Nanakshahi] worship in these countries, there are not now four daily assemblies; but it is said, that formerly these meetings were regular, and when no offering was made by any of the laymen, the Mahanta defrayed the expense; but Govinda Das considers this as unnecessary, and no meeting takes place, but when some person makes an offering.

Buchanan also noted that inclusion in the Nanakpanthi community as lay followers did not necessarily involve an abandonment of prior religious practices and convictions: devotees "follow exactly the same customs that they did before their admission" and "observe the same rules of caste, employ the same Brahmans as *Purohits* [ritual officiants] in every ceremony, and in all cases of danger worship exactly the same gods." However, while Govinda Das asserted that "Vishnu, Brahma and Siva are gods [and that] he occasionally makes them offerings," he claimed to do so "merely in compliance with the custom of the country." By contrast, in personal spiritual instruction Govinda Das acknowledged "only one supreme God (*Parameswara*)" who "ought to be the only object of worship," to the exclusion of the secondary Hindu deities listed above. These latter admissions by Govind Das would seem to imply a conscious recognition on his part of the divergence that had developed between the normative dictates of religion set out by Guru Nanak in the sixteenth century and Nanakpanth religious practice extant in the early nineteenth century.[54]

Though he did not remark upon it, Buchanan's descriptions of Dasnamis and Nanakpanthis reveal interesting similarities, particularly with respect to social exclusivity in matters of monastic recruitment and a general impression of laxity in religious observances.[55] Today there is little question of the strong affinity between Dasnamis and Nanakpanthis (or Udasins). Ghurye noted in the 1950s that "the philosophy of the Udasi ascetics is the same monistic Vedanta as that of the Dasanamis," and that "whenever there is any quarrel with the Vaishnava ascetics, they [Udasins] are always to be found on the side of the Saiva sadhus."[56] The anthropologists Baidyanath Saraswati and Surajit Sinha recorded in Banaras in the 1960s an Udasin tradition that the first person to take initiation from Shri Chand was Bhakta Giri, a Dasnami sanyasi of Bodh Gaya.[57] And Udasins assert that not only was Shri Chand an avatar of Shiva, but that Shri Chand and Guru Nanak only articulated Udasin truths that had existed since time began.[58]

Though measuring sectarian prosperity and decline is exceptionally difficult, it would appear that the proximity to Shaivism and the rise of khalsa politics conspired to diminish the institutional fortunes of the Nanakpanthi community in Bihar by the end of the nineteenth century. Such a conclusion is at least suggested by the meager returns for Nanakshahis of any kind, particularly as compared to Ramanandi bairagis and Dasnami sanyasis, in the census figures for the years 1891 and 1901 in the Bihar districts of Patna, Gaya, and Shahabad (roughly congruent with Buchanan's Patna, Bihar, and Shahabad districts).[59] In retrospect, Nanakpanthis in Bihar may be understood to have experienced what Richard Eaton has described as a process of "accretion": Udasins in Bihar, by gradually approximating Shaiva beliefs and practices, came to be regarded (and, indeed, regarded themselves) as Hindu by the early twentieth century.[60] This process would have been spurred as well by khalsa Sikh reforms emanating from the Punjab after the middle of the nineteenth century, which were designed to purge from Sikhism "corrupt" Hindu practices, establish for Sikhs a distinct, non-Hindu religious identity, and bolster khalsa Sikh institutional fortunes in the twentieth century at the expense of Udasins.

Perhaps not unlike khalsa Sikhs in the Punjab, Ramanandis in the early nineteenth century were exceptional for their unwavering, aggressive moral posture in the Gangetic core districts surveyed by Buchanan. This was coupled with, and possibly contributed to, the improving material fortunes of the sampraday in the central Gangetic region during the eighteenth and nineteenth centuries, the evidence for which exists in the history of the major pilgrimage centers of Banaras and Ayodhya. In their anthropological survey of Banaras carried out in the 1960s and '70s, Baidyanath Saraswati and Surajit Sinha discovered that the two most prolific monastic communities were the Dasnami and the Ramanandi. That Dasnamis predominated in Banaras is not at all surprising given that the city, as Kashi, was long regarded as Shiva's place, but the rise to prominence of Ramanandis there is a fact worthy of note. Even more remarkable is that, according to Saraswati and Sinha, of the forty Ramanandi institutions in Banaras, two were claimed to have been founded by Ramanand himself in the fifteenth century, while the remaining thirty-eight were founded between 1700 and 1968 (with over half founded after 1900).[61] Likewise, in his own very different anthropological exploration, van der Veer observes that "there can be no doubt about the fact that Ayodhya became an important pilgrimage centre only in the eighteenth century," and that Ramanandis rose to dominate the religious topography of the town at the expense of an established Dasnami presence and with the patronage of Awadhi nawabs headquartered in Lucknow.[62]

Hence, the eighteenth and nineteenth centuries should be seen as a time of expansion for Ramanandi monasticism vis-á-vis the competing religious orders, and not merely in terms of enlarged monastic endowments but numbers of lay and ascetic adherents as well. This trend did not escape the notice of observers, both Indian and European. H. H. Wilson noted in the late 1820s that

the ascetic and mendicant followers of Ramanand, known indiscriminately as *Ramanandis* or *Ramawats,* are by far the most numerous class of sectaries in Gangetic India: in Bengal they are comparatively few: beyond this province, as far as to *Allahabad* [i.e., in what is now Bihar and eastern Uttar Pradesh], although perhaps the most numerous, they yield in influence and wealth to the *Saiva* branches, especially to the *Atits* [Dasnamis]: hence [i.e., west of Allahabad], however, they predominate, and either by themselves, or their kindred divisions, almost engross the whole of the country along the *Ganges* and *Jamna:* in the district of *Agra,* they alone constitute seven-tenths of the ascetic population. The *Ramanandis* have very numerous votaries, but they are chiefly from the poorer and inferior classes, with the exception of the *Rajaputs* and military *Brahmans,* amongst whom the poetical works of Sur Das and Tulasi Das maintain the pre-eminence of *Rama* and his *Bhakts* [devotees].[63]

One large agricultural community of Bihar that increasingly patronized Vaishnava monks, according to Herbert Hope Risley, the celebrated ethnologist-anthropometrist of the late nineteenth century, were Kurmi peasants. This is a remarkable transformation, given Buchanan's observation eighty years earlier that the vast majority of Kurmis in Bihar looked to Dasnami sanyasis for religious guidance.[64] An important observation made at the end of the nineteenth century by Jogendra Nath Bhattacharya, president of the College of Pandits in Nadia (in Bengal), helps to put these changes in religious-historical perspective: "the Vaishnavas are very fast extending the sphere of their influence, and many of the *Tantrics* [Shaivas and Shaktas] are now espousing Vaishnava tenets in order to have the advantage of enlisting among their followers the low classes that are becoming rich under British rule."[65] That such a process was already under way in the early nineteenth century is suggested by Buchanan's surprised observation that Vaishnava images were installed in a prominent Dasnami math in northern Gorakhpur and were receiving the undivided attention of the gosains there.[66]

These religious transformations may help explain, in turn, the terminological ambiguities that plague any historical discussion of monasticism in the Gangetic north. Perhaps the best example of such ambiguity is the term *gosain* itself, which even in the early nineteenth century had begun to lose its specific Shaiva and Dasnami connotations in the Gangetic core of Bihar and eastern Uttar Pradesh to become a general term denoting sadhus.[67] Prior to 1800, "gosain" in the Gangetic core referred primarily to Dasnami nagas. This continued to be the case in the vicinity of Patna as late as 1810, during Buchanan's visit: describing the mutual enmity felt by monks in the various orders in Patna and Bihar (later Gaya) Districts, he remarked that "the title Gosaing, which the Brahmins of the sect of Vishnu adopt in Bengal, is considered by the followers of Ramananda as highly disgraceful, and as appropriate to the Dasnami-Sannyasis, their most bitter enemies." However, upon heading west from Patna and crossing the Son river, which separated Shahabad from Patna and Bihar (later Gaya) Districts, Buchanan found that the usage of the term gosain began to alter: in the town of Ara, less than ten miles west of the Son, the principal Ramanandi referred to himself as *Gosaing*. As Buchanan moved further west into Gorakhpur, he observed that "here the term Guru is not very commonly used, and that Gosaing is applied as synonymous, and is applied to the sages of all castes and sects." By the close of the nineteenth century, Risley found that the term in Bihar also applied to house-holder Vaishnavas, in addition to being employed as a synonym for bairagi.[68] By 1910 the term gosain had become fully applicable to both Shaivas and Vaishnavas, even in Patna and Gaya Districts. Hence, local subdistrict officers conducting village-by-village surveys in Bihar were describing *thakurbaris,* or Vaishnava temples, erected or inhabited by gosains.[69] However, the term "gosain" also continued to refer to Shaiva monks throughout Gangetic south Bihar, as illustrated by the existence of "a *pucca Shivalay* [brick-built Shiva temple] built by Gosain Bisun Puri 30 years ago at the cost of about Rs. 2000/-."[70] Conversely, there were no references to bairagis having constructed Shaiva temples or tending to Shaiva images in the village notes of Patna, Gaya, and Shahabad Districts; furthermore, the term "bairagi" continued throughout the nineteenth century (and continues today) to refer specifically to Vaishnava sadhus.

Given the increased applicability of the term "gosain" and the general impression among nineteenth-century observers of the spread and dominance of Ramanandis in the Gangetic north, it seems likely that as non-Vaishnava sadhus increasingly adopted Vaishnava tenets or melted into Ramanandi institutions, the terms that had heretofore described those sadhus began to be lose their specific sectarian associations. An additional factor that has already been noted was that in the eighteenth century Ramanandis had gained control of major monastic centers in the Gangetic north, such as Ayodhya; consequently, much of the terminology and religious practices associated with those places would have been absorbed by the Vaishnava newcomers.[71] These explanations, if correct, would imply that the terminological shift would have already begun by the early nineteenth century in regions considered Vaishnava strongholds, and indeed, Buchanan's observation (noted above) on the loose applicability of the term "gosain" in Gorakhpur and, to a lesser extent, Shahabad Districts seems to bear this out. This explanation is further supported by a consideration of the term *atit* (literally, detached) which, in the early nineteenth century, referred specifically to the less orthodox ranks of Dasnamis who made up the vast majority of Shaiva sanyasis in the north.[72] Atits, according to Wilson, were not nearly so strict in their ascetic practices as *dandi* (orthodox) sanyasis, and consequently could engage in business transactions, own property, and officiate as temple priests; many atits, then, would have been far more susceptible to popular religious attitudes than their dandi counterparts. By the late nineteenth century, Risley observed that the term applied both to Vaishnava sadhus and to "degraded" Shaiva sanyasis, which for Risley meant those who had "succumbed to the temptations of the flesh"; meanwhile, William Crooke, who directed the census in Uttar Pradesh, argued that a distinction needed to be drawn between householder (or married, *gharbari*) and sanyasi atits, and that while the latter were generally regarded as Shaiva, they were addressed with the Vaishnava invocation, "*Namo Narayanaya*," or "bow to Narayana."[73] By the mid twentieth century, "atit" (like gosain) had ceased to have a specific Shaiva connotation.[74]

An unfortunate consequence of this growing terminological imprecision is that it renders useless from the ascetic perspective much of the strictly quantitative data generated by the colonial censuses of the late 1800s and early 1900s. This is because far more individuals in Patna District referred to themselves in the 1891 census as gosain (3,438) and atit (1,218) than as bairagi (546) or sanyasi (621); likewise a decade later, in the 1901 and 1911 censuses for Patna District, there were many more gosains than atits, bairagis, and sanyasis combined.[75] Shahabad District, by contrast, showed large returns (around 7,000) for atits in all three censuses, on average nearly three times that of all other sadhus combined. In addition, the population figures referring to one or another ascetic identity were highly aberrant over the three censuses in Bengal province (which included Bihar), rendering any interpretation virtually impossible. Indeed, so pronounced were the aberrations in the first large-scale British-Indian census in 1872 that census officials decided to omit the returns for the relative numbers of "various religious sects" in the province of Bengal.[76] The situation had not improved even by the 1911 census, the director of which noted that "it was decided not to attempt to obtain a record of Hindu sects, previous experience having shewn that the results are so inaccurate or incomplete as to be of little or no statistical value."[77]

The interpretive problems were particularly pronounced in Bihar, and one source of confusion for census officials there may well have been the general terminological fluidity noted above, which in all likelihood enabled sadhus to refer to themselves in a variety of ways depending on the phrasing of census inquiries regarding identity.[78] Another factor that would have further complicated the task of interpreting the aggregate data was the very size and diversity of the province of Bengal, which until 1912 included the culturally distinct regions of Bihar, Bengal, and Orissa. Though those regions possessed a shared religious vocabulary, that vocabulary did not necessarily refer to comparable religious phenomena. The situation was less complex to the west, in Uttar Pradesh, which was not only more homogeneous culturally but, especially in the western plain between Banaras and Agra, predominantly Vaishnava.[79] However, as we shall see in the next chapter, by the early twentieth century the Vaishnava ascendancy over sectarian rivals was of less significance than internal distinctions among Vaishnavas themselves, particularly among Ramanandis.

Religion and Social Change

For the historian, religion cannot not be understood independently of status and the social order, however these are expressed. Thus far I have concentrated on the social dimensions of monastic sampraday in the Gangetic core as revealed in Vaishnava and Shaiva soldiering prior to the nineteenth century, in the religious networks described by Buchanan in the early nineteenth century, and in random observations up to 1900. My primary aim here has been to describe the presence of a Vaishnava reform-mindedness in the Gangetic north, rooted in the greater social openness and broader socioreligious vision evident in the Ramanandi sampraday as compared with the other major monastic communities. My discussion reflects approaches to social relations either implicit in religious tradition (particularly with regard to monastic soldiering) or, more particularly, explicit in the opinions articulated by gurus, particularly in Buchanan's accounts. Hence, thus far, the discussion reflects the views of sadhus. By contrast, it is much more difficult to discern for this period—even in Buchanan's rich prose—the opinions that low-status people (whether shudra or untouchable) may have held on issues of status, religious identity, and monastic recruitment. As we shall see more clearly in chapter 2, sadhus were often self-conscious social actors, accustomed to offering guidance based on their worldviews and to having their opinions solicited and registered with care. By contrast, the opinions of shudras and untouchables (whether cultivators, artisans, or laborers) were generally unsolicited, and as a result their voices were not heard—at least, not until the early twentieth century when, abruptly, many erstwhile shudras emerged as able social activists and vociferous articulators of kshatriya (and decidedly non-shudra) status.

I take up in detail that early twentieth-century "kshatriya reform" history and historiography, and the ways in which it drew on and intersected with the religious institutions in the Gangetic north, in chapters 3 and 4. However, it is important to note here a key element of those chapters so as to place the present discussion in broader perspective. The success of kshatriya reform movements depended on the ability of popular intellectuals (who, in most cases, were not sadhus) to initiate new kinds of religious discussions as a basis for social change. Kshatriya reform did, at times, benefit from the intellectual contributions of individual sadhus and, more frequently, from the authoritative opinions of prominent swamis recorded in regional publications. However, it did not depend upon the leadership of monks or even the active complicity of monastic institutions. The fact that peasant and artisan intellectuals could initiate a religious discourse to advance a specific social agenda meant that religion for them (the intellectuals, if not all peasants and artisans) had become, at some fundamental level, a more private affair, and that the sadhu either as holy man or as guru and counselor was no longer as crucial a component of popular religious life. This should not, I would argue, be taken to signify the decline of monasticism in north Indian peasant life as such. However, the increasing "laicization of religion" should be understood as one among several challenges facing Indian monasticism, particularly after the middle of the twentieth century.[80]

CHAPTER 2

Ramanand and Ramanandis, ca. 1900–1940

> *Don't ask about caste.*
> *If you love God, you belong to God.*
> —attributed to Ramanand,
> ca. 1350

Sectarian traditions associated with precolonial Vaishnava and Shaiva soldiering and, more particularly, colonial sources describing monasticism in the nineteenth century confirm that the history of monasticism reflected social and ideological change in north Indian society. Likewise Ramanandi hagiography, read carefully, can reveal a great deal about popular ideological change in the Gangetic north, both within and without monastic life. This was true in the fourteenth century, when Ramanand is believed to have uttered the words quoted above; it continued to be true in the early 1600s, when Nabhadas listed in the *Bhaktamal* ("the garland of devotees") the five brahman men, the two women, the kshatriya prince, the weaver, the cobbler, the peasant, and the barber who represented the first generation of Ramanand's disciples.[1] However, of fundamental importance to present-day Ramanandi identities are the first four decades of the twentieth century—and in particular the years 1918–1921, when "radical" Ramanandis decided to reject any institutional monastic connection between Ramanand and Ramanuja, the twelfth-century theologian of south India who had long been regarded as the originator of Vaishnava bhakti and, hence, a prominent figure in Ramanandi tradition. Needless to say, the Ramanandi

48

conception of Ramanand would undergo fundamental, and controversial, change as a result of this decision. This chapter examines the ideological debates in the early twentieth century that occasioned this new vision of Ramanand, and the social and historiographical causes and consequences of those debates.[2] The object is to bring the social and ideological dimensions of twentieth-century Ramanandi egalitarianism into better focus.

On the margin of Ramanandi history there has existed an ongoing European and American historiography of Indian religious belief, which has occasionally, though unevenly, touched on Ramanand and Ramanandis. Though this historiography has not yet altered in any substantial way the trajectories of ideological change in Gangetic society, it has on occasion come into sharp focus in the eyes of monks and lay devotees. This point was reinforced for me recently (18 October 1994) in Jaipur: while we were discussing the role of the Galta *pith* (religious center) in the history of Vaishnava soldiering in the eighteenth century, the Galta mahant's eldest son and heir apparent to the mahantship, Avadesh Kumar Mishra, suddenly produced copies of two articles, Peter van der Veer's "Taming the Ascetic" and Richard Burghart's "Founding of the Ramanandi Sect." The pages were worn and the margins full of handwritten commentary. We proceeded to discuss the contents of both articles for over an hour; Burghart's piece was of particular interest to Avadesh Kumar Mishra, since (as we shall see in the pages below) it contains arguments that implicitly favor the Ramanuji side (favored by Galta) of a debate that began in 1918 and continues to influence the structure of the Ramanandi sampraday.

It is appropriate, then, to begin this chapter on the historiographical margin, by way of introducing the interpretive dilemmas occasioned by the study of Ramanand and Ramanandis, for academics as well as monks.

Ramanand Obscured

Notwithstanding the importance of the Ramanandi sampraday as the largest Vaishnava monastic order in north India (and perhaps the largest monastic community, Shaiva or Vaishnava, in India), Ramanand and Ramanandis have gradually receded from the pages of historical scholarship on India. One reason is an increasing scholarly interest in the *sant* tradition, since about 1400 an important literary-*cum*-religious movement in north India that until recently was regarded as the heir to Ramanand's broadly articulated *bhakti-sadhna* message of "disciplined love for god."[3] Indeed, it can be argued that the increasing interest in sant studies has pushed Ramanand and Ramanandis into the background.[4] Guru Nanak is included among the sants, as are several figures claimed by Ramanandis as members of Ramanand's original circle of disciples, most notably Ravidas and Kabir. Sants are bound to each other in the clarity of scholarly hindsight by a disdain for brahmanical knowledge and ritual, an outspoken disregard for idols and images, and a dedication to egalitarian poetic verse—all of which lends to the study of sant literature a distinctly counter-elitist, folk-culture appeal.[5] In addition, many scholars have been drawn to the uncompromising criticism of caste hierarchy common to sant rhetoric, not to mention the "low-caste" origins of most sant practicioners.[6] Also a factor is the chronological implausibility of Ramanand's life when viewed from the perspective of his main sant disciples. Charlotte Vaudeville, a pioneer in the field of sant literary and historical scholarship, calculated that Ramanand "would have had to live more than 118 years in order to be the real Guru of all the twelve disciples" attributed to him.[7] The consensus among sant scholars today is that later sant traditions created a guru-disciple link with Ramanand in order to afford the sant poets greater social and political respectability.

However, the relative paucity of scholarship on Ramanand must also stem from the mixed social and political message sent by his life, as it is remembered. As both a Sanskrit-educated brahman and a Vaishnava-bhakti visionary, Ramanand is believed by many to have occupied an important and neglected space between two competing "Hinduisms": one composed of sophisticated pandits, the other of radical poets. For Indologists reared on the basic structural oppositions of caste hierarchy, the difficult question is, can one life occupy both ends of the spectrum? So little of a reliable nature is known about Ramanand that the question cannot be answered with certainty. The multiple and seemingly contradictory meanings of this important life, in addition to the relative lack of "hard" biographical data regarding it, have inspired one scholar to cast doubt on Ramanand's authorship of the famous verse discounting caste and to argue that Ramanand did not intend at all for a community, or sampraday, to gather around him and his message.[8] Indeed it would require little in the way of argumentation to suggest further that Ramanand never even existed but was conjured up by monks at a much later date to satisfy a drive for brahmanical respectability within the order. With the thorny problem of Ramanand out of the way, it would be much easier to understand Indian social and cultural history as an ideological struggle ranged above an uncompromising caste divide. But Ramanand, shadowy and mystifying though he may be, has been kept alive by the force of Ramanandi tradition, although that tradition itself has undergone dramatic change.[9]

Ramanand tends to be eclipsed in particular by Kabir and Ravidas, two figures who from the Ramanandi point of view were among Ramanand's inner circle of disciples and whose ideologically potent verse, therefore, finds frequent expression in Ramanandi tradition. Kabir and Ravidas flourished in the fifteenth and early sixteenth centuries and are remembered for the steadfast challenge they posed to the very idea of varna and jati as systems of human classification. Based on the rhetorical structure of his verse, Kabir appears to have hurled his invective from a self-imposed perch well beyond the social system; Ravidas, by contrast, spoke from deep within society, focusing on his own lowly status as a cobbler to better apprehend and articulate the injustices of varna.[10] Kabir questioned the very foundations upon which varna and jati rested, entreating the learned brahman to "look in your heart for knowledge. Tell me where untouchability came from, since you believe in it."[11] He assaulted the sensibilities, interspersing direct insults with stark depictions of the blunt corporeality of human existence and thereby entering into an immediate and passionate dialogue with the listener.[12] Kabir's object was to lay bare human conceits, which he did by aiming sharply worded barbs at the brahman pandits who thronged the steps leading down to the Ganga in Banaras or at lecturing *qazis* (scholars of *sharia,* or Islamic law), comfortably ensconced among legal tomes. Though Ravidas did not utilize invective and shock tactics to make his point, he nonetheless urged his listeners, in a passage reminiscent of Ramanand's couplet, to "ask not about caste,. . . . What is there in clan or caste? Brahmin, Kshatriya, Vaishya, and Shudra, all belong to the same caste."[13] He insisted, "A family that has a true follower of the Lord is neither high caste nor low caste, lordly or poor."[14]

The followers of Kabir and Ravidas who do not consider themselves Ramanandis have used varying strategies to pursue their goal of a more equal and just society. For example, there is the wide discrepancy between the original message of Kabir and the methods of his present-day devotees, noted by David Lorenzen: "The songs of Kabir himself display such a militant iconoclasm that it is quite consistent to assume that he meant to break with both Islam and Hinduism and establish an independent religious tradition. His followers, however, seem to have soon brought their sect into the orbit of non-caste Hinduism."[15] By "non-caste Hinduism" Lorenzen means to evoke a religious strategy that accepts "many of the behavioral forms or structures of caste Hinduism while at the same time infusing them with an ideological content that is in direct opposition to basic socioreligious values characteristic of caste Hinduism."[16] While Kabir's present-day followers ultimately embrace varna, then, they manipulate it to suit the social needs of their own shudra and untouchable constituents. The full historical irony of this doctrinal-behavioral strategy was particularly evident in Patna during the 1987 all-India conference of the Kabirpanth. Notwithstanding the strident anti-varna pronouncements of modern-day Kabirpanthis, this conference was held under the auspices of the national headquarters of the *Yadava Mahasabha*, the political heir to the Yadav-kshatriya movement of the pre-1947 era and currently a major caste organization deeply involved in state and national politics.[17]

But while the followers of Kabir seemed to have moderated his radical anti-establishment message, a process of radicalization seems to have occurred among followers of Ravidas. The modern *Chamar* (untouchable leatherworker) followers of that sant have developed a clear social agenda and are in no way reluctant to seek reform openly. A Chamar leader of Lucknow struck a militant pose by reinterpreting Ravidas as among those who "demolished the philosophical fort of the Brahman's culture by denouncing unequivocally the distinctions of caste, sect, sex, and special privileges, and by downgrading sacrificial rituals, temples, and bibliolatry."[18] Similarly, today's Chamars of Shri Govardhanpur, on the southernmost edge of Banaras, "have no intention of accepting their lot as if it were decreed by fate or religion" and have been working since 1967 to erect a large Ravi Dasi temple in the hope that "their four-story edifice will rival temples in other sectors of the city and become a familiar part of the pilgrims' circuit."[19]

Though it is a much larger, wealthier, more powerful, and socially more mainstream monastic community, attitudes in the Ramanandi sampraday bear striking similarity to the modern ideologies espoused by the Ravidasi and Kabirpanthi communities, no doubt because of the importance of both Ravidas and Kabir to Ramanandi tradition. Indeed, the disagreements that would come to divide the sampraday after 1918 indicate that many Ramanandis believed that Ramanand—presaging Kabir—had intended all along to destroy the edifice of caste through concentrated polemic and vitriolic attack; others depicted Ramanand—like Ravidas—as a saint who rose above the injustices of caste and sought its atrophy through disuse. Ranged against them, however, was a strong subgroup of Ramanandis who felt that there was a place for both religious and social hierarchy within the sampraday—that some sadhus, by virtue of their sectarian pedigree, were "purer" and worthy of greater respect than others, and that some sadhus, by virtue of their caste background prior to entering the sampraday, were deserving of better treatment in the monastic community.

The Ramanandi Past: Hagiography, Lineage, and Doctrine

Ramanand is today held by Ramanandis to have been an avatar of Ramchandra, the god-king of epic Ayodhya, returned to earth to rescue Hinduism from the corrupting effects of human divisiveness. The institutional centrality of Ramanand has long been reflected in the *guru parampara* (preceptor lineage) that connects every Ramanandi through an unbroken succession of gurus with Ramanand himself and, eventually, Ramchandra. The details and meanings of Ramanand's life, which were the subject of heated controversy in 1918–1921, emerge from commentaries on the *Bhaktamal,* a verse compendium describing important devotees authored by Nabhadas, himself a Ramanandi, in the early seventeenth century.[20]

The beginning of the twentieth century did not mark the first time Ramanandi memory was hauled up for inspection, and a review of an earlier controversy confirms that efforts to manipulate the institutional memory of Ramanand reflects changing attitudes toward caste in the sampraday. According to orthodox Ramanandi tradition, an important gathering of Vaishnavas took place in the Galta region of Jaipur in the early 1700s, the ostensible purpose of which was to organize a defense against attacks by Shaiva gosains.[21] The less-heralded agenda was the elevation of Ramanand to a level equal to that of Ramanuja, the twelfth-century Tamil theologian long considered the founder of Vaishnava bhakti, in north Indian Vaishnavism, and the delimitation of thirty-six legitimate "gateways" through which a Ramanandi could claim a guru-disciple link to Ramanuja.[22] Those thirty-six gateways descended only through the twice-born (i.e., brahman, kshatriya, and vaishya) male disciples of Ramanand and excluded his shudra, untouchable, and female disciples. Though the latter (including, importantly, Kabir and Ravidas) were still considered followers of Ramanand, they "lost their role as a transmitter or preceptor of the tradition"; their disciples, in turn, who may have considered themselves Ramanandis, "now found themselves outside the Ramanandi sect." Nevertheless, "other genealogies indicate that male and female Hindus of servant [shudra] and untouchable birth were still being admitted into the Ramanandi sect"—and, hence, that the corporeal fact of being shudra, untouchable, or female was not what offended Ramanandis in the early 1700s, but the staunch anticaste ideology articulated by those "tainted" members of Ramanand's inner circle.[23] Thus while prior to Galta Ramanandis may have denied outright the relevance of caste (not to mention gender) distinctions, after Galta they moved toward an ambiguous ideological position: they chose to "recognise the category of caste but adopt an entirely neutral attitude toward it with reference to their sectarian recruitment."[24]

In addition to ushering in what was the first major ideological transformation in the Ramanandi sampraday, the Galta meeting also represented the historical context for the composition of the first major addition to the Bhaktamal, entitled *Bhaktirasbodhinitika* and authored by Priyadas in 1712.[25] Priyadas would add 634 verses to the extant 214-verse Bhaktamal, and his work would be included with almost all subsequent commentaries.[26] His substantive contribution was to append the miraculous legends that have become commonplace today concerning many important figures in Nabhadas's Bhaktamal, including Tulsidas, Mirabai, Kabir, Ravidas, and, of course, Ramanand.[27] This process of hagiographical accretion continued into the nineteenth and twentieth centuries, particularly after 1918 when a group of sadhus from Ayodhya would take up, once again, the question of Ramanand's relationship to Ramanuja.

In the nineteenth century, however, a major change would take place in the way Ramanandis (indeed, all Indians) communicated religious tradition, which in itself may have contributed to (and certainly shaped the logistics of) the unfolding of the 1918–1921 controversy. This change was manifest in the printing press, which was gradually popularized throughout north India in the latter half of the nineteenth century.[28] The result of this popularization, I would argue, was an increasing doctrinal self-consciousness among literate Ramanandis, and a hagiographical text as central as the Bhaktamal would not be immune to such a process.[29] The rendering of the verse and commentary of the Bhaktamal into a form accessible to early twentieth-century Vaishnavas would have been a task that required constant oral exposition. In the major Vaishnava establishments throughout the Gangetic region, Ramanandi scholars were thus constantly engaged in exegesis of the Bhaktamal as a matter of experiencing and expressing faith, guiding lay Vaishnavas and young Ramanandis, and articulating a universal moral code. The relatively autonomous nature of those establishments had meant (prior to the arrival of printing presses) that local exegeses of the Bhaktamal hagiography could conflict and still not threaten the overall ideological integrity of the sampraday.

By the nineteenth century, however, with the spread of presses throughout the Gangetic north, this was increasingly no longer the case. A widely known commentary of the Bhaktamal was a Persian manuscript by Tulsiram, entitled *Bhaktamalpradipan* (Bhaktamal illuminations). Tulsiram was a highly esteemed rasik Ramanandi scholar of Ambala, a sizable town north of Delhi in what is now the state of Haryana. Two important Hindi translations of Tulsiram's commentary were published in 1867, marking in all likelihood the first time this text had been rendered in multiple copies by a printing press. One translation, by Hari Baksh Ray, was produced fairly close to Tulsiram's home in the town of Solma.[30] The other translation (with minor additions), done by Pratap Sinha of Muzaffarpur District in north Bihar and entitled *Bhaktakalpadrum* (or, the tree of devotees), was so popular that by 1874 a third edition had been issued by the respected Naval Kishore Press of Lucknow; by 1952 a twelfth edition was published by its offspring, the Tejkumar Press.[31] The next major Bhaktamal commentary to emerge, entitled *Shri Bhaktamal: Tika, Tilak, aur Namavali Sahit* and authored by Sitaramsharan Bhagvan Prasad (a nephew of Tulsiram) in 1903, would be reissued several times.[32] The cumulative effect of the appearance in print of multiple Bhaktamal editions must have been dramatic—not because of any partisanship Bhagvan Prasad, Tulsiram, or any other scholar-devotees may have evinced on the issue of Ramanand's identity, but because the representations and interpretations of Ramanand's life could now not only confront one another in print but, inevitably, would encounter the variety of local, unpublished interpretation.

Of the three published Bhaktamal commentaries just noted, the most recent—Bhagvan Prasad's—would increasingly be regarded as the most authoritative. Bhagvan Prasad was a well-known Ramanandi scholar-devotee and a resident of Kanak Bhavan in Ayodhya, an influential rasik establishment. He was also deeply engaged in the British-Indian intellectual exchange of the late nineteenth and early twentieth centuries, and his treatment of the life of Ramanand reflected this intellectual milieu, right down to his textual critique of nineteenth-century British scholarship.[33] Bhagvan Prasad's account relied for the most part on earlier versions of the Bhaktamal, including especially another Persian-language version by Tapasviram entitled *Ramuze Mihovafa*.[34] Tapasviram (1815–1885) was Bhagvan Prasad's father and Tulsiram's brother.[35] Hence, Bhagvan Prasad was in all likelihood regarded as the scion of north India's first family of Bhaktamal exegesis. In addition to drawing on his family's expertise, however, Bhagvan Prasad cited a Hindi document entitled *Shri Ramanand Yashavali* [The eminent renown of Ramanand], which was said to be based on a portion of the *Agastyasamhita* that detailed events said to be destined to occur in the future—thereby lending the account an unimpeachable Sanskrit, Vaishnava authority.[36] It is likely that the details of Ramanand's life as depicted in Bhagvan Prasad's commentary (given below) derived primarily from this latter source, since his version conforms in all particulars to that given in a Hindi translation of the *Agastyasamhita* by one Ram Narayan Das in 1904, rendered in English by R. G. Bhandarkar in *Vaishnavism, Saivism, and Minor Religious Systems* in 1913.[37]

What emerged as a result of Bhagvan Prasad's exegetical labors was a critical examination of the fundamentals of Ramanandi tradition, an account of a life of unparalleled importance that tried to reconcile a variety of proto-doctrinal opinions through exhaustive scholarship. Was Bhagvan Prasad conscious of the cultural and historical import of his work? Certainly he understood its significance as a document of sampraday record. It is for this reason that he began the text with what he called *Shri Vaishnava Namavali*, a list of 108 prominent Vaishnavas throughout the central Gangetic region. The Namavali is more than just a list, however, for it supplements names, dates, and places with a confirmation of each individual's contribution to the sampraday. It represented a way of commemorating the breadth of Ramanandi achievement, both geographically and intellectually; it also allowed Bhagvan Prasad to express his own personal religious roots within the Ramanandi universe.

Bhagvan Prasad's account of the life of Ramanand spans approximately eighteen pages.[38] It begins with the list of twenty-two gurus, starting with Ramanuja, who is referred to here only as "*shri 108 swami*," and ending with Ramanand, whose name is preceded by the phrase, "*ananta shri bhagvan*," or eternal God.[39] This represented what would have been the generally agreed upon (if not official) spiritual lineage of Ramanand and therefore was a crucial element of Ramanandi guru parampara in the early twentieth century. Ramanand's immediate guru was Raghavanand, who, in addition to being accorded the honorific "shri 108," is given the suffix *acharya,* or virtuous leader. The reader is told that prior to meeting Ramanand, Raghavanand (whose name, like Ramanand's, can be translated as "bliss in God") gathered about him a multitude of devotees and traveled the length and breadth of India, finally settling in Kashi (Varanasi), where he became a well-known teacher and "initiated people from all four varna [brahman, kshatriya, vaishya, shudra] and four *ashrami* [student, householder, retiree, and ascetic] as fervent devotees of *Ram.*" This phrase is significant because Raghavanand's varna-blind guru style emerges as a precursor to Ramanand's own, for which the latter is so famed.[40] Bhagvan Prasad then goes on to remark that Ramchandra became manifest as a disciple to Raghavanand in the avatar form of Ramanand. "In this manner," he continued, "the glory of the auspicious path of Shri 108 Ramanuja spread and continues to spread like nectar all over earth."[41] The next five-and-a-half pages focus on the great significance of Ramchandra's decision to descend to earth in the body of Ramanand, the description of which repeatedly employs the metaphor of a "bridge spanning the ocean of the world of mundane existence"; to the twelve main disciples of Ramanand, plus an additional two, Galabanand and Yoganand; and to a chart that lists the deities that took up residence in each of the bodies of these disciples. Five further pages trace Ramanand's birth and childhood, and, most importantly, the circumstances of his discipleship to Raghavanand, which led ultimately to the creation of the Ramanandi sampraday as a distinct body of devotees. Bhagvan Prasad encapsulates the essentials of that account as follows:

Ramanand (originally Ramadatta) was born into a respectable kanyakubja brahman household in Prayag in 1300. He began schooling at the age of four and proved to be such a promising student that by the time he was eight there was nothing more the scholars of Prayag could teach him. At the age of twelve he took up residence in Kashi, where he became the student of an [unnamed] dandi sanyasi and lived according to *smarta* doctrine.[42] He one day encountered Raghavanand in Kashi, who immediately foresaw his destiny and prophesied that young Ramadatta's body was on the verge of expiration, and therefore urged him to take refuge in *Hari* (Vishnu). Ramadatta referred the details of Raghavanand's outburst to his dandi sanyasi guru, who confirmed the prophecy but could offer no remedy. The sanyasi

therefore urged Ramadatta to save himself ["protect your body"] by taking refuge with the great seer [i.e., Raghavanand]. The youth went to Raghavanand, prostrated before him, and said, "*hé* great master, consider this body
and soul an offering and protect it in this world and the next." Having performed the initiatory mantras and bestowed the name Ramanand upon him,
Raghavanand then instructed his new disciple in the techniques of controlled
breathing [*pranayama*] and deep meditation, so that when death [*kal*] came
to spirit Ramanand away, he appeared already corpse-like. Ramanand eventually emerged from this death-like trance chanting the "shri mantra" and
immediately became absorbed in serving his new guru.[43]

At this juncture, Bhagvan Prasad remarked that Ramanand's yogic abilities were only to be expected, inasmuch as "he is himself in reality the
avatar of the great master [i.e., Ramchandra]; in any event [he contin-
ues], this is all a big *lila* [sport] and therefore proper."[44] Bhagvan Prasad's
comment here seems gauged to forestall the criticism that an avatar of
god should not have to suffer such human frailties as mortality and waste
meditative effort in cosmic subterfuge. Bhagvan Prasad then took special pains to point out the circular elegance of Ramanand, the very image of god, going about his menial duties as a disciple to Raghavanand,
who is depicted in the same breath as both guru and devotee of Ramanand. The author picks up the thread of Ramanand's life at a later
date: "Ramanand then undertook a series of long pilgrimages that led
him all over the subcontinent. Upon returning to Kashi, Ramanand approached Raghavanand to perform the appropriate ritual guru *darshan*
[literally, viewing] of reunion. Ramanand's codisciples meanwhile had
been demanding that Raghavanand punish Ramanand for having not paid
close enough attention to commensal restrictions while away on pilgrimage.[45] Raghavanand perforce ordered Ramanand to "go forth and
propagate your own sampraday."

One or two points need to be emphasized here. First, Bhagvan
Prasad's edition of the Bhaktamal should be understood not simply as
a scholarly tour-de-force and a concrete example of deep faith, but as a
commemoration, indeed celebration, of the Ramanandi sampraday.[46] At
the heart of that commemoration lay the divine figure of Ramchandra
as lived through the avatar Ramanand. This important life is thus retold
as *lila,* cosmic sport, an expository mode that allows the narrator to reconcile Ramanand's godliness with the all-too-human predicaments in
which he finds himself. Indeed, such predicaments are an essential part
of lila, because they allow the audience to elicit human meaning from
the behavior of gods on earth; were gods to refrain from becoming mortal and engaging in human activity, with mortal circumstances, lila would

lose the inner logic that fuels it—hence the epic, heart-wrenching tale of Ramchandra exiled from Ayodhya and beset by the forces of evil. Ramanand is thus presented not only as a disciple in a religious community that descends from Ramanuja, but is portrayed as a humble student in performance of *guru-seva* (service). The crucial moment of the lila, of course, occurs when Ramanand is expelled from the discipleship of Raghavanand and the guru-brotherhood of his codisciples, an event that then enables him to complete the drama by creating the Ramanandi sampraday. Nothing in this account would have appeared problematic to Bhagvan Prasad, who in 1908 traced his own guru parampara back through forty-two generations of discipleship to Ramchandra of Ayodhya; in this parampara, Ramanuja was tenth in descent and Ramanand thirtieth.[47] It would, however, prove offensive to a younger generation of Ramanandis a decade later.

Other Ramanands

Varying conceptions of Ramanandi *parampara* (tradition) both prior and subsequent to Bhagvan Prasad's Bhaktamal commentary in the first decade of the twentieth century suggest that ambiguity on the question of Ramanand's life tended to be the rule rather than the exception, a fact that enabled Ramanand to be all things to all Ramanandis. That this was no longer the case by 1918 is evidenced by the rancorous dispute that erupted over a new Ramanandi ideological orthodoxy that conceived of Ramanand as entirely independent of Ramanuja. The versions of Ramanand's life that I present in brief below have in common a Ramanand that hails not from Prayag, the heartland of the Gangetic north, but from the peninsular south. First among these is a highly rudimentary biographical sequence that had been dictated to Francis Buchanan in the early nineteenth century during his tour of South Bihar. This version, as told by Jagannath Das, a Ramanandi of wide renown in Bihar and a main informant of Buchanan regarding Ramanandis, described Ramanand as a *Dravira,* or south Indian, brahman and disciple of Vedant Acharya, a Ramanuji and also a southerner. Though Jagannath Das understood Ramanand as fundamentally important to his own religious identity, Ramanand was nevertheless an intermediate link in a religious tradition that began with Ramanuja five or six guru-generations earlier.[48]

Over a century after Buchanan's tour a different version of Ramanand's life appeared in the *Journal of the Royal Asiatic Society*, authored by the well-known missionary and Indologist, J. N. Farquhar.[49] Farquhar began his 1920 consideration of the life of Ramanand by acknowledging his good fortune at having the opportunity to attend the *kumbh mela*, India's largest pilgrimage festival, at Allahabad (Prayag) in 1918, where he met with many Ramanandis, including no doubt some younger sadhus who would soon lead the call for a new, more stringent Ramanandi tradition. Based on encounters with Ramanandis at the Prayag kumbh, Farquhar theorized that Ramanand was a south Indian who migrated northward around 1430, took up residence in Kashi, and flourished there until about 1470.[50] Notwithstanding this southern connection, which he would eventually abandon in any case, Farquhar contended that Ramanand was completely unconnected to Ramanuja or any Ramanuji gurus, but acknowledged that he nevertheless borrowed liberally from the qualified monism of Ramanuja; only in later generations would Ramanandis and Ramanujis begin to associate with each other because of the proximity of their philosophical doctrines.[51]

By 1920, of course, the question of Ramanand had already erupted into a full-blown controversy within the Ramanandi community itself, and the issue of the *Journal of the Royal Asiatic Society*, which no doubt was as closely read in Allahabad, Banaras, and Patna as in London, was sure to spark many responses. That of Rai Bahadur Lala Sita Ram is of particular importance, because of an extensive correspondence he carried on with the eminent linguist and Indologist Sir George Grierson from about 1904 until the mid 1930s.[52] Sita Ram was a retired magistrate and deputy collector of Uttar Pradesh who became associated with Allahabad University and eventually authored the definitive, Vaishnava history of Ayodhya.[53] In a letter sent to Grierson at the end of June 1920, Sita Ram expressed his strong objections to several points in Farquhar's essay and offered a number of corrections to it, arguing in no uncertain terms that Ramanand was originally a guru in the Ramanuji tradition who later branched off to develop his own teachings of boundless love that refused to countenance the narrow-mindedness of caste and ritual.[54] Interestingly, however, Sita Ram raised no objection to Farquhar's original contention that Ramanand was a brahman from the south. Grierson received this particular correspondence two years after his essay on "Ramanandi, Ramawat" for the *Encyclopaedia of Religion and Ethics*. Nevertheless, the imprint of Sita Ram's Ramanandi views on the social implications of Ramanand's bhakti tenacity, along with Bhagvan Prasad's Bhaktamal-derived narrative of Ramanand's life, emerge clearly in Grierson's article.[55]

The representations of Ramanand by Grierson and Sita Ram on the one hand and by Farquhar on the other reflect the determination of each party to offer a complete and static view of a Ramanandi sampraday that was in reality experiencing the throes of dramatic change. Grierson and Sita Ram's Ramanand was a disenchanted Ramanuji who tried to span the caste divisions of fourteenth-century Gangetic society with a message of love and equality. Farquhar's Ramanand, by contrast, was completely independent of the Ramanujis; Farquhar even argued, based both on his experience with Ramanandis and on his perception of the orthodoxy of a number of prominent "medieval" disciples, that "there is no evidence that [Ramanand] modified the social rules of caste in the slightest."[56] In retrospect, Farquhar's presentation of the historical question of Ramanand reflects his attempt to reconcile the many different (and often conflicting) opinions he must have encountered during his discussions with Ramanandi sadhus at the 1918 kumbh. Grierson, by contrast, left India in the mid 1890s; his presentation of Ramanand's life, therefore, reflects his connections with an older generation of Ramanandi scholars in closer contact with colonial officialdom, such as Lala Sita Ram and Sitaramsharan Bhagvan Prasad, the Bhaktamal exegete.[57]

These local variations on the theme of Ramanand's life were no doubt supplemented by numerous others through the course of the nineteenth century, versions that differed not only in relatively minor details but on the overarching question of Ramanuja. The variety and fluidity of parampara in the pre-1918 phase serves to highlight again the most salient organizational feature of the sampraday, namely, the many-centered nature of Ramanandi authority. A product of the constantly shifting fortunes of powerful monasteries in local settings, this diffuse populism meant that the only opportunity for reconciliation of ideological differences (and perhaps the only occasion that required any reconciliation) in the sampraday occurred approximately once every three years on the occasion of the kumbh mela (held by turns in Nasik, Ujjain, Allahabad, or Haridwar)—and then only among those sadhus who chose to attend.

The Rise of Radical Ramanandis

The quest for power and influence in the Ramanandi sampraday took place on the ground of the past, and those best able to ne-

gotiate that ground ultimately dictated the immediate social and political dimensions of the monastic community. The major transformation
in the institutional memory of the sampraday occurred between 1918
and 1921: an extended moment, focused on Ayodhya in what is now
eastern Uttar Pradesh, but concluded at the Ujjain kumbh in what is
now western Madhya Pradesh. The events of 1918–1921 extended thus
to the southwesternmost edge of the Hindi-speaking north, to Malwa,
the Vindhya Range, and the headwaters of the Chambal River—a region that represents for many the border between south and north India. The location of Ujjain was geoculturally appropriate for the denouement of the crisis, given the implications of the debate for southern
influences in the Ramanandi sampraday. While the object in the early
1700s in Galta was to elevate the status of Ramanand vis-à-vis Ramanuja
while restricting the entry of radical anti-varna sentiment into the sampraday, the motive in 1918–1921 seems to have been to loosen that social stricture by making Ramanand altogether supreme and eliminating
all mention of Ramanuja.

Though Ramanand's divine status was practically assumed by Ramanandis at the turn of the century (at least, judging by Bhagvan Prasad's
Bhaktamal commentary), by 1918 a group of Ramanandis rejected vehemently the possibility that Ramanand was a member of someone else's
(i.e., Ramanuja's) sampraday and insisted instead that he single-handedly founded the order. At stake, it was argued, was Ramanand's position as the unequivocal proponent of Vaishnava *bhakti* (love for god) in
the north, an issue that naturally would have some bearing on his status
as the originator of the sampraday that took his name. However, while
many conceded that Ramanand was an important link in the descent of
Shri Vaishnava belief, they held Ramanuja to be the original earthly fount
of knowledge and devotion.[58] Conversely, the radical Ramanandi element could stomach no presentation of Ramanand that compromised
in any way his complete and total control over his own destiny and the
destiny of his religious community. I favor the term "radical" to describe
these sadhus because they chose to elevate a core article of faith to force
a reconstituted Ramanandi memory. The radical position demanded either allegiance or refutation: a Vaishnava was either a *Ramanuji* or a Ramanandi. Those who chose to retain the Ramanuja link—regardless of
their opinion regarding Ramanand's divinity—found themselves accused
of opposing the avatar status of Ramanand and were labeled (and stigmatized) accordingly. After 1921 both sides would seek the moral high
ground by claiming the appellation "Shri Vaishnava."

Much of the resentment on the part of this new radical element stemmed from the association of Ramanuja and Ramanuji-oriented Vaishnavas with elitist attitudes and commensal practices. For instance, Shivnandan Sahay (Bhagvan Prasad's first biographer) noted in 1908 that among the many differences between Ramanujis and Ramanandis, the former "only allow initiation to brahmans and kshatriyas."[59] In fact, such attitudes were not new. As noted earlier in the discussion of the Galta conference in the early 1700s, there had been a long-standing desire among elements within the order to limit (or at least control the ideological effects of) the entry of low-status individuals. We noted in the previous chapter as well the presence of elitist pockets in the Ramanandi sampraday in the early nineteenth century: Buchanan had observed in 1812 that though the terms Ramanandi and Ramawat were "applicable to either Brahman or Sudra, and in general both live together and are called Avadhut . . . , some Brahmans affect superior purity, will not eat with the Sudras, and are called Acharyas."[60] (By 1918 the term *acharya*, which refers to a person of virtuous conduct, would come to be associated with Ramanuji elements in the sampraday; by contrast, *das*, which means servant or slave, was symbolic of one's Ramanandi status.) Finally, it may be noted that the perceived elitism of Ramanuji circles in the north was generally consistent with the historian Burton Stein's conclusions (albeit for an earlier period) regarding the marked "Brahman-dominated Hindu orthodoxy" of south Indian Shri Vaishnava institutions, especially at Tirupati and Srirangam, which prohibited the infiltration of shudras.[61]

While social and religious elitism was not a new phenomenon in the sampraday, the emergence of a widespread and coordinated opposition to that elitism was. In retrospect, one early indication that a major shift in attitudes was in the air may have been evident in the 1911 census returns for religious sect in Uttar Pradesh. The first response of a sizable number of Vaishnavas, when asked their sect (i.e., Vaishnava or Shaiva) by census officials in 1911, responded that they were "Ramanandis."[62] Given the subsequent conflict, it is likely that this response was provoked by increasing resentment felt by Ramanandis in their relations with elitist acharya elements in the order. The catalyst for the conflict was provided in 1918 by a visit to Ayodhya by the head of the Shri Vaishnava Totadri math in south India. Particularly galling to many Ramanandis was the fact that the *Anantacharya* (eternal leader) from the south refused to prostrate before Sita and Ramchandra images in two major Ramanandi temples, refused to accept *prasad* (a ritual offering of food or drink), and in general "behaved like a strict Brahman who thought the Ramanandis an inferior community."[63]

These angry recollections stand in sharp contrast to those of Swami Dharnidharacharya, a rising young Bihari intellectual of Ayodhya who drew close to the visitor from the south during his brief visit in 1918. Dharnidharacharya, looking back in the 1930s, was so impressed with the philosophical and moral discourses by the Anantacharya held regularly in Kanak Bhavan that, as he put it, "my heart was cleansed and I realized that there would be no better opportunity to become his disciple."[64] When he became the *chela* (disciple) of the Anantacharya, he was given the name "Dharnidhar Ramanujadas," or Dharnidhar, slave of Ramanuja. This choice of names could not have failed to irritate those radical Ramanandis who had begun associating the elitist elements in the sampraday with the figure of the south Indian theologian, Ramanujacharya. However, the use of "das" as a suffix suggests as well that the Ramanuji-Ramanandi battle lines were not firmly marked out at that time (1918), and that many Ramanandis accepted a servile position with respect to the acharyas in the order.

The radical Ramanandi opinion that began to solidify after 1918—much to the dismay of Dharnidharacharya and similar figures—was characterized by its proponents as *svatantra* (sovereign or free) and held essentially that Ramanand had originated a religious tradition wholly independent of any connection with Ramanuja and the Shri Vaishnavas of the south.[65] Central to the propagation of this view was another young Ramanandi sadhu, one Bhagavad Das (later Bhagavadacharya), who had become a disciple of a prominent rasik guru in Ayodhya in 1919.[66] To redress the many injustices and insults that he felt were being heaped upon Ramanandis by Ramanujis in the sampraday, Bhagavadacharya formed two committees: the "Shri Ramanandi Vaishnava *Mahamandal,*" a "supra-council" that directed the svatantra movement, and the *Puratatvanusandhayini Samiti,* charged with identifying and studying historical documents associated with Ramanand.[67] Both were devoted, ultimately, to purging the sampraday of Ramanuji elements. Bhagavadacharya was soon challenged to a debate, which took place in the Hanumangarhi, the main naga fortress of Ayodhya. After it became apparent that no one had the rhetorical skills to defeat Bhagavadacharya, his guru and reportedly the most powerful intellect in Ayodhya, Mahant Swami Rammanoharprasadacharya of *Bara Asthan* (big place), was persuaded to oppose him in debate. According to recent Ramanandi recountings of these events, it was felt that since there was no one in Ayodhya who possessed the courage to face Rammanoharprasadacharya, the Ramanuji side would emerge victorious.[68] In the end, and contrary to all expectations, the young disciple won the day.

The Ayodhya debate, which occured in 1919 or 1920, did not in any way signal the end of the matter. Indeed, according to Ramanandis it only created the need for the more august "historical" debate at the 1921 Ujjain kumbh. The specific question to be addressed was whether the sacred books of the south Indian Shri Vaishnavas offended Ramchandra; implicit to the debate was whether Ramanuja was regarded by Ramanand as a monastic predecessor. The Ramanuji side was defended by Swami Ramprapann Ramanujadas of the Totadri math; Bhagavadacharya argued on behalf of the radical Ramanandi position.[69] The jury took little time in deciding in favor of Bhagavadacharya and stating that henceforth the Ramanandi sampraday was to be independent of Ramanujacharya and south Indian Shri Vaishnavas. The new guru parampara placed Ramanand twenty-second in descent from Ramchandra and included no mention whatsoever of Ramanuja.[70] Crucial to the Ujjain victory was the discovery of a fifteenth-century guru parampara that made no mention of Ramanuja; this parampara was said to have been authored by Agradevacharya, a grand-disciple of Ramanand, and was uncovered by the aforementioned research committee (*Puratatvanusandhayini Samiti*).[71]

Even the conclusion reached at Ujjain did not completely resolve the dispute, and those Ramanandis who are today thought of as Ramanujis continue to reject the validity of the 1921 Ujjain debate. Among their objections are the charges that the fifteenth-century guru parampara was forged by Bhagavadacharya, and that the juries for both the Ayodhya and Ujjain debates were strategically loaded with prominent naga mahants and others sympathetic to the radical postition.[72] Indeed, it would take years of writing and propagandizing before Bhagavadacharya's position would be regarded as "orthodox" by Ramanandis themselves. In a 1924 contribution to a major Hindi-language journal of Banaras, one Shyamsundardas continued to insist that the "thread of descent [in the Ramanandi sampraday] began with Ramanuja."[73] Three years later Bhagavadacharya would publish his first major work, *ShrimadRamanand-Digvijayah* (The World-Conquest of Ramanand), a four-hundred-page treatise in Sanskrit and Hindi on the life of Ramanand, thus correcting the hagiographic "deficiencies" of Ramanandi tradition. In the introduction to that work, Bhagavadacharya rearticulated his position on Ramanuja, focusing in particular on the narrative of Ramanand's life found

in the Bhaktamal: "The intention with which Nabha-ji composed his poetic verse is a point of great dispute. There is no harm in suggesting that
Nabha-ji's intent was to show that Shri Ramanandacharya used the very
same philosophical system that Shri Swami Ramanujacharya had used to
propagate religious ideas. . . . However, it would constitute a great error to suggest that he intended to depict Shri Ramanand Swami-ji as a
disciple of the sampraday and tradition of Shri Ramanuja Swami-ji."[74]
In the same year (1927), another debate would be held in Vrindaban;
according to a recollection of these events by one late twentieth-century admirer of Bhagavadacharya, the Ramanujis were said to have behaved so disrespectfully that, henceforth, they would no longer be considered part of the fourfold division of Vaishnavas (known as the
chatuh-sampraday) and would no longer be allowed to share ground with
Vaishnavas at the major festivals.[75] The extent to which the radical position came to dominate Ramanandi attitudes throughout the north is
reflected in the fact that Ramanujis failed to take part in the ceremonial
procession of the monastic orders at the 1932 kumbh held in Ujjain.[76]

Many scholars continued to assert into the 1930s, however, that Ramanand was not the sole, independent originator of the sampraday. In
the early 1930s, *Kalyan* (Benediction), a widely distributed monthly
magazine published in Gorakhpur, brought out a special number on the
lives of famous yogis and swamis, entitled *Yogank*. This issue described
Ramanand as a follower of Ramanuja who had been excommunicated
for careless commensal behavior while on pilgrimage. Avadh Kishor Das,
a supporter of the radical position and the editor of a 1935–1936 collection of essays on Ramanand and the Ramanandi sampraday, responded
by attacking the editors of *Kalyan:*

We have nothing whatsoever in common with the Ramanuji sampraday. We
disagree with them on every point. Ramanand a follower of a sampraday
which we do not even accept as legitimate? How many hearts burn with this
statement? But it does not end there. This enemy of the Ramanandi sampraday has launched a heavy attack. . . .

The editor and author of *Kalyan* should realize that *jagat-guru* [lord-
of-the-world] Shri Ramanandcharya-ji was never a follower of the Ramanuji
sampraday but was rather according to the eternal proof of the *shrutis* [re-
vealed wisdom] and *shastras* [legal texts] the leader of the Shri sampraday,
which later became known by his name. No one excommunicated him and
he was not any common devotee, but was the leader of countless devotees
and the avatar of lord Shri Ram.[77]

Avadh Kishor Das concluded by exhorting Ramanandis to confront those
responsible in Gorakhpur and demand an explanation and an apology.

Eventually the views of the radical faction came to dominate the Ramanandi sampraday. Ramanandis became those who adhered to the svatantra, or independent, position and refused all links with the Ramanuja heritage, while those who retained those links were known as Ramanujis. Since guru parampara represented a fundamental element of Ramanandi identity, the dispute was certain to affect everyone in the sampraday. Even Sitaramsharan Bhagvan Prasad, who by all indications endeavored to remain aloof from Ayodhya politics and left little in the way of comment on the radical interpretation of Ramanand's life, seems to have been touched by the controversy. In 1908, a decade prior to the eruption of the dispute, Bhagvan Prasad's guru parampara had placed Ramanuja tenth and Ramanand twentieth in descent from Ramchandra.[78] Bhagvan Prasad passed away in 1932, over a decade after the Ujjain decision. In a 1940s memoir written by one of his admirers and dedicated to explicating the subtleties of Bhagvan Prasad's teachings, a guru parampara is given that is said to have been taken from the pages of Bhagvan Prasad's 1928–1929 diary.[79] This guru parampara makes no mention whatsoever of Ramanuja. Likewise, in subsequent editions of Bhagvan Prasad's commentary on the Bhaktamal, a guru parampara of Ramanand is given that places Ramanand twenty-second in descent from Ramchandra, again omitting mention of Ramanuja.[80]

There remain, however, pockets of Ramanuji strength throughout north India. Vaishnava centers today dominated by Ramanujis include the Janaki-asthan in Sitamarhi, north Bihar (said to be the exact location where Sita was discovered emerging from the furrow left by her father's plowing), and the Galta Pith on the outskirts of Jaipur. Indeed, even Ayodhya continued to harbor many sadhus who chose not to accept the parampara advanced by Bhagavadacharya. Among them was Dharnidharacharya, who returned in 1924 despite bitter memories of Ayodhya as the center of the movement to repudiate Ramanujacharya. Indeed, as far as he was concerned (writing in the 1930s), a final decision was never reached regarding the official guru parampara.[81]

Bhagavadacharya himself would rise, in the 1970s, to the very pinnacle of Vaishnava monastic authority as a result of his lifelong efforts. His was a circuitous route to the top, however, and along the way he would alienate many within and beyond Ayodhya, including his own guru, Mahant Rammanoharprasad, whom he defeated in debate.[82] Even though his *ShrimadRamanand-Digvijayah* was published in 1927, and despite the fact that his radical position was gaining increasing acceptance among Ramanandis through the 1920s and 1930s, it would appear that Bhagavadacharya was regarded as something of a revolutionary for many years. Indeed, in 1929 Swami Raghuvaracharya of Bara Asthan (the math in Ayodhya that Bhagavadacharya had joined in 1919 and had been obliged to leave after defeating his guru in debate soon thereafter) authored a commentary on the *Anandabhashya* (Discourses on Bliss), which was purported to be the specific teachings of Ramanand; this text would remain unchallenged through the 1930s and 1940s as the authoritative statement of Ramanandi doctrine.[83] Following the tumultuous 1920s, Bhagavadacharya would retire to a cave at Mount Abu and begin formulating his scholarly campaign; he would eventually shift his base of operations to the city of Ahmedabad in Gujarat and begin writing in earnest.[84] In 1955 Bhagavadacharya publicly took issue with the way Ramanandi doctrine was being taught, denounced Raghuvaracharya's *Anandabhashya* commentary as completely devoid of any connection to Ramanand's true teachings, challenged all comers to a debate on the veracity of the sources for that text, and promised to produce a document of his own. His opponents remained (according to him) silent, so in 1958 he published *ShriJanakikripabhashyasya* (The Discourses of Shri Janaki, or Sita).[85] In 1963 Bhagavadacharya authored yet another treatise, entitled *ShriRamanandabhashyam* (The Discourses of Ramanand), which created considerable consternation among major sampraday figures in Ayodhya and Banaras.[86] In 1967 his first major work, *ShrimadRamanand-Digvijayah,* was reissued (as *ShriRamanand-Digvijayah*) by the Adhyapika Shrichandandevi Press, Ahmedabad, signaling the consolidation of his position as India's preeminent Ramanandi intellect.

By the late 1960s Bhagavadacharya was approaching his hundredth year and presumably had outlived most if not all of his opponents from the 1920s; indeed, his very longevity may have contributed to his ascent in sampraday politics by the 1970s. More important, however, were his organizational and literary energies, which during the 1940s, 1950s, and 1960s were manifest in social reform efforts to eradicate untouchability, in his authorship of more than forty articles and books in both Sanskrit and Hindi on Ramanandi doctrine, and in his editorship of a journal, *Tatvadarshi* (Reflections on the Supreme Spirit).[87] In 1971 his centenary was celebrated with great fanfare in Ahmedabad. Judging by the hundreds of luminaries in attendance, Bhagavadacharya had attained great stature both within and outside the Ramanandi sampraday—particularly in Gujarat state politics and in the all-India associational politics of the *Bharat Sadhu Samaj* (or Indian Sadhu Society).[88] Finally in 1977, at the Prayag kumbh, a wide array of sampraday leaders would declare him the first *jagadguru-Ramanandacharya* (universal leader [wearing the mantle of] Ramanandacharya) since Ramanand himself, and the twenty-third in descent from Ramchandra, in gratitude for his life-long service to the sampraday.[89] Not only would this mark the pinnacle of Bhagavadacharya's career, the granting of such an honor to the fire-brand of the 1920s would signal that the radical Ramanandi view had achieved wide acceptance in Vaishnava circles by the 1970s.

In a variety of ways, then, the concerns expressed in Ayodhya in 1918–1921, which continue to ripple through north India today, mir-rored those of the early eighteenth century in Galta. The important difference, however, is that in the early twentieth century the side gen-erally perceived to have predominated—the radical Ramanandi faction—favored a radicalization of the meaning of Ramanand's life with respect to Ramanuja and varna.[90] By articulating a guru parampara free of any mention of Ramanuja, radical monks were in effect rejecting the very notion of social superiority which, in their view, fueled the Ramanuji "acharya" avowals of religious exclusivity. Given the details of Ra-manand's contested life and the core Ramanuji assertion that Ramanand was expelled from the society of monks for careless eating practices while on pilgrimage, an opinion after 1918 on the question of Ramanuja as a spiritual antecedent of Ramanand could only be articulated with refer-ence to caste and commensality. While this question is taken up in greater detail below ("Caste and the New Ramanandi Order"), it should be noted that van der Veer has argued (rightly) that caste was not the only consideration in an individual's decision to support either the Ramanuji or the Ramanandi position. Van der Veer cites as evidence the fact that "even abbots of *Kurmi* and *Barhi* [cultivator and carpenter] castes chose to become Ramanuji."[91] While I agree generally with van der Veer's position, I disagree with two assumptions that are implicit in his obser-vation. The first is that the low ascriptive status of Kurmis and Barhais was self-evident (to observers and to the subjects themselves) and re-mained unchanged through the twentieth century. While this assump-tion was shared by the brahmanical and colonial elite in the early twen-tieth century and appears commonplace in the discourse of backward classes of the late twentieth century, it was probably not an assumption shared by many Kurmis and Barhais themselves in the 1920s. For Kur-mis, Barhais, and others, caste in the first half of the century was very much in the eye of the beholder, and many in those communities held themselves to be of high-caste status and were actively promoting pro-grams of varna reidentification in an effort to claim for themselves a noble, kshatriya past.[92] And, I would argue, whether they considered themselves high caste in the 1920s depended very much on whether they conceived of varna merely as a social idea to be manipulated or as a fundamental, essential, and all-encompassing mold from which there was no escape—in a word, as caste.

Van der Veer's second assumption, which emerges out of the first, is that given a low ascriptive status, Kurmis and Barhais should have supported Bhagavadacharya's radical position, thus demonstrating a disdain for caste hierarchy. While quite plausible at first glance, this assertion should raise a logical query: if in fact Kurmis and Barhais indeed believed themselves to be of low status, how could they possibly evince a disdain for caste in the first place? The answer, of course, is that while they were no doubt aware of the many assertions that they were socially inferior, they did not necessarily consider themselves to be of low status. Rather, the overt Kurmi and Barhai support for the Ramanuji position should be read as a conscious expression of their own perceptions of themselves as high status, which would be consistent with peasant attitudes toward caste and status that were coalescing outside the sampraday. And again, a belief in one's high status requires a commitment to the very idea of hierarchy.

Varna, jati, and caste are slippery concepts under the best of circumstances. This is in part because the very idea of status had long been a matter of contention in north India. Crucial to my understanding of caste is the examination from within of all casual assertions of ascriptive status, including caste. I would argue that the success of the radical Ramanandi faction in the Gangetic region after the 1920s (and particularly by the 1970s) signifies that caste no longer represented an all-encompassing, unquestioned social code for a critical mass of Vaishnava sadhus. Discerning what such ideological shifts may have meant for "ordinary people" outside the sampraday is a task for chapters 3 and 4.

New Hagiography, New History

The altered mythology of Ramanand's life imposed by the radical sentiment entailed the evolution of a new and more socially and religiously aggressive Ramanandi history.[93] In the early 1930s a group of influential Ramanandis, tacitly supported by Bhagavadacharya, formed the Ramanandi Literature Publication Committee whose goal was the publication and propagation of Ramanandi books.[94] The founding members of the committee included Sitaramiya Mathuradas, who had played a leading role in the 1918 committee that investigated the tradition of the Ramanandi community; Ramballabhasharan, a leading rasik of Ayodhya; and Bhagvandas, a prominent mahant of a naga akhara in Ayodhya. The committee provided an important forum for the articulation of the wider social and religious concerns of Ramanandi history, conceived almost entirely in terms of two broad historical themes: caste elitism and the coming of Islam to India. Ramanandi concern with caste elitism focused on the restrictive recruitment practices of the major historical rival to Vaishnava monasticism, the Dasnami organization said to have been established by Shankaracharya in the beginning of the ninth century. The Ramanandi history of Islam in the subcontinent depicted Ramanand as the champion of a Hinduism that had been weakened by internecine struggle with Dasnamis and therefore vulnerable to violent Muslim persecution.

Much like their perception of Ramanuja's Shri Vaishnava practices, radical Ramanandis understood brahman elitism to be the defining feature of the Dasnami order. Bhagavadacharya described the exclusivity of Shankaracharya's Dasnamis as the religious and social antithesis of core Ramanandi teachings:

Having overcome Buddhism, Swami Shankaracharya-ji established his own monastic society. But in this he was not entirely successful. His insipid monism was incapable of drawing any followers. It was also heretical and mean-spirited. His path was only open to the brahman jati; it was difficult for others to enter. As a result, brahmans [given their small numbers] could not enlarge this community, and others were not given the opportunity to try. Ramanand understood the precise nature of this dilemma. He was well-acquainted with the consequences of parochialism.[95] From its very inception the sampraday was egalitarian. Swami Shri Ramanand was not at all reluctant to place its egalitarianism before the world. The result was that one huge community was formed, and this was the equivalent of a holy boon for the spread of religion.[96]

Ramanandi hindsight in the twentieth century decried the Vaishnava-Shaiva rivalry as "Hindu versus Hindu" conflict. In order to endow the narrative of this internecine strife with dramatic force, the new Ramanandi historiography relied on a depiction of Muslims as unidimensional villains bent on the destruction of a divided Hindu society. In the words of Sitaramiya Mathuradas, Shaivas stood by opportunistically "while Vaishnavas were butchered by Muslims."[97] Bemoaning the caste-mindedness that was thought to have fed rival monastic antipathies and Hindu decline vis-à-vis Islam in this period, another author wrote, "This was not a time to bicker about jati differences, this was a time to 'worship god and be part of god.'"[98] The egalitarian presciptions of radical Ramanandis in the 1930s relied, then, on a new Ramanandi view of the past rife with distinctly anti-Muslim rhetorical tones.

It should be noted that Ramanandis in early twentieth-century Ayodhya struck this ardently anti-Muslim pose despite the fact that much of the land with which the various orders within the sampraday enriched themselves was given to the Ayodhya monasteries by Shuja ud-Daula (the Nawab of Awadh) in the late eighteenth century. Judging from Buchanan's description, written in the second decade of the nineteenth century, an antagonism toward things and people Islamic at that time could not have been further from the minds of Ramanandis: "The Ramanandis or Ramawats [of Gorakhpur district] have very numerous establishments, and a great deal of land free of revenue, the greater part of which I am told, they obtained from Suja ud Doulah, to whom they contrived to render themselves very agreeable. They are indeed skilful courtiers. Most of the lands were therefore granted to the convents of Ayodhya, near where this prince resided."[99] Nevertheless, the radical Ramanandi view in the twentieth century broke with its eighteenth-century antecedents and held that fourteenth-century north Indian Hindu society had been embroiled in internecine squabbles and had suffered the relentless persecution of Muslim tyranny.

A vision of Muslim persecution in the past did not mean, however, that the Ramanandi sampraday had no room for some Muslims in the present. The radical vision articulated by Bhagavadacharya included the careful reiteration that the "first generation" of Ramanand's followers emerged from virtually all sections of society—especially, in the person of Kabir, Muslim society. Ramanand's first circle of disciples represented an ideal model for coexistence in the present, but on Ramanandi terms: Bhagavadacharya laid great stress on the assertion that "Vaishnava religion is not reserved for only one certain jati and only one lineage; rather, any jati, any lineage, any class, and any person can find a place in its huge domain." And not only was Kabir the quintessential example of devotion and diversity in this paradigmatic vision of society, along with the other disciples he was thought to have been a manifestation of Vaishnava divinity: "Much as the community of gods took the form of monkeys and aided Ramchandra when he was an avatar, many liberated souls took earthly form in the age of avatar Ramanand. Narad, Bhisham, Bali and others became brahmans, kshatriyas, vaishyas, shudras, Muslims, etc. and carried out fully the wishes of Ramanand." In much the same way that the radical Ramanandi vision deemed varna insignificant in matters of belief, Islam too was conceived as but a minor impediment to participation in a community driven by Ramanandi love. If "thousands of brahmans, kshatriyas, vaishyas, shudras, and untouchables fell in love with the beauty of Vaishnavism," why exclude Muslims? Indeed, according to Bhagavadacharya, Ramanand invited such a diverse range of devotees to be his own disciples precisely so he could "through them cleanse *Bharat* [India] all at once in the unremitting current of the Ganga." The exact dimensions of the "cleansing" process were left to the discretion and imagination of the reader.[100]

Caste and the New Ramanandi Order

Bhagavadacharya's strident reiteration of Ramanand's fourteenth-century liberalism signified the reemergence of the view that caste status could constitute neither an obstacle nor an asset to full participation in the sampraday. The experiences of other Ramanandis of the late nineteenth and early twentieth centuries confirm this general disdain for commensal restrictions according to caste, but at the same time reflect a fundamental equivocation on the issue of varna differentiation. Perhaps no individual better reflects the Ramanandi disdain for caste than Bhagvan Prasad, the Bhaktamal exegete who ranked among the top intellectuals of Ayodhya at the turn of the century.[101]

Bhagvan Prasad was born in 1840 into a family of scholarly, well-to-do Kayasths, already noted for their long-standing contributions to Ramanandi literature.[102] Much of his childhood was spent in Mubarakpur, a prestigious Kayasth enclave near the town of Chapra in Saran District. In Mubarakpur a local Ramanandi named Shivcharan Bhagat—a *Koiri* (vegetable gardener) "whose knowledge of Persian was so great people addressed him as *munshi* (scribe)"—had an early influence on Bhagvan Prasad's religious education.[103] In 1858, one year after his marriage, Bhagvan Prasad became a disciple of Swami Ramcharandas, of Parsa village, Chapra District, who bestowed upon him the name Sitaramsharan, a typically rasik title that connotes taking refuge (*sharan*) in the conjoined deity of Sita and Ramchandra.[104] In 1863 Bhagvan Prasad became a subinspector of schools, and his subsequent employment in this line took him all over Bihar. It was not until 1881, however, that Bhagvan Prasad was introduced to the famous rasik of Bhagalpur, Shri Ramcharandas Hanskala, and was granted the title *Rupkala,* which may be translated as "manifest beauty." Bhagvan Prasad never had children, and between the years 1885 and 1895 his mother, father, and wife all passed away; left with no immediate family ties to Bihar, Bhagvan Prasad, like his father and uncle before him, retired to a contemplative life in Ayodhya.

In addition to earning a broad reputation as a rasik poet and Ramanandi scholar, Bhagvan Prasad gained a certain notoriety during his government service as one who was only too willing to flout the norms of public decency. While in Patna as Deputy Inspector of Schools, as biographer Shivnandan Sahay noted with reluctant admiration, Bhagvan Prasad frequently "attended to the personal religious needs of his palanquin-bearing Kahar, his servants, and his shoe-repairman as Vaishnavas, one and the same."[105] Bhagvan Prasad's blatant disregard for caste in the pursuit of the Ramanandi ideal of religious devotion aroused the consternation of many of his peers, who complained that ministrations to people of shudra and untouchable status would only result in a depletion of the economic and social services provided by those segments of society. In particular, respectable people were greatly put out by what appeared to them a presumption of dignity on the part of lowly shudras. According to Sahay, many of them raised objections to Bhagvan Prasad's ministrations to mere laborers—in this case Kahars—on the grounds that the latter would develop ideas about proper and improper work and eventually refuse to perform the back-breaking task of palanquin-bearing.[106] While the fears of respectable society may have been real, it is also extremely likely that Bhagvan Prasad's close religious interaction with shudras and untouchables evoked a more visceral response, quite apart from any impending scarcity of laboring Kahars. Even Sahay himself felt obliged to apologize for his subject's behavior, explaining that "as far as I understand, his idea was that by ministering to these people they would be more attentive to the salubrity of their meals and would thereby not be faced with any obstacles en route to salvation."

Bhagvan Prasad's ministrations reflected his own personal interpretation of the social mandate implicit in the religious message of Ramanand. However, Ramanandi ambivalence toward caste emerged in discussions about the prescribed stages of a sadhu's entry into the sampraday. In his biography of Bhagvan Prasad, Sahay expressed the view that originally anyone (including untouchables) could have become Ramanandi sadhus, but that by his time (the early 1900s), "Ramanandis bring disciples from only those jatis from whom water can be taken."[107] For those designated shudra by the elite, this phrase, "from whom water can be taken," was a common enough euphemism for a person of "pure shudra" status, with whom restricted physical contact could be made. From the elite perspective, such physical contact would have occurred in the course of consuming goods and services common in everyday life; the designation "pure shudra" implied a substantial body of "impure"—hence untouchable—people with whom physical contact was both unnecessary and improper. Buchanan, in the early nineteenth century, had included in the term "pure shudra" the well-known designations of Kayasth, Koiri, Kurmi, Kahar, Goala, *Dhanuk* (archers, cultivators, palanquin bearers), *Halwai* (sweets vendor), *Mali* (flower gardener), *Barai* (cultivator and vendor of betel-leaf), *Sonar* (goldsmith), *Kandu* (grain parcher), and *Gareri* (blanket weavers and shepherds).[108]

By the late nineteenth century Kayasths had begun organizing a movement to reject their ascribed shudra status in favor of a kshatriya one; by the early twentieth century, many others—particularly Kurmis, Koiris, Kahars, and Goalas—followed the Kayasth lead (although each utilized distinct arguments) and defined for themselves similar kshatriya identities.[109] All these reform movements, however, had in common serious attempts at the redefinition of physical labor in terms that reflected the newfound desire for respectability. Shivnandan Sahay's observation that "Ramanandis bring disciples from only those jatis from whom water can be taken" reflects a subtle but important equivocation on the issue of caste, an equivocation that spelled the difference between those who were able to join the ranks of Ramanandi sadhus and those who could only benefit from the teachings of Ramanand and Ramanandis.

Furthermore, the fact that an initiate had gained entry into the sampraday did not necessarily mean he was guaranteed equal treatment irrespective of varna status. According to Lala Sita Ram, author of an important Vaishnava history of Ayodhya, numerous exceptions were made for high-caste novitiates of a major naga akhara (the *Hanuman Garhi* in Ayodhya). Those exceptions included a waiver of the thirteen-year age limit for initiation as well as freedom from having to perform "any lowly tasks," i.e., having to prepare meals, clear and clean dishes, carry wood, and draw water from the well.[110] It is worthwhile noting, in this context, that present-day Ramanandis claim that prior to 1921 all Ramanandis had to perform these lowly tasks for the acharyas among them—who were exempted from such work and whom the Ramanandis would label "Ramanuji" after 1921—and that this was one of the main reasons that Bhagavadacharya strove to repudiate all connections with the south Indian Ramanujacharya.[111] And despite the apparent victory of Bhagavadacharya and the rise to orthodox status of his views, in areas where Ramanujis remain strong Vaishnava sadhus are fully cognizant of and responsive to caste distinctions. According to Burghart, who worked primarily in Janakpur in Nepal's eastern terai,

[The sadhus] claim that one's mind and body are formed of one's caste, and since the soul dwells within one's mind and body until death, caste rules of commensality must be observed within the sect. For this reason Ramanandis of male Twice-born body do not accept 'imperfect' (*kacca*) food or initiation from Ramanandis of Once-born [shudra] body. Even the Ramanandi Renouncers and Great Renouncers . . . who dress in bark, roam in itinerant monasteries and smear ashes on their body observe caste rules of commensality amongst themselves.[112]

While Lala Sita Ram candidly accepted the fact of such caste distinctions in the process of training monks, he nevertheless defended what he saw to be the progressive attitude of the Ramanandi sampraday in the early twentieth century. For instance, he noted in his correspondence with Sir George Grierson that "a visit to any of the akharas of Ramanandi bairagis will convince that Sudras of all classes are as freely admitted and invested with the sacred thread as the twice born."[113]

Investiture with the sacred thread conferred, by definition, elite "twice-born" status and was theoretically reserved for vaishyas, kshatriyas, and brahmans. By performing this ceremony on behalf of shudras, the Ramanandi sampraday (or some in the sampraday) effectively undermined the hierarchy implicit to caste through the adroit application of varna ideology. The practice of sacred thread investiture in Ramanandi akharas should ultimately be understood in the context of the kshatriya identity movements of the early twentieth century, inasmuch as it encapsulates in a single ritual the entire thrust of the kshatriya campaigns. Lala Sita Ram's assertion of Ramanandi progressivism in this regard would suggest that the sampraday was involved, at least tangentially, in the process of varna reidentification. It should be added that the willingness to countenance varna distinctions in monastic recruitment and training and the recognition of the varna systemics implicit to sacred thread investiture as a strategy for shudra social advancement are both entirely consistent with the essentially Ramanuji position expressed by Sita Ram in his reaction to Farquhar's 1920 presentation of Ramanand.

Hence the Ramanandi sampraday in the early twentieth century did not (and still does not, if we accept the arguments of Burghart and van der Veer) constitute a monolith of opinion on the relevance of caste rank in monastic life. That a debate was emerging at this time in the sampraday, with varna and status as the central issues, is clear; it is also clear that the debate was closely linked both chronologically and thematically with the divisiveness over guru parampara in 1918–1921. Hence the position taken by Shyamsundar Das in 1924, who (like Sita Ram) has already been cited for his Ramanuji stand with respect to Ramanand's guru antecedents: in the pages of north India's most respected Hindi-language periodical, the *Nagaripracharani Patrika*, Shyamsundar Das disputed the contention that "Ramanand broke *completely* with the strictures of *varnashramdharm* [living according to the dictates of varna and one's stage of life]" even though "there is no doubt that in choosing his disciples he gave no thought to considerations of jati."[114] Questions of caste propriety were inescapably linked to the issue of guru parampara, inasmuch as the choice of one's disciples (or, conversely, one's guru) represented the most concrete expression of social ideology.

By the 1930s three discernible factions appear to have emerged around the issue of caste status in the sampraday.[115] Again, disagreement revolved around whether an individual—in this context a shudra individual—retained his varna status after becoming a Ramanandi monk. The egalitarian view, favored by a group led by Bhagavadacharya, held that "amongst sadhus there is no varna system at all" and that "someone of shudra origins can be considered just as pure upon becoming a Vaishnava ascetic as a Vaishnava from a brahman family." In opposition stood Swami Raghuvaracharya (the author of *Anandabhashya*, theologically dismissed by Bhagavadacharya in later years) and his adherents, who maintained that "the varna system does in fact exist amongst sadhus and upon becoming a Vaishnava ascetic a brahman remains a brahman and a shudra remains a shudra," and thus "the two could never eat together." A third view, maintained by "Udasin"[116] scholars of Ayodhya, occupied the middle ground between the two opposing factions by arguing that though "the shudra Vaishnava who exhibits all the qualities of a good Vaishnava can be considered pure in all respects . . . , this [purity] is only ornamental; in reality, he is not the same as everyone else."[117] Because of the multiplicity of authoritative voices in the sampraday, the question of varna would prove to be difficult to resolve. Bhagavadacharya would himself take up the cause of untouchables after his move to Ahmedabad.[118] Apprehensive of the potential divisiveness of the controversy, particularly given the increasing influence of monks like Bhagavadacharya, one Ramanandi urged "all the scholars of the sampraday

[to] convene and issue a judgment." Whether such a meeting ever took place is not known, though it is clear that the conflicting attitudes continued to thrive.[119]

Conclusion

The belief in a glorious past in which persecutions by both Muslims and Dasnamis were overcome, the devotion to the central figure of Ramanand (and through him Ramchandra) unfettered by an association with the south Indian brahman Ramanuja, and the dedication to an egalitarian social order that invited the participation of elite, shudra, and untouchable alike—these constituted the core reference points for a radical Ramanandi after 1921. The following poem by Ramavatar Yadav, entitled "Yatindra-stav" (Hymn to a Great Sadhu) and featured prominently in a 1935–1936 publication honoring the reinvigorated conception of Ramanand, brought these three elements together to glorify the living past of the sampraday:

> Though Hindu jati was lost in a fog of ignorance,
>   you shined a light on the right path.
> Though we endured many blows at every step,
>   you nourished us with great support and wisdom.
> Though some fled the battleground of their fate,
>   you injected vitality back into their veins.
> You cleansed the holy ground once again,
>   and showed the world the one-ness of Vishnu.
>
> Who could have exposed the fallacy of high and low
>   if such a sadhu had not entered the world?
> Who else could have inspired the notion that no one is
>   impure amid the tranquility of God's realm?
> Who else could have drawn so many across the ocean
>   of existence in the sparkling moment of Ram-mantra?
> Who else could have inspired Kabir and Ravidas to
>   liberate the oppressed with but a bit of verse?
> Who else could have comforted the fallen souls who flocked
>   to them beneath a shower of resplendent love?
> Who else could have banished the evil notion that
>   "he who can be cut and wounded must not be Hindu?"
> Who else could have shown such valor destroying the
>   monolith of sin and expelling narrow-mindedness?
> Surrounded by enemies everywhere, who would have preserved
>   the name "Hindu" had such a sadhu not arrived?

In their reconstructed hagiography radical Ramanandis viewed Ramanand, like Ram himself, as the savior of Hindu India. Ayodhya, as north India's center of Ram worship and, hence, the main geographic focus of Ramanandi devotional attentions, could only grow in stature along with Bhagavadacharya during the twentieth century—and, not coincidentally, at the expense of older centers, such as Galta, dominated by Ramanujis. And as Bhagavadacharya's stature grew, so did the new Ramanandi emphasis on a history of Muslim tyranny as both a catalyst and a backdrop for Hindu decline prior to the arrival of Ramanand. In retrospect, then, some of the factors that would combine to render Ayodhya a political flash point in the late twentieth century were already coming into place after 1918. As we shall see in the following chapters, Ayodhya would be reinforced as a central place in the popular imagination of north Indians through other, nonmonastic means.

From the mid-nineteenth century onward, the increasing use of print by Ramanandis would create new strains in the sampraday, simply by bringing into focus the varying versions of tradition extant in the community of monks. Hence, print technology would help to intensify the transformation of long-held hagiographical differences into full-fledged ideological battles. That such battles were fought prior to the arrival of the printing press—though perhaps with less frequency—seems clear from the decisions taken at Galta in the early eighteenth century. Because many important monastic centers tended to be far apart and off the beaten track, rendering long-distance communication difficult, such periodic meetings were crucial to the resolution of sampraday conflicts. The kumbh mela would answer this need in the eighteenth and nineteenth centuries, by serving as a periodic—but not too frequent—forum for settling internal as well as intersectarian disputes and for making major sampraday announcements. As a medium for the articulation of sectarian views, however, the kumbh would be supplemented and, increasingly after 1921, superceded by the printed word. Bhagavadacharya's investiture as jagadguru-Ramanandacharya in 1977 at the Prayag kumbh itself, an honor that capped a five-decade torrent of publications, is the strongest example of this new monastic reality.

The existence of the office of jagadguru Ramanandacharya after the 1970s should not be taken, however, as an indication that a supreme monastic authority can now quash doctrinal dissent in the sampraday. To the contrary, the creation of the position has resulted since the death of Bhagavadacharya (in 1981 by most accounts) in multiple claims to the title, most of which recognize Bhagavadacharya as the first jagadguru-Ramanandacharya since Ramanand himself.[120] Hence, despite the dom-

inance of radical Ramanandi views, the sampraday still does not constitute an ecclesiastical monolith with one group of religious leaders dic-
tating religious opinion for the rank and file to follow. The sampraday
remains, fundamentally, a populist organization, the monastic systemics
of which depend on the recognition, respect, and support individual gurus and swamis receive in villages, towns, and cities throughout north
India. An important consequence of this institutional flexibility is that
multiple views on guru parampara and caste can continue to coexist in
the twentieth century, without necessarily threatening the overarching
integrity of the sampraday. Indeed, the fact that there existed a mediat-
ing, "Udasin" view on the issue of caste in the sampraday in the 1930s
is of great significance here, suggesting that the contending factions in
the sampraday were not involved in a damaging, two-party conflict. Indeed, it is possible to argue that this represented the institutionalization
of ambiguity on the question of caste, which in turn has allowed the
sampraday to contain a broad array of social ideologies through much
of the twentieth century and, thereby, to continue to broaden its appeal
in north Indian society.[121]

To what extent did the campaigns for peasant-kshatriya status outside the sampraday, discussed in the following chapters, contribute to or
inform the varna debate among Ramanandis, and vice versa? Given the
intricacy of monastic networks in peasant society and the nineteenth and
twentieth-century interests of monks in social reform, there should be
no doubt that the two worlds spoke to each other in myriad ways. However, as has been noted in the conclusion to the previous chapter, a new
feature of religious and social discourse in peasant society in the early
twentieth century was the initiative taken by local intellectuals beyond
the arena of monastic sampraday. In other words, the relationship between peasants and monks, and the popular conception of religion in
day-to-day affairs, was undergoing change in the early twentieth century. Discerning that change and its social, political, and economic implications is a task for the following chapters.

CHAPTER 3

Being *Vaishnava*,
Becoming *Kshatriya*

According to the 1901 census, Bihar and Uttar Pradesh combined contained about 72 million people. Of that number, over 44 million were officially classified as *shudra*, untouchable, or, more precisely, according to the very limited degree of social contact they were allowed with the twice-born.[1] The Ramanandi sampraday provided in the nineteenth and twentieth centuries an institutional context within which members of those stigmatized communities could acquire a modicum of social and religious dignity. By the late nineteenth century a parallel and qualitatively different brand of social reform had begun to emerge that was, strictly speaking, independent of any direct institutional connection to the Ramanandi or any other Vaishnava sampraday. Rather, this new reformism originated in the jatis assigned shudra status and was for the most part spearheaded by articulate, educated members of those stigmatized communities.[2] Whereas shudra and untouchable involvement in Vaishnava religiosity, whether as lay devotees or as sadhus, was predicated on a Ramanandi disdain for status, these new jati reformers sought personal and community dignity on their own by the unqualified assertion of status. Such assertions occurred among a broad range of agricultural and artisanal jatis who had in common an ascriptively shudra past, and the discussion in this chapter reflects that socio-occupational variety. Of particular interest, however, given their centrality to Gangetic agriculture and relative demographic strength, were the kshatriya campaigns mounted by Kurmi, Yadav, and Kushvaha peasants.[3] Hence, I pay particular attention to these groups.

Though the various new kshatriya organizations that began to appear after the late nineteenth century were institutionally separate from the Ramanandi or any other Vaishnava sampraday, they did evince, as I will argue, a distinctly religious character in both form and content that can only be described as Vaishnava. This is most evident in the very strategy employed in claiming high status: the ex-shudras asserted kshatriya status on the basis of genealogical ties to either Ram or Krishna, the well-known avatars of Vishnu. In addition, much of the reform urged upon the jati communities by their leaders involved abstinence from meat and intoxicants so as to inculcate a "pure" lifestyle, tactics which echoed those utilized in Buchanan's day as the hallmark of Vaishnava (particularly Ramanandi) respectability.[4] The language and rhetoric of kshatriya reform also reflected an unmistakable Vaishnava texture, which I explore in some detail. Finally, though Vaishnava monasticism was not integral to kshatriya reform, Ramanandis, and particularly Ramanuja-oriented Ramanandis, did on occasion become involved as proponents of kshatriya identity. The intersection between Vaishnava monasticism and kshatriya reform is particularly revealing given the disputes over caste and tradition in the Ramanandi sampraday in the twentieth century.

The most broad-based kshatriya reform movements occurred among Kurmi and Yadav peasants. Yadav and Kurmi-kshatriya advocates maintained important roots in the Gangetic core of Bihar and eastern Uttar Pradesh, but gained wide support throughout northern and western India. The less well-known Kushvaha-kshatriya movement, meanwhile, experienced its greatest successes among peasants in the Gangetic core; other analogous peasant and artisan-based reform programs experienced similar regional concentrations of activity. Notwithstanding their broad regional appeal, the Kurmi and Yadav movements have received only limited, descriptive attention in the historical literature.[5] By contrast, more attention has been given to the movement to inculcate a kshatriya identity among the smaller but more influential Kayasth community, which has been well represented in the professions, the civil service, and politics.[6]

Because many jati reformers encouraged vegetarianism, abstinence from spirituous liquors, Sanskrit education, and wearing of the sacred thread among their members, it is possible to see in the kshatriya reform movements a significant degree of what the anthropologist M. N. Srinivas has called "Sanskritization."[7] However, it can be argued that the focus on Sanskritization has led scholars to emphasize the cosmetics of ritual and behavioral transformation and obscured from view the more significant, underlying meanings of ideological change implicit in social reform.[8] Underpinning the ceremonial concerns, emphasis on classical education, and advocacy of pure living that characterized these reform efforts was, I argue, a complex and highly ramified Vaishnava discourse that extended throughout and beyond Gangetic India. Indeed, the history of kshatriya reformism described here suggests that a Vaishnava ethic of reform had become institutionalized in the everyday lives of ordinary people by the turn of the century. Examining the nineteenth-century antecedents of kshatriya reformism, exploring its complex dimensions in the twentieth century and its occasional intersections with Ramanandi monasticism, and discerning some of its broader political and cultural implications, are the objectives of the remainder of this book.

Status and the Nineteenth Century

The concern with personal dignity, community identity, and caste status reached a peak among Kurmi, Yadav, and Kushwaha peasants in the first four decades of the twentieth century. But widespread, though sporadic, apprehensions over such issues extended well beyond those who cultivated the soil and emerged well before 1900. That a concern for status and dignity was not restricted to peasants is evident from the official record: by the end of the nineteenth century two influential, landed communities of ambiguous social rank in the Gangetic core, Bhumihars and Kayasths, had already made claims to superior status, and as a result their official position was in doubt. While the 1901 census was in the compilation stage, Bhumihar associations filed numerous representations with E. A. Gait, the director of census operations for Bengal and Bihar, which argued that, for the purposes of the census, the term "Babhan" should not be used to describe them and instead they should be classified as *Bhumihar*, or landed, brahmans.[9] Ninety years earlier, in his survey of what later became Patna and Gaya Districts of Bihar, Buchanan had noted with some disdain that Bhumihars (to whom he referred as Magahi and military brahmans) "have betaken themselves entirely to agriculture and arms, and cannot be considered as belonging to the sacred order."[10] He consequently ascribed to them kshatriya status. Gait followed suit in his census report at the turn of the century, though he left the question of Bhumihar status officially unresolved: "The best opinion at the present time is perhaps in favour of the Brahmanical origin of the Babhans, but it would be incorrect to say that they are, therefore, Brahmans still. In the eyes of the general Hindu public they constitute a separate caste, which is generally, but not always, regarded as slightly superior to that of the Rajputs [regarded as kshatriya]."[11] By contrast, Kayasths had been classified as pure shudras by Buchanan in the beginning of the nineteenth century.[12] As a result of their very public campaign for kshatriya status in the last quarter of the century, not to mention their substantial economic and political clout, Kayasths were classified along with "Babhans" and Rajputs as "other castes of twice-born rank" in the 1901 census hierarchy for Bihar.[13] Herbert Hope Risley, who devised the hierarchy, noted elsewhere that "the social position of the Behar Kayasths is unquestionably a high one," inasmuch as "popular opinion ranks them next in order to the Babhans and Rajputs."[14]

The problem of ambiguous status implicit in the many claims for high caste was not restricted to Bihar. Risley also designed a complex hierarchy guide for the Uttar Pradesh census that acknowledged disputed claims by delineating such intermediate categories as "Castes allied to Brahmans and who are considered to be of high social standing"; "Castes allied to Kshatriyas, though their claim is not universally admitted"; and "Castes allied to Vaishyas, but their claim is not universally admitted."[15] Additional intermediate categories reflected the broader incongruity between social practice, particularly regarding the consumption of food and water, and varna theory. Such categories included "Castes of good social position, superior to that of the remaining classes"; "Castes from whom some of the twice-born would take water and *pakki* [prepared food], without question"; "Castes from whom some of the twice-born take water while others would not"; "Castes from whose hand the twice-born cannot take water, but who are not untouchable"; "Castes that are untouchable, but do not eat beef"; and "The lowest castes eating beef and vermin."

Indeed, Risley's hierarchy for Uttar Pradesh was far more elaborate than that for Bihar, suggesting that contending claims of social respectability may have been more deeply entrenched in the western half of the Gangetic Plain.[16] In any case, it is clear from a perusal of Buchanan, writing ninety years before Risley, that status claims predated the creation of the Indian census; neither were they restricted to the powerful landed and professional jatis. For instance, Buchanan observed that in south Bihar,

Although the Rajputs are here universally admitted to be Kshatriyas, there are, as in Bhagalpur, other pretenders to that rank whose claim is not generally admitted . . . *by those who are not in their power.* It must however be observed, that their claims to a descent from the original regal tribe is probably as well founded as those of the Rajputs. . . . In fact, every military tribe that had sufficient power, seems to have been admitted *by the Brahmans* into the regal caste, so soon as it became subject to their authority, and betook itself to a pure life.[17]

These "other pretenders" to rank included, most prominently, Kurmi and Goala peasants. The two italicized phrases point out not only Buchanan's awareness of the influence of brahman opinion in his depiction of Gangetic social differentiation, but the awareness among those aspiring to elite status that the complicity of brahmans (as venerated scholars) was a valued requisite. Perhaps to redress the brahmanical weight of his own presentation, Buchanan was willing to cite (often with considerable sympathy) cases of dissenting claims to status in the regions he surveyed, noting especially the religio-mythical account given by "Goala" peasants (who would later claim Yadav-kshatriya status) regarding their own origins: "These people, however low they may be held by the Brahmans, pretend to considerable dignity on account of their connection with the god Krishna, who, although a Kshatri of the family of the moon, was adopted by a Goyala, and many of his wives (1600) are said on some authorities to have been of the Goyala tribe."[18]

Buchanan observed similar localized claims to high status among Kurmis in the Gangetic core, based on an Ayodhya-centered consciousness. The significance of Ayodhya here derives not so much from the importance of that site as a growing Ramanandi monastic center as from its position as the mytho-historical kingdom of Ramchandra (though of course the two are closely related) and hence as an increasingly important geocultural hub of Vaishnava belief. Buchanan noted that so-called *Ayodhya Kurmis*, especially in the Bhojpur region of western Bihar and eastern Uttar Pradesh, claimed superior status and even spurned certain economic and agricultural roles on the basis of that assertion.[19] One case dating from the late eighteenth century concerned a group of influential, land-controlling Ayodhya Kurmis who lived in the Parraona environs of northeast Gorakhpur District and upon whom Asaf ud-daula, the fourth Nawab of Awadh, attempted to bestow the title of "Raja" and thus kshatriya status.[20] The Kurmi avowal of noble status ultimately seemed to fail due to united Rajput opposition in Asaf's court. Ironically, the Rajput constituency of Awadh itself composed a "group of newcomers to the court, who had been peasant soldiers only a few years before. They were called, half sarcastically, the '*Tilangi* Rajas' [or] 'trooper rajas'—the people described by the shocked Muhammad Faiz Baksh as the new Nawab's courtiers: 'Naked rustics, whose fathers and brothers were with their own hands guiding the plow . . . , rode about as Asaf ud-daula's orderlies.'"[21] In other words, the Rajputs of Awadh, who along with brahmans constituted the main beneficiaries of what historian Richard Barnett characterizes as "Asaf's permissive program of social mobility," were not willing to let that mobility reach beyond certain arbitrary sociocultural boundaries.

Notwithstanding a lack of success at the nawabi court, however, Kurmis still managed to craft for themselves a sophisticated identity. Indeed, Buchanan's description indicates that some wealthy Kurmis in the early nineteenth century were on the verge of rejecting entirely the physical labor inherent in a peasant-cultivator existence:

The families most nearly connected with the chiefs of Parraona, and some others, who were *Chaudhuris* [chiefs] of *Pergunahs* [precincts], are reckoned *Ashraf* [high class], and scorn the plow. While a great many of [them] have become ashamed of the term Kurmi, and reject all additions to the names above mentioned, . . . many of them are not ashamed of this name. . . . The families reckoned Ashraf, perhaps 110 houses, can read and write [and] unless exceedingly poor, will not hire themselves as plowmen, nor on any account act as domestics.[22]

Later data, from early twentieth-century village note surveys in Patna District, suggest that Kurmis in Bihar possessed an Ayodhya-centered consciousness as well. According to this detailed survey, *Awadhia* (a Persianized version of Ayodhya) Kurmis were the dominant community in a large tract of villages in the Barh precinct of northeast Patna District; as an example, in one village the surveying officer noted that "there are 9 families / 60 people of Awadhia Kurmis who wear the sacred thread since a long time."[23] Likewise, according to officials northwest of Patna in Saran District, among Kurmis "Ayodhias were particularly singled out as the 'substantial farmers and . . . the most influential sub-caste.'"[24]

Similar claims to status prevailed among many Muslim peasants in Bihar, who appropriated the title *Shekh*, implying highly coveted Arab origins. Buchanan remarked that "even though every low fellow assumes this title, . . . he is [nevertheless] not admitted to any rank."[25] Purnea District, in the northeasternmost section of the Gangetic core, possessed the greatest concentration of Shekhs claiming "descent from the gentry of Arabia." Buchanan insisted, however, that "a few alone can boast of this distinction, and the greater part are not to be distinguished from the Hindu peasantry of the vicinity. These Sheykhs are in general cultivators, and seem much fonder of the plough than of any other profession."[26] Shekhs were more evenly spread throughout the Gangetic dis-

tricts to the west of Bihar, and here similar doubts were raised by colonial observers as to their exact history. Of particular note were concerns
not unlike Buchanan's raised in the late 1860s by Henry Miers Elliot.[27]
Elliot divided Muslims into two large categories, viz., the nobility descended from "foreign invaders" and the commoners who descended
from or were themselves Hindu converts, whom he referred to as "Ma-
hommedans." The nobility comprised four ethnic groups, "Sayyid,
Mughal, Pathan, and Shaikh"; but for Elliot, the last of these terms represented a conceptual, classificatory stumbling block: "Any ordinary
Musulman who belongs to none of the three above-named classes
[Sayyid, Mughal, and Pathan], is called Shaikh. A vast number of the
converts from Hinduism give themselves this title, which from being so
promiscuously used has long ceased to have any special meaning or value
as a title of honour."[28] In a later, more detailed consideration of the
subject, Elliot confessed an inability to pinpoint the "true" identity of
Shekhs, observing that while many were descended from low-caste
Hindu converts, many others could be regarded as "the lowest class of
the descendants of the invaders." Like Buchanan, Elliot was forced to
base his conclusions on information provided by informants and on his
own first-hand observations of the apparent racial stock of a given community. Hence Elliot observed that "[the Shekh] is often of Affghan
descent, though his forefathers were not of sufficient social standing to
acquire the title of Khan. There is also much Persian, Bokhariot, and
Turki blood in his veins. Judging from the appearance of this class on
the whole, one would say that the non-Aryan element preponderated
considerably."[29]

Claims of this sort, grounded in the racial assumptions of the nineteenth century, were resorted to as a way of resolving the inevitable ambiguities that plagued colonial classification. In this case, those ambiguities indicate that a significant number of Muslim peasants sought to
achieve a modicum of self-respect through the articulation of a noble
past, expressed here as an identity with the Arab crucible of Islam, regardless of whether that identity was called into question by colonial
observers. This process, boiled down to its essentials, is analogous to the
changing identities among Kurmi, Yadav, and Kushvaha peasants, aspirations that begin to crystallize into full-fledged movements by the 1890s.

The divergent claims to status in the nineteenth century (and earlier)
illustrate the point that for non-Muslims, while varna was generally accepted as the basis for identity, on the whole little agreement prevailed
with respect to the place of the individual and the jati within a varna hierarchy. Srinivas, describing social relations in the mid-twentieth cen-

tury, regarded such a "lack of clarity in the hierarchy" as "one of the most striking features of the caste system," adding that "it is this ambiguity which makes it possible for a caste to rise in the hierarchy."[30] Such ambiguity only becomes a striking feature, however, when observers expect to see the opposite, that is, a complete congruity between theory (varna) and practice (jati). Such expectations were increasingly palpable in the late nineteenth and early twentieth centuries, when India became for nascent (imperial) anthropology a "laboratory of mankind," wherein scientific methods of observation (anthropometry among them) were expected to produce clear and straightforward sociological (and racial) patterns that conformed to varna-derived theories.[31] But if the claims to status confronted by Buchanan were at all remarkable, it is because they appear so commonplace, as if they were not at all unexpected given the all-too-obvious dysfunctions between theory and practice.

What is perhaps more significant, given the foregoing, is that a popular concern with status predated the rise of an imperial census apparatus and the colonial obsession with caste. Rather, claims to personal and community dignity appeared to be part of a longer discourse that did not require European political and administrative structures. This should not be taken to imply that the role of the state generally was of no significance. Status predicated on the presence of an interested state as arbiter was clearly evident in the political culture of Mughal India and Awadhi north India, but only served to give added political credence to attitudes that already possessed substantial popular appeal.[32] The role of the British in the late nineteenth and early twentieth centuries was to further solidify the discourse of caste into a hierarchical "caste of mind," at least for those on the perceiving end.[33] Even as this occurred, however, kshatriya identities were coalescing in peasant society that would, ultimately, threaten to undermine the systemics (if not the principle) of hierarchy by the middle of the twentieth century.

Building a Kshatriya Past, ca. 1900–1940

"The world is full of change!" declared Dilipsinha Yadav in 1914, as he exhorted his jati brothers to reform their lives.[34] The early twentieth century was an age of change indeed, as sporadic and localized claims to status coalesced into regional and national peasant organizations in cities and towns across north India. Such organizations met annually to define their community identities and espouse their reformist causes. Leading members would give speeches in festive gatherings, contrasting past glories with their degraded present; the assembled congregation would pass resolutions expressing the urgent need for social, religious, and educational reform; occasionally a peasant jati *mahasabha* (great association) would mobilize enough funds to build a school to educate its sons (and, sometimes, daughters) or build a press to publish a jati newsletter. Despite their diverse jati nomenclature, most of these organizations articulated a common historical vision: an ancient past of kshatriya distinction that had long since deteriorated into present-day shudra dishonor. The vision for the future was embodied in appeals for a return to the heady days of the kshatriya past.

A striking feature of these peasant-based social movements in the late nineteenth and early twentieth centuries is the quality of their leadership. A new educated elite, which had begun to penetrate the lower and middle rungs of government service, provided the organizational frame for the status claims among communities formerly identified as servile. This is most evident among Kurmis, the first peasant community to organize a campaign for kshatriya identity. By the 1890s the Kurmi-kshatriya movement was being coordinated on a broad, transregional level. The mantle of leadership in this phase befell the well-connected Ramdin Sinha, a government forester who had gained notoriety by resigning from his official post to protest a provincial circular of 1894 that included Kurmis as a "depressed community" and barred them therefore from recruitment into the police service.[35] The governor's office was flooded with letters from an outraged Kurmi-kshatriya public and was soon obliged to rescind the allegation in an 1896 communiqué to the police department: "His Honor [the governor] is . . . of the opinion that Kurmis constitute a respectable community which he would be reluctant to exclude from Government service."[36] Ten years later, Devi Prasad Sinha Chaudhari, a Kurmi-kshatriya writer and lecturer, would make a special point of acknowledging in his work the sponsorship of a large number of wealthy Kurmi kshatriyas, including Kashi Ram Varma, a zamindar of Unnao District on the southwest border of Lucknow; Amarnath Sinha, a zamindar and municipal commissioner in the town of Barh, south of Patna; and Ramkishor Sinha, subinspector of police in Tikari thana, Patna District.[37]

Though the official government recognition in 1896 of Kurmi respectability represented a major, and early, victory for the Kurmi-kshatriya movement, especially vis-á-vis its critics, it represented only one component of the complex history of kshatriya identity. The close ties between the new kshatriyas and the colonial government were not restricted to the Kurmis, nor was the battle for respectability fought solely with government petitions and interdepartmental circulars. The peasant communities that would begin to articulate formal kshatriya identities in the early twentieth century had also developed through the nineteenth century distinct ties with the local apparatus of empire. *Gopas, Goalas,* and *Ahirs,* who would by the early 1900s begin referring to themselves as Yadav kshatriyas, had long sought and attained (after 1898) recruitment as soldiers in the British Indian Army, particularly in the western Gangetic Plain.[38] *Koiris* and *Kachhis,* who would identify themselves as Kushvaha kshatriyas after about 1910, had long been the preferred cultivators of government poppy (and consequently the recipient of many interest-free government loans) for the production of crude opium in the Patna and Banaras regions through the nineteenth century.[39]

Kurmis, whose local conferences in the 1870s and 1880s coalesced into a pan-Gangetic phenomenon in the 1890s, expressed kshatriya status in terms of Vaishnava mythology.[40] At an 1895 meeting in Lucknow, for example, one Ganesh Swami Sadhu traced the genealogical descent of Kurmis from his study of the *Skanda Purana* and argued that the terms *Kurmi, Kunbi,* and *Kanbi* all derived from the name *Kurm,* the tortoise incarnation of Vishnu who supported the earth while the gods churned the ocean of milk for the nectar of immortality.[41] Unlike Yadav and Kushvaha kshatriya reformers, the Kurmi reformers in the early twentieth century did not specify a single genealogical line but rather many lineages through which Kurmi kshatriyas could have descended. Thus Devi Prasad Sinha Chaudhari, an early Kurmi publicist of Lucknow, listed in 1907 over sixty kshatriya lineages denoting Gangetic and Maharashtran lineages "in which Kurmis are found." Chaudhari based much of his discussion of what he termed the "famous kshatriya branches" almost entirely on "Kitts' Compendium of Hindu Castes and Tribes and other English books."[42]

Advocates of Kurmi-kshatriya identity broadened their social base to include influential agricultural communities throughout India, most notably *Kunbis, Kulambis,* and *Marathas* of Maharashtra; *Patidars* and *Patels* of Gujarat; and even *Naidus, Reddis,* and *Okkalingas* of South India.[43] Chaudhari maintained in his 1907 tract that most Kurmis descended from Ramchandra's two sons, Kush and Lav. He added, however, that some Kurmis were descended from Krishna and other notable chiefs involved in the epic Mahabharata wars.[44] Given the relatively early date (1907) of Chaudhari's booklet and the emergence as early as the 1870s of diverse Kurmi organizations, it is likely that Kurmis were simply amassing the maximum number of possible routes to kshatriya status. In later years, Koiris, Kachhis, and Muraos (as Kushvaha kshatriyas) would assert genealogical links with Ramchandra via his son Kush, while Goalas, Ahirs, and Gopas (as Yadav kshatriyas) would likewise affirm a descent from Krishna.

As with Kurmis and the early expression of an Awadhia/Ayodhya consciousness, the Goala association with Krishna and his Braj homeland was evident long before the formal articulation of a Yadav-kshatriya movement in the early twentieth century.[45] By the 1910s, however, the diffuse assertions of Krishna kinship had coalesced into a concerted call for kshatriya status based on a claim of descent in the ancient lineage of Raja Yadu (hence Yadav), of which Krishna was the most famous progenitor.[46] As with Kurmis, the newly delimited Yadav-kshatriya community expanded its geographical horizons to incorporate not only Goalas of Bihar and eastern Uttar Pradesh, but Ahirs, Gops, Gopals, and Sadgops—closely related and/or synonomous jati communities throughout the Gangetic north that combined cultivation with the herding of cattle and dairy farming.[47] By the 1930s, Yadav-kshatriya historians held that "Yadavs [were] the ancient citizens of the land of the Aryans [and] have their origins in the main *Chandravamsh* [lunar line] branch of kshatriyas, . . . and as the *Suryavamsh* [solar line] is known for its original ancestor Ramchandra, the Yadu line is famous for its original progenitor Lord Krishna."[48] In the reconstructed history of the Yadav kshatriyas, the devastation of the Mahabharata wars signaled the onset of jati decline, Yadav unity began to give way to factionalism, and drinking and gambling corrupted once-noble jati morals. The standard Yadav-kshatriya account concluded with the final stages of cultural decline, marked by mass conversions to Buddhism and the requisite repudiation of the sacred thread.[49]

The Kurmi and Yadav-kshatriya movements of the twentieth century both possessed distinct early nineteenth-century antecedents in the form of a geocultural association with historical manifestations of Vishnu—Ramchandra and Ayodhya in the case of Kurmis, Krishna and Mathura-Vrindaban in the case of Yadavs. By contrast, the nineteenth-century antecedents of the Kushvaha-kshatriya movement reveal distinct cosmological associations with Shiva and his divine consort, Parvati. Kushvaha-kshatriya identity was espoused by agricultural communities well known throughout the Gangetic north for an expertise in small-

scale vegetable and (to an increasingly limited extent after the turn of
the twentieth century) poppy cultivation. Prominent among them were
Kachhi and *Murao* agriculturalists of central Uttar Pradesh, *Kachhvaha*s of western Uttar Pradesh, and *Koiri*s of Bihar and eastern Uttar
Pradesh.[50] Made up of such skilled agriculturalists, these communities
had long since come to the attention of colonial administrators and eth-
nologists. Both W. W. Hunter in the 1870s and H. H. Risley in the 1890s
recorded the legend that Koiris and Kachhis were created by Shiva and
Parvati to tend the vegetable (Risley mentions in particular radishes, *mu-
rai,* hence *Murao*) and flower gardens of Banaras, a mythological reflection of the importance to their identity of both agricultural skill and
Shaiva belief.[51] Indeed, Risley characterized the majority of Koiris in Bihar as Shaiva or *Shakta* (followers of *shakti,* the female personification
of cosmic energy) and observed that "Vaishnavism has hitherto made
little progress among them." Buchanan, eighty years earlier, had noted
that most Koiris in Bihar followed Dasnami sanyasis, while many in the
Gorakhpur region adjacent to Ayodhya as well as in Purnia in the east
had already begun to look to Ramanandis for spiritual guidance.[52]

By the early 1920s, the ideology of social reform began to displace
the commitment to Shaiva-Shakta origins and replace them with a kshatriya identity based on an historical association with Ramchandra. According to Gangaprasad, a resident of Banaras and an outspoken proponent of reform, Koiris, Kachhis, Muraos, and Kachhvahas were
inexorably connected to the roots of Vaishnava history through linear
descent from *Kush,* the son of Ramchandra. Gangaprasad argued therefore that the proper designation of the greater north Indian jati should
be *Kushvaha* kshatriya.[53] The early twentieth-century reconstruction of
the past, here recounted by Gangaprasad, linked the history of the jati
with the ill-fated cause of the defense of Hindu India. The descendants
of Kush, the reader was told, eventually found military service in the
courtly ranks of Raja Jaichand, whose north Indian armies were subsequently defeated in battle by Sultan Shahabuddin Ghuri at the close of
the twelfth century, during the consolidation of Muslim rule based in
Delhi. Gangaprasad blamed all the ills of the subsequent eight centuries
on Muslim persecution, citing particularly the fear of Muslim atrocities
as the sole reason Kushvaha kshatriyas fled to the forests in disarray, dis-
carding their sacred threads, so as not to be recognized as erstwhile de-
fenders of the "Hindu" faith. The jati history concludes with a rueful
account of social degradation, disorganization, and dispersal throughout north India; Kushvaha kshatriyas then became known by the more
familiar local designations of Kachhvaha, Kachhi, Murao, and Koiri.

Movements for kshatriya identity were by no means restricted to the major peasant jatis, but included a wide range of less populous communities that often combined "traditional" occupations with agriculture. Examples include *Kahar*s (palanquin bearers and household servants), *Tanti*s (weavers), *Sonar*s (goldsmiths), *Mali*s (flower-gardeners), *Tambuli*s (betel-leaf traders), *Kalwar*s (distillers), and numerous others.[54] This fact was not lost on Nirgun Sinha "Khali," author of several Yadav kshatriya tracts, who by the end of the 1930s called repeatedly for greater ideological flexibility in allowing these claims on the grounds that an augmented kshatriya population would "bolster the defense of Hinduism."[55] His comments on the plethora and diversity of jati reform movements in the early twentieth century give some indication of the heady transformations that marked this period: "In these changing times jatis that we would have considered shudra twenty or twenty-five years ago are now educating scholars who are proving that their communities are not only vaishya and kshatriya, but even brahman! Only a few jatis today fail to become agitated when called shudra; most become quite stern and angry at the mere mention of the term."[56]

A heightened sensitivity to caste, identity, and the past marked the social and cultural transformations of this period. A popular verse of the time, attributed to one Bharat Bharati and cited in at least two reform pamphlets, urged its audience to reflect,

> Who were we, what has happened, and where are we going now?
> Gather round everyone and ponder these questions together.
> If we fail to appreciate the entirety of our past,
> we may never realize who we really are.[57]

Jati reformers of the early twentieth century took this poetic counsel particularly seriously and spent endless hours reconstructing, indeed reinventing, the pasts of their communities. But what they were saying and the ways in which they were saying it are two distinct and equally significant phenomena. On the surface these publicist-reformers understood, or at least represented, the past in terms of a familiar Vaishnava mythological framework; the myth-history that resulted began with the primeval battle between good and evil that set the groundwork for the cosmological origins of the Hindu world, continued with the epic lineages of Vishnu's avatars, and concluded with the alleged civilizational chaos that accompanied the Muslim invasions and the rise of British power. However, the rhetoric beneath the profusion of mytho-historical detail can tell us a great deal more about the quality of social and cultural change in this period.

Rhetoric and Reform

Kshatriya reform depended not simply on a Vaishnava mythological framework, but on the institutionalization of a belief in Vaishnava morality, pervading day-to-day affairs. The repeated references in kshatriya reform literature to Vishnu, Narayan, Rama, Krishna, and related Vaishnava personages (such as Lakshmi, Sita, Radha, Hanuman, etc.), the frequent use of Vaishnava terms in common discourse, and the occasional allusions to the changing institution of Vaishnava monasticism (particularly the Ramanandi sampraday), all reflect this institutionalization process. And from the perspective of the new kshatriyas, the central social imperative of Vaishnava morality was caste reform. An example of this can be seen on the cover of a 1920 pamphlet advocating the kshatriya status of Kahars, where the maxim, "This world faces innumerable challenges, but no one of them is greater than jati reform," is attributed to Ramchandra himself.[58]

The lives of Ramchandra and Krishna were frequently held up by jati reformers as the standard for morally correct attitudes and behavior, even at the risk of criticizing contemporary Vaishnava institutions. A didactic technique often utilized by the jati publications was a mock dialogue between two or more people. One particularly telling "conversation" was contributed to the *Kurmi Samachar* ("Kurmi Newspaper") by a correspondent in 1895. The piece portrays a discussion between a social critic by the name of Vichar Sinha and one Bhagat-ji, meant to represent mindless obedience to religious custom.[59] The dialogue begins with Bhagat-ji's enthusiastic description of a lavish wedding he has just had the pleasure of attending. Sinha responds by attacking the "foolish expenditures" and "corrupt practices" seen during marriages, such as the spectacle of fireworks and, especially, dancing girls:

VS: You surely have read in the Ramayan that all the gods, sages, seers, and great men came and attended the grandeur of Raja Ramchandra Maharaja's wedding. Well how could they possibly stomach seeing those prostitutes flaunt themselves and hearing those filthy songs they sing at our weddings today?

Bh: I suppose you're right. But nowadays people even arrange for dancing girls in the temples. In fact, they even perform on the birthday celebrations of Krishna and Ramchandra. Nobody goes if there aren't any dancers.

VS: Exactly. By constantly allowing these dancers to perform we have allowed our judgment to become perverted, and now we can't seem to enjoy worshipping God without them. Oh, what a state our country is in!

This portrayal of the corruption of temple worship, whether real or imagined, was gauged to shock the Kurmi kshatriya readership into promoting prudent expenditures during family ceremonies such as weddings; the financial savings that would thus accrue could then be directed toward the betterment of the jati as a whole. The editor of the *Kurmi Samachar,* Babu Bhagvandin, may have been troubled by the risqué content of the criticism and prefaced the dialogue with the cautionary note that "the editor chooses to make no comment here." Nevertheless, the puritanical Vaishnava tenor of the piece reflects the willingness of kshatriya reformers to address religious issues directly, even to the extent of caricaturing contemporary religion itself as little more than mindless custom.

Also typical of kshatriya reform were frequent textual allusions to Vaishnava festivals and Ram and Krishna bhakti. For example, Nauvat Ray, a proponent of Kahar status in western Uttar Pradesh, noted the significance of the publication day of his 1920 jati-reform booklet with the declaration, "Today is the great day of *vijay dashmi*—this is our special festival, the auspicious day that commemorates the victory of the stately and revered Bhagvan Ramchandra-ji. It was on this day that he killed Ravana, the very embodiment of evil, and hoisted the banner of victory."[60] *Vijay dashmi,* literally "victory on the tenth," also refers to the tenth day of the moonlit half of the lunar month of *Ashwin* when, during the annual performance of the Ram Lila, or the "play of Ram," Ramchandra destroys the evil king Ravana in a dramatically reenacted battle.[61] Nauvat Ray and his publisher, Fakirchand, incorporated the historic meaning of Ramchandra's epic battle against the forces of evil directly into the struggle for kshatriya status. In a supplicatory aside, the publisher also noted the auspicious date and prayed to Ramchandra to support their cause, identifying the opponents of the Kahar movement for kshatriya status with the evil Ravana:

Then [when Ramchandra defeated Ravana] it was *tretayug,* now it is *kaliyug.* Since then our condition has deteriorated. At that time you killed the evil Ravana, freed the world from sin, restored the dignity of dharma, and spread contentment and tranquility. Why will you not come back now, when dharma has all but disappeared from the world and we are oppressed by Ravana in the form of our detractors? Bhagvan! Please come, slay the demon, and restore completely the dignity of dharma and hoist the banner of victory. Unite through love brahman, kshatriya, vaishya, and shudra, fulfill your own visions, and everyone will extol you and abide by your directives.[62]

The commitment of Kahars to Ram was equally powerful in south Bihar. In 1906, the Kahars of Gaya—who styled themselves *Ramani* Kahars—organized a *Ramani Dharma Pracharani Sabha* (Association for the Spread of Ramani Dharma) and, under its auspices, produced a short pamphlet of rules, regulations, and fines to counter the "many crude practices that had, over time, corrupted the jati."[63] More interesting than the elaborate punishments prescribed for offenders of jati dignity are the names printed on the register of officers and members of the jati sabha itself.[64] Listed as vice-chairman of the organization was one Ram Das, "a noted resident of the neighborhood of Geval Bigha in Gaya." Others included a bookseller named Ram Kishan Das who was listed as the consultant for the association, and *Chhote* Ram Das,[65] both of the same neighborhood. As noted in chapter 2, "das" means "servant" or "slave" and was commonly assumed as a suffix by many Ramanandi sadhus (especially prior to 1918) to signal their symbolic relationship to Ramchandra; here it would appear that Kahars had begun adopting the suffix for their own purposes, regardless of any connection to the sampraday. Even more remarkable were the names of many of the remaining members. The associate chairman, his assistant, and fully forty-nine of the fifty-eight general and associate members possessed the surname *Ram*.[66]

The institutionalization of Vaishnava language was not restricted to personal nomenclature, however. The author of a 1924 publication, again from Gaya, which advocated the Kanyakubja-kshatriya status of Sonars (goldsmiths), pointed out that the universal importance of Vaishnava belief could even be seen by the frequent colloquial use of the names of Vishnu's avatars in popular language: "Let us now turn to the subject of popular language. Even the most boorish peasants, who don't know anything, immediately cry out 'Ram Ram' upon meeting one another. The Thakurs say 'Jay Radho-ji ki' [victory to Radha]. When this spread into popular usage among the four varnas is not in fact known. . . . If someone stumbles while walking along, "*aré* Ram" [oh Ram] immediately escapes from his lips."[67] Such terms were also brought to bear in peasant politics, most notably during a tense three-year period of peasant activism in Awadh beginning in 1919. Baba Ramchandra, who both espoused Kurmi reform and came to lead the peasant outcry against landlord tyranny, introduced the language of Vaishnava devotion in Awadh peasant politics to advance the notion of a just political economy crafted around the ideal of Ramchandra's Ayodhya. According to historian Gyanendra Pandey, Baba Ramchandra recalled some years later that he actively promoted the use of the egalitarian greeting, *Sitaram*, in the place of the hierarchical *salaam*, an act that was soon to earn him the ire of "many of the praiseworthy and respectable folk of the upper castes."[68]

Similarly, Vaishnava symbols and vocabulary adorned the textual frame of jati reform literature, including such literary constructions as the names of publishing houses, illustrations, dedications, and prefatory benedictions. A typical example was a collection of exhortational songs and prayers on the subject of social reform among Goalas. This short tract, entitled *Jatiya Sandesh* (Jati Message), was published by one Swami Nathu Bhagat Yadav and printed by the *Haribhakt Narayan Raja* Press in Darbhanga, North Bihar.[69] The facts that the publisher was himself a Yadav and a religious figure (as reflected in the title "Swami") and that the name of the press was composed of a phrase signifying devotion to Vishnu (*Haribhakt Narayan*) only serve to underline the complementarity of peasant-kshatriya reform and Vaishnava rhetoric. Inscribed on the cover page is the initiatory *mantra* or chant for worshipping the conjoined image of Radha-Krishna (*Shri Radhokrishnabhyanamah*) followed on the inside cover by a picture of the divine couple. Likewise, a compendium of social rules for Yadav kshatriyas was published in 1928 from the *Gokul* Press, Gokul being the remembered home of Krishna, Radha, and the cowherds around Vrindaban and Mathura in western Uttar Pradesh. And, as a final example, separate editions of a prominent historical tract on Yadav-kshatriya history were published in Etawah and Lucknow from the Krishna Press.[70]

The reformist kshatriya dedication to a Vaishnava ethic even extended, in some cases, to pugnacious attacks against competing religious traditions. Jamuna Prashad Yadav, in a 1927 pamphlet published in Jhansi and directed at caste members in his native Chhattisgarhi region as well as "for the benefit of the entire Ahir jati," condemned what he termed the "lewd, sex-ridden" rituals and practices of "*vam margis*" (a pejorative term for practitioners of a particular kind of Shaiva-Shakta tantra) and exhorted Yadavs to follow the correct worship of the Vaishnavi *devi* (goddess).[71] Although Chattisgarh in what is now Madhya Pradesh is some distance removed from the Gangetic core, J. Yadav's remarks mirrored in tone as well as content a Ramanandi polemic directed against the so-called vam-margis published in Prayag (Allahabad) ten years later and widely available in north Bihar. In this publication, entitled *Devivali Pakhand* (The Heresy of Sacrifice to the Goddess), Janki Ballabh Das launched a thoroughgoing invective against Shaiva-Shakta tantra, with particular criticism of the worshipers of the goddess Durga (the main proponents of which he alleged were *Maithil brahmans*, that is, belonging to the dominant land-controlling jati of North Bihar) for their animal sacrifices, but shifted quickly to accusations of everything from pedophilia, ritual sex, and incest to the consumption of beef, alcohol, and far more reprehensible substances, all allegedly performed during tantric rituals.[72]

However, the most explicit indication of the Vaishnava rhetoric of social reform in the early twentieth century was the affirmation by kshatriya ideologues of the upright morality of their jati constituents. This was best expressed by Gangaprasad, the Banaras-based proponent of Kushvaha-kshatriya identity, who described his jati brothers as "followers of the Vaishnava path" and noted that "devotees made certain their children received proper spiritual initiation and education."[73] Gangaprasad added that all Kushvahas "receive the mantra from their family gurus and sing those verses every morning and evening" and that "in the month of *Kartik* or *Shravan* they worship *Mahabir* [Hanuman, the embodiment of true devotion to Ram and Sita], wear the sacred thread, and offer bread and sweets." Similarly, Baijnath Prasad Yadav's compendium of rules for Goalas not only prescribed upright decorum and proper methods of celebrating a variety of household and public festivals, but also condemned the various "evil" attitudes and practices of caste members such as illiteracy, child marriage, drinking, gambling, and wasteful expenditures.[74]

When reformers were not citing the extensive Vaishnava credentials of their jati members, they were marshaling a wide array of sectarian institutional sanction to back their claims of kshatriya status. In Maharashtra and Gujarat, associated Kunbis and Kanbis solicited and received this certification from the head abbot of the Dasnami order in Nasik, northeast of Bombay, and from his Ramanuji counterpart in Kanchi, southwest of Madras.[75] Kurmis of the Gangetic north, however, sought the Vaishnava backing of Radhacharan Goswami of Vrindaban, who presided over a debate of Banaras scholars on the subject of Kurmi status that took place under the auspices of the Kurmi association of Bharehta village south of Banaras in 1907.[76] In defense of the Kurmi claim to kshatriya status, Radhacharan Goswami cited a range of positive attributes, including the fact that "this jati has built many temples in which brahmans have performed the image consecrations and wherein all people pay respectful homage to God by taking the water with which the feet of the image has been washed."[77] Caste-based temple construction occurred most prominently in the major Vaishnava pilgrimage centers. In Ayodhya, for instance, a multitude of "caste temples" erected in this century would buttress the kshatriya status claims of jati organizations; these include temples built by Kurmis, Yadavs, Kahars, Kayasths, Barhais, Malis, Murais (Kushvahas), Sonars, and many others.[78]

Kshatriya Reform and Ramanandis

Kshatriya reform in the early twentieth century was built on a Vaishnava mythological foundation, espoused a strict Vaishnava morality, employed a rich Vaishnava symbolic vocabulary, and even contributed materially to the success of Vaishnava pilgrimage centers. Taken as a whole, then, the history of kshatriya reform in the late nineteenth and early twentieth centuries reflects the institutionalization of Vaishnava belief as a generally agreed-upon Hindu framework for social change, regardless of one's specific sectarian commitments. In this sense, the kshatriya reform campaigns as a whole can be seen as ideological heir to the Vaishnava reform mentalities of the nineteenth and twentieth centuries, particularly as manifest in Ramanandi liberalism with respect to caste. But while the Ramanandi sampraday has long evinced a marked disdain for questions of status, particularly in the twentieth century, the whole point of kshatriya reform campaigns was the enhancement of status. This major ideological difference, I would suggest, explains the unevenness of Ramanandi participation in the forefront of kshatriya reform campaigns.

However, as I have noted in the previous chapter, the Ramanandi sampraday was not ideologically monolithic, and many Ramanandis harbored views on caste wholly divergent from what became the dominant position in the sampraday in the twentieth century. More precisely, those sadhus who chose not to accept what I have termed the "radical" Ramanandi guru parampara after 1921 and who consequently were labeled Ramanuji, not only took a conservative approach to the question of Ramanand's monastic antecedents by insisting on the retention of Ramanuja in their guru parampara, but insisted on the maintenance of caste boundaries in monastic life. Based on their willingness to admit the relevance of varna in religious affairs, it would not have been ideologically inconsistent for a "Ramanuji Ramanandi" to promote the pursuit of status implicit in movements for kshatriya reform. In this section I examine two such individuals, kshatriya ideologues with Ramanuji links to the Ramanandi sampraday, to throw light on how the travails of being Vaishnava informed the politics of becoming kshatriya, and vice versa.

The first of the two, Raghunandan Prasad Sinha Varmma, a proponent of kshatriya status for Sonars (goldsmiths), published a booklet from Gaya in south Bihar in 1924, three years after the Ujjain decision, which declared that Ramanuja was not included in the guru parampara of Ra-

manand. Even though his name suggests a nonascetic status, Varmma's
lay partisanship in the parampara dispute is made immediately clear in
his work: both above the title on the cover page and prior to the introduction are dedications to Ramanujacharya.[79] In addition, he notes that
he received the help of one Babu Aditya Narayan Sinha (of Chaudha-
rani Tola, Village and Post Office Mokama, District Patna), a devotee
of Swami Ramprapann Ramanujadas.[80] Ramprapann Ramanujadas, it
may be recalled, represented the south Indian Shri Vaishnava side in the
debate against Bhagavadacharya at the Ujjain kumbh in 1921. Varmma
also assured the reader that in addition to shedding light on the "ancient pedigree of the Sonar jati," he would "elaborate some of the mys-
teries of Shri Vaishnava dharma."[81] After devoting the next forty-six and
a half pages to the "Kanyakubja-kshatriya" identity of Sonars, Varmma
turned to "the importance of Shri Vaishnava dharma," prefacing his remarks with the core Ramanuji tenet that "the swami of Shri Vaishnava
dharma is Vishnu and the acharya is Shri Lakshmiji."[82] This was certain
to enrage any radical Ramanandis who happened to read the tract, inasmuch as the 1918–1921 dispute was sparked by the unwillingness of Ramanujis to worship the images of Ram and Sita.

Varmma was only warming to his Ramanuji task, however; he next
made reference to the universal acceptance of Shri Vaishnava symbols
by "other sampraday": "Regardless of membership in any particular sampraday, the obligation of any auspicious ceremony, such as marriage or
the birth of a child, requires the correct application of *tilak* [a marking
of vermilion or sandal] powder in a vertical fashion [on the forehead].[83]
This is inevitably called the marking of Shri Vishnu. When followers of
other sampraday follow such obligations they take that very name, they
wear his very sign."[84] Varmma chose not to mention Ramanandis here
by name; however, since Ramanandis and Ramanujis employ nearly iden-
tical tilak markings, it is clear that this was a calculated affront and that
radical Ramanandis were the main target. His objective was to position
those loyal to the memory of Ramanuja as "high" Vaishnavas, within
which exist the various—and by implication hierarchically inferior—
sectarian divisions. To this end, Varmma hypothesized that since "so
many other sampraday rely on our literature (Gita, Ramayan, Bhagvat,
etc.) and we read or take no interest in the literature of any other sampraday, we must be the most superior."[85] He asserted, in addition, that
no other sadhus were so pure, a reference no doubt to the "acharya"
status long maintained by Ramanujis and to the commensal restrictions
that were alleged to have been the cause of Ramanand's expulsion from
the fraternity of Raghavanand's disciples in the fourteenth century.

Far more detailed mention was made of Ramanandi-Ramanuji divisiveness by Swami Dharnidharacharya, the author of a 1930 history of Bihar-based Kurmis who styled themselves "Awadhvamshiya" (of the lineage of Awadh) kshatriyas. Prior to addressing the subject of kshatriya identity in his booklet, Dharnidharacharya focused on "sampraday matters," citing his guru-given name as Dharnidhar Ramanujadas, his guru's place as the Totadri Math (the center of south Indian Vaishnavism), and finally his guru-parampara, which includes Ramanuja but makes no mention whatsoever of Ramanand. The actual text begins with supplications to Ramchandra and Ramanuja, followed by a few words on the author's name and village; Dharnidharacharya then takes up a detailed disquisition on the history and religious dimensions of the Awadhia kshatriyas. Included here are such topics as the origin of kshatriyas; the genesis of the kurmm vamsh; the spread of the kshatriyas from Ayodhya to modern Bihar and eastern Uttar Pradesh; the tale of Ramchandra's birth and the birth of his two sons, Lav and Kush; the correct ritual observations for pregnancy, birth, menstruation, eating, sacred thread investiture, marriage, and death; and the traditional roles of each of the four varna.[86]

The author then returns to matters of personal and sampraday concern, the narrative of which I shall recount here in some detail.[87] Dharnidharacharya was born in 1891 to an Awadh-kshatriya family of Patipur village, not far from the town of Nandalalabad in Patna District, south Bihar. He reveals little of his youth, aside from the fact that his given name was Dhanraj Sinha Varmma and that he was married at the age of fourteen. Soon thereafter and against the wishes of his parents, Dhanraj (the young Dharnidharacharya) left home. Crossing the Ganga, which forms the northern border of Patna District, he wandered northward for about one hundred miles and eventually found himself in a village near the town of Sitamarhi in north Bihar; there he remained for six months, in a small establishment of a local naga *jatadhari* (a sadhu who wears long, matted hair). Finally, afraid that his parents would be able to locate him and force him to return home, Dhanraj set off for Nepal with a group of wandering monks and from there undertook a lengthy pilgrimage route that led him all over north India. He visited such sites as Mukti Narayan, Damodar Kund, Tansen Pahar, Gangasagar, Puri, Prayag, Chitrakut, and finally ended up in Ayodhya, by then well known as one of the most important pilgrimage centers in the Gangetic region. At this point in his life, probably around 1910, Dhanraj decided to remain in Ayodhya and began the study of *nyaya* (logic, one of the six traditional schools of Indian philosophy) and related subjects under the tutelage of Saryudas, a noted Ramanandi scholar.

Dhanraj passed the next several years furthering his studies under various teachers connected to the rasik strain of Vaishnava bhakti, when in 1918 the controversy over Ramanuja and the Ramanandi parampara erupted in Ayodhya and, subsequently, throughout north India. The ensuing debates were particularly all-consuming in Ayodhya, and few if any there remained aloof from the turmoil. The author was certainly no exception: the ties Dhanraj formed with individuals in the south Indian Vaishnava tradition at this time ensured that he would be caught in the throes of sampraday discord. Dhanraj eventually supported the Ramanuji view and even went so far as to become the disciple of a major Shri Vaishnava figure from south India visiting Ayodhya at the time; indeed, it was during his initiation that he even was given the name *Dharnidhar Ramanujadas,* or "Dharnidhar, slave of Ramanuja." If Dhanraj had achieved by this time a fraction of the scholarly respect he was to garner in the 1930s, the new title of this young Vaishnava intellectual—not to mention his recent initiation with a south Indian guru—was sure to have raised the ire of more than a few Ramanandis. Dharnidhar itself means "mountain"; as a result of the author's growing prominence in the 1930s, he became regarded generally throughout Bihar and eastern Uttar Pradesh as Swami Dharnidharacharya.

By the 1920s prevailing opinion in Ayodhya had tipped in favor of the radical Ramanandi view, and the memory of Ramanuja was being purged (at least officially) from sampraday records. Naturally, Dharnidharacharya was deeply disturbed by this development, and his recollections of Ayodhya in this period are full of bitterness. But it is his response to the radical position that is of particular interest, because the evidence he marshaled to prove that Ramanuja, and not Ramanand, was the founder of the Shri Vaishnava sampraday consisted primarily of prophetic Sanskrit hymns composed by ancient *rishis* (seers) well before the advent of either Ramanand or Ramanuja. These texts shared in common the prediction that the four main divisions of Vaishnava sampraday, or *chatuh-sampraday,* would be founded by Vishnuswami, Madhvacharya, Ramanujacharya, and Nimbarkacharya.[88] Dharnidharacharya warned that "anyone who opposes such proof would in the end come to ruin."[89] In response to the Ramanandi claim that the literature of the Ramanujis offended Ramchandra, he asserted, on the authority of the *Brihadbrahm Samhita* (part 2, section 7, verses 1–71), that "it is well known that Shri Ramanuja Swami is the originator of the *Ramtarak* mantra [an invocation to Ram as savior]." Dharnidharacharya urged Ramanandis to "renounce obstinate factionalism. . . . If not, the loss will be on their own heads, since it is well known that 'the mantras of the man who is without a sampraday will bear no fruit.'"[90]

Notwithstanding these remonstrations, however, there was little Dharnidharacharya could do to check the gradual rise to prominence of radical Ramanandis in Ayodhya. In fact, he was so dismayed by the turn of events that at some point in the early 1920s he contemplated leaving Ayodhya altogether and undertook another lengthy pilgrimage to put the controversy behind him. Again his travels took him all over the northern half of the subcontinent, but also to Totadri and Venkatesh, the former his guru's place and both important Ramanuji sites in the southern peninsula. Nevertheless, Dharnidharacharya found himself yearning for Ayodhya, which had become a home to him notwithstanding the many reminders of the quarrel that had disrupted his life, and he returned there in 1924. Eventually, with the assistance of a friend, Dharnidharacharya took up residence at the *Uttar Totadri Math* (the northern branch of the south Indian Totadri math) in Ayodhya, an institution clearly in sympathy with the Ramanuji position. Ensconced in the idyllic setting of the monastery's *Venkatesh* temple bordering on *Vibhishan* pond, and thereby insulated from the haughtiness of predominantly Ramanandi Ayodhya, the author gained a reputation of high scholarly ability and began to accept students, to whom he devoted his full attention.[91]

It was in all likelihood the reputation as an energetic young Vaishnava intellectual of Ayodhya that attracted to Dharnidharacharya the attention of kshatriya ideologues in the late 1920s, and by 1930 he had published his jati study. The boy who had run away at the age of fourteen or fifteen thus found himself returning home, both geographically and genealogically, in his thirties and forties. Dharnidharacharya's role as a monk addressing issues of caste status for individuals outside the world of sampraday was an appropriate one and, indeed, was endorsed and even emulated by a number of Dharnidharacharya's peers throughout the Gangetic region. Three individuals in particular who appear in the prefatory pages of Dharnidharacharya's *Shri Awadhvamshiya Kshatriya Martandah* merit a brief mention here: Ramtahaldas, Hanuman Sharan, and Videhanandani Sharan. The first, Ramtahaldas, in a letter expressing his deep appreciation for the work that Dharnidharacharya had done in advancing the cause of the Awadhvamshiya kshatriyas, described himself as a "Shri Vaishnava pandit" of Daraganj near Prayag.[92] The others, Hanuman Sharan and Videhanandani Sharan, were described in an adjoining felicitation as the successive heads of the Rajapur *Thakurbari* (abode of god) in Patna and praised for their work on behalf of both Vaishnava belief and the Awadhvamshiya kshatriya sabha; the former, Hanuman Sharan, was in all likelihood born an Awadhvamshiya kshatriya. It is also worth noting that Hanuman Sharan claimed guru-parampara descent from Swami Balanandacharya, the eighteenth-century Ramanandi of Jaipur who is credited with organizing the Vaishnava naga armies.[93] This conforms, incidentally, with the suggestion (see chapter 1) that soldier monasticism in the eighteenth century drew on a nonelite, shudra base; in the early twentieth century, Awadhvamshiya kshatriyas would refute the imputation of shudra-ness and, indeed, would use the Rajapur Thakurbari in Patna (along with the Uttar Totadri Math in Ayodhya) as informal distribution centers for Awadhvamshiya-kshatriya propaganda.[94]

Besides providing a recollection of the Ramanandi crisis of memory and ensuing Ramanandi-Ramanuji animosities that bears striking, if predictable, contrasts to that given by the radical Bhagavadacharya (recounted in the previous chapter), Swami Dharnidharacharya's reminiscences afford a sense of the networks that allowed him and others of the north Indian Ramanuji mold to remain active in Gangetic Vaishnava culture. Perhaps more importantly, the experience of Swami Dharnidharacharya leads to broader speculation regarding the intersections of sampraday and caste in the Gangetic region. According to Dharnidharacharya, an extensive Ramanuji network spanned the religious topography of Bihar and Uttar Pradesh, a network that eventually supported and sharpened the identity of reformist kshatriyas claiming Awadh as a place of origin. Indeed, a similar network seemed to be in place as well to nurture a Kanyakubja-kshatriya identity for Sonars, and it is likely that there were other examples of Ramanuji sadhus involved in kshatriya reform, because those Vaishnava monks who became Ramanuji by force of circumstance after 1921 were by definition more attuned in general to the ideological demands of varna commensality. While all Ramanujis were not invariably enmeshed in the kshatriya campaigns of the early twentieth century, Ramanujis were more likely to respond positively to the concerns being raised by the widespread kshatriya movements of peasants and artisans long labeled shudra by the social elite. Others less concerned about jati, varna, and personal purity—whatever their imputed status—and more interested in developing an aggressive, egalitarian social vision within the dominant monastic order of Gangetic India (the Ramanandi sampraday) could be expected to have sided with Bhagavadacharya and the radical wing. These latter, of course, would not be and were not precluded from advocating the cause of jati reform in the late nineteenth and early twentieth centuries, but they would have been less likely to do so given their disdain for issues of status in general.[95]

While I have argued that the crisis of tradition that divided the Ramanandi sampraday after 1918 can only be understood in terms of caste in colonial India, it would be difficult to make a related argument, namely, that kshatriya reform in the early twentieth century can only be understood in terms of caste attitudes expressed in the Ramanandi sampraday. However, it is clear from the foregoing that attitudes toward caste expressed in north Indian Vaishnava monastic circles were not restricted to the realm of sampraday but were applied to the "outside" world. Hence, not only was an institutionalized Vaishnava discourse inherent in the dialogue of social change, certain Vaishnava monks were willing and able to act as intellectuals on behalf of agricultural and artisan communities. Indeed, kshatriya identity seemed at least as important to Dharnidharacharya and his associates as their status as Ramanuji Vaishnavas. The eventual dominance of radical Ramanandis in Ayodhya may also help to explain the overt dedication of Ramanujis to the cause of kshatriya campaigns. Men like Dharnidharacharya probably saw the growing kshatriya movement as an outlet for political and intellectual expression, which for them had been quashed to a large extent within the sampraday by the group of young Ramanandi radicals spearheading the "Gangeticization" of Vaishnava tradition. Kshatriya reform gave Dharnidharacharya and other Gangetic Ramanujis the opportunity to organize, to espouse a group identity, and perhaps most significantly, to express their own opinions regarding the crisis in the sampraday itself through the forum of local jati publications.

Before concluding this section, it is important to note that the involvement of Vaishnava monks in kshatriya reform was not restricted to the Ramanandi sampraday. The other mainstream Vaishnava orders in Gangetic north India were oriented primarily toward the worship of Radha and Krishna and included the relatively small Radhaballabhi community and the more populous Gauriya (followers of Chaitanya) and Nimbarki sampraday. These sampraday were concentrated in western Uttar Pradesh, particularly the Mathura-Vrindaban region, and Bengal proper and were only very sparsely represented in the central and eastern Gangetic districts between Lucknow and Patna, what I have referred to generally as the Gangetic core.[96] If kshatriya reformers, particularly those claiming descent from the chandra-vamsh (lunar lineage) of Krishna in western Uttar Pradesh, wished to enlist the intellectual and religious sanction of Vaishnava sadhus, they would have been as likely to turn to these sampraday. However, if kshatriya reformers in the Gangetic core required Vaishnava monastic confirmation of their kshatriya status claims, they would have to seek out sadhus from what was essentially the dominant Vaishnava order there: namely, the Ramanandi sampraday.[97]

Likewise, there is no reason to presume that Ramanandi devotion to Ram and Sita would have restricted their kshatriya reform activity to those movements that sought a genealogical link with Ramchandra's suryavamsh (solar lineage). Though Ram and Sita were central to Ramanandi identity, Radha-Krishna bhakti also figured prominently in Ramanandi worship and literature. Buchanan noted on several occasions that Ramanandis were willing to instruct lay followers in the worship of any of Vishnu's avatars, most particularly Ram and Krishna.[98] Such devotional flexibility was evident even in Ayodhya itself, where, Buchanan observed, the Ramanandis "do not scruple to deliver the form of prayer, by which Krishna is addressed."[99] The Ramanandi focus on Krishna extended as well to hagiographic and mythological literature; for example, the Bhaktamal, a text of major importance for all Vaishnavas, recounts numerous stories and legends pertaining to saints famous for their vigorous devotion to Ram as well as Krishna and their attendant pantheons. The main Bhaktamal scholars in the nineteenth and early twentieth centuries, as noted in the previous chapter, were associated with the Ramanandi sampraday, most notably, at the turn of the century, Sitaramsharan Bhagvan Prasad. Indeed, Bhagvan Prasad was also well known for his poetry describing the life of Mirabai, the legendary Rajput princess whose adorations of Krishna superseded her matrimonial obligations. In addition, Ramanandis in Bihar have long considered the *Bhagavata Purana,* which among other things recounts the life of Krishna, and the *Bhagavad Gita,* comprising Krishna's discourses to Arjuna on the battlefield, texts of major doctrinal importance.[100]

Hence, chandra-vamshiya kshatriya reformers could partake of the monastic and religious world of Ram without compromising their commitments to a social identity focused on a descent from Krishna and his historical antecedents. The most articulate, numerous, and best-organized kshatriya reformers claiming descent from Krishna in the early twentieth century were Yadavs, and indeed there are indications of strong Yadav involvement in both Ram worship and the Ramanandi order after 1900. For example, van der Veer lists a number of "caste temples" built in Ayodhya in this century, among which is one founded by Yadavs. Freitag notes that during the annual Ram Lila festival in Banaras in the early twentieth century, Yadavs were prominent among those who served to carry the huge images of Ram and his brother Bharat in the *Bharat Milap* (reunion with Bharat) procession.[101] And I have cited in the conclusion to the previous chapter a 1935–1936 poem published in a Ramanandi magazine and authored by one Ramavatar *Yadav* "Shakta" Visharad (or Ramavatar Yadav, learned in Shakta doctrine), which praises Ramanand's efforts on behalf of the downtrodden masses.

The Ancient Present:
Race, Dignity, and Labor

A compelling theme addressed by much of the kshatriya reform literature through the early twentieth century was the redefinition of agricultural labor in terms of ancient pedigree and personal dignity. The ideas formulated in this literature challenged the brahmanical notion of physical work that girded the notion of a "plowman boundary" separating the shudra and untouchable mass from the varna elite. The rhetoric employed by the jati reformers bore a relationship to that devised by Swami Dayanand in his attempt to cast a new *Arya Samaj* (literally, "Aryan society") according to what he saw as the "original" meaning of the ancient Vedic corpus. Dayanand posited a varna system based not on birth but merit that, according to the historian Kenneth Jones, held great attraction for those "frustrated by the conservatism of the Hindu world."[102] However, notwithstanding these and other shared themes (most notably around the idea of an "Aryan" people) between kshatriya reform and Arya Samaji ideology, the relationship between kshatriya reformers and the Arya Samaj was often troubled.

For kshatriya reformers, the arguments for a reconsideration of social differentiation and dignified work were woven together with protohistorical accounts of the influx of an Aryan race into the south Asian subcontinent. As a Kushvaha-kshatriya ideologue put it,

The country we live in is named *Aryavarta;* it is called Aryavarta because in the beginning the Aryas settled here. . . . The place of origin of the Aryas is Tibet, and the Aryas that crossed the mountains did not discriminate among themselves. Rather, those who worshipped and sang hymns to god received great respect and were called rishis. There were also those who ruled, handled administrative affairs, and fought wars, and those who practiced agriculture, while those who were stupid did daily work. *They were chosen to serve.* Over time the priests were called brahmans, the rulers were called kshatriyas, agriculturalists were called vaishyas, and the stupid who could not learn *were given the name shudra*. However, they were all sons of the same father, and to facilitate the smooth functioning of Aryan society the names of these four varna—brahman, kshatriya, vaishya, and shudra— were institutionalized.[103]

The articulation of Aryan racial origins would commingle with that of Vaishnava genealogies and would vary only in detail, not in scope. Hence the reconstellated Kurmi-kshatriya identity of the 1920s extended the genealogy back into the Vedic age to include descent from the so-called *Indra* jati, that is, partisans of the Vedic god Indra. The Indra jati, it was contended, was one among several semidivine communities who in- habited the Tibetan plateau in the north and fought incessant wars against hideous demons to the west.[104] The conclusion inevitably reached fol- lowing this representation of the "golden age of Aryavarta" held that originally one's varna was determined by one's abilities, not by one's deeds in a previous life (*karma*).[105]

This rendering of "Hindu" history and the aggressive interpretation of varna in racial terms were hallmarks of Arya Samaji reform in late nineteenth and early twentieth-century Punjab and western Uttar Pradesh.[106] In fact, one such Kushvaha-kshatriya pamphlet was authored by a teacher of the local Dayanand Anglo-Vedic high school in Ba- naras.[107] Not surprisingly, that work's overtly Arya Samaji stance in no way contradicted the standard Vaishnava conception of varna and labor outlined in the jati reform literature of the early twentieth century. Sig- nificant inroads had been made by Arya Samajis into the Yadav-ksha- triya movement as well, especially in western Uttar Pradesh and Delhi, where many villages and towns with large Yadav populations came to have Arya Samaji temples, priests, schools, and publicists.[108] A close in- spection of the Gangetic reform literature reveals, nevertheless, a great ambivalence on the part of most jati reformers regarding the proper role of the Arya Samaj in Indian society in general and in social and religious change in particular. The comments of two jati reform authors reveal the conflicts between what they and others were beginning to define as *sanatan dharma*, the "eternal religion" to which they avowedly sub- scribed, and what was increasingly being characterized as the offensive, "non-Hindu" programs of the Arya Samaj. Dilipsinha Yadav, whose writings were influential among Yadav kshatriyas throughout U.P, at- tacked Arya Samajis as "Vedic believers in name only, who have, for the sake of their own greed and self-aggrandizement, granted initiation to Chamars and Muslims."[109] While the propagation of Arya Samaji ideas by men like Swami Krishnanandji, a self-described Yadav kshatriya, who toured the Punjab, Uttar Pradesh, and Bihar, certainly must have had a significant impact on jati reform rhetoric, it would be an overstatement to contend that the Arya Samaj was a leading force in kshatriya reform.

Raghunanandan Prasad Sinha Varmma, the Kanyakubja-kshatriya ideologue on behalf of Sonars (cited in the previous section for his views on Vaishnava sampraday), was more explicit in his condemnation of the followers of Dayanand:

These days Dayanandis, also known as Arya Samajis, are secretly gaining entrance into all jati mahasabhas, are gradually scandalizing the sanatan dharma, and are devoting all their efforts to the subversion of the varna system. The varna system is the very foundation of sanatan dharma. The important point is that these atheists have even worked their way into the Kanyakubja-kshatriya jati society and are very influential; their articles have already been published, the name of one is *"Svarnakar Koi Jati ya Varna Nahin Hai* [Sonar is not a Jati or Varna]." It is with great sorrow that I must report that . . . our Kanyakubja-kshatriya brothers pay not even the slightest heed to this [threat]. It is impossible to gauge the effect these godless essays will have in the future. We hereby inform our Kanyakubja-kshatriya brothers—whosoever should read such an article or hear such a speech should immediately refute it![110]

From the tone of these remarks, published in 1924, it is clear that while the Arya Samaj had made significant inroads into the jati reform movement, those inroads were severely resented by what had become, by the early twentieth century, "orthodox" opinion. This, of course, begs the questions of what constituted orthodoxy and how certain elements of Hindu belief came to be considered orthodox. In partial answer, Philip Lutgendorf has recently described the bland, universally acceptable Hinduism that was being promoted as sanatan dharma in north India by such men as the Hindu nationalist Madanmohan Malaviya, the publicist Din Dayal Sharma, and the *Ramayana* scholar Pandit Jwalaprasad Mishra.[111] Lutgendorf's main emphasis here is on the overriding importance of the immensely popular *Ramcharitmanas* of Tulsidas to the success of the sanatan dharma agenda, an agenda closely allied to the desire to create an Indian identity built on Hindu ideas. Tulsidas' *Manas* thus became

the Sanatani scripture par excellence—a devotional work which still preached reverence for cows and Brahmans; offered a veritable catalogue of sacred rivers, pilgrimage sites, and popular rituals; presented a harmonious synthesis of Vaishnavaism and Shaivism; and in the minds of devotees managed at one and the same time to stand for religious egalitarianism, the maintenance of the social status quo, and (later on) even nationalism and swadeshi (the boycott of British products, especially textiles), since it offered an inspiring vision of a powerful and self-sufficient Hindu state.[112]

Sanatan dharma was (and remains) a loose enough amalgam of religious concepts to represent all things to all Hindus, for Lutgendorf an "old-time religion" of sorts, self-conscious, conservative, vague, and, most importantly, exclusivist, by enabling adherents to delimit those who were not "orthodox."

On the question of the acceptability of certain forms of labor, however, kshatriya reformers unambiguously asserted that actual agricultural work was in no way undignified, a conclusion of no small significance given the elite aversion for physical labor—an aversion only reinforced by colonial replications of varna as irrefutable caste hierarchy. Ascriptive caste based on a principle of social hierarchy was attacked in the name of a distinct kind of racial equality, the logic of which dictated that since all Hindus are of the same race (i.e, Aryas), all Hindus are equal. Devi Prasad Sinha Chaudhari asserted in 1907 that "Kurmi kshatriyas practice agriculture as a livelihood and since it is associated with the earth it is therefore a noble vocation." According to the *Rgveda,* he continued, "in ancient times well-born men took up the plow, cultivated, and were known as Aryas."[113] Swami Abhayananda Saraswati elaborated on this sentiment twenty years later when he noted that according to the *Ramayana,* "Maharaja Janak and his queen [i.e., Sita's foster parents] practiced agriculture and protected their subjects" and that therefore farming "cannot be considered an obstacle to being kshatriya."[114] J. Chaudhari of the Anglo-Vedic High School in Banaras insisted that "there is nothing undignified about plowing a field," and suggested that people who argue otherwise are either exposing their ignorance of the ancient texts or, more likely, "simply do not want to work." He further noted that "in Bihar Rajputs and in some places even Bhumihars plow the fields. Konkani brahmans and farmer brahmans of Mewar also work the plow. Rajputs plow in Rajputana [Rajasthan] and Garhwal as well. . . . So long as these brahmans and kshatriyas don't become shudra by plowing, Koiris will not relent [in their demands for kshatriya status]."[115] At the 1907 debate over the viability of a Kurmi-kshatriya identity, the Vrindaban scholar Radhacharan Goswami even cited the fact that Kurmis were "almost entirely landowners and cultivators, and are quite powerful," as evidence of their kshatriya status.[116]

Similar arguments were constructed for nonagricultural and marginally agricultural communities claiming professional dignity in this period. Raghunandan Prasad Varmma urged his jati brothers not to be at all ashamed of their scientific and technical skills as goldsmiths and pointed to the scientific achievements that made America and Germany great. He added that three out of four of Kush's sons (i.e., Ramchandra's grandsons) were said to have become skilled in handicrafts and architecture.[117] Lalji Lal of the Tanti (weaver) community in Bihar argued that cloth production was a noble occupation, especially given the efforts by Mahatma Gandhi to elevate the practice of spinning to a patriotic pastime—a campaign that made the spinning wheel the symbol for the nationalist movement.[118] Likewise, the tedious profession of hauling water received critical consideration by Kahar reformers. Nauvat Ray refused to refer even to water-hauling as an occupational birthright (*pesh*) but insisted on it as professional wage labor (*mazdur*) because he did not consider it an act that only a certain section of society had the ability to perform. His argument employed and inverted classic varna logic:

These days, a section of uneducated people in this jati provide the service of drawing and carrying water, and this is a kind of task that everyone in Hindu society himself must perform every day to some extent at one time or another. . . . And yet this is not even degraded work, because high jatis in Hindu society also perform this very mazduri. On railway station platforms and in temple water-booths one can hear the pandit calling for water. How could a brahman perform this task if this is such lowly work?[119]

This argument may appear simplistic, but its implications were to prove enormous for the political economy of varna in the village: by consciously rejecting the assumption that the physical act of hauling water (or palanquins, for that matter) was an inherent corporeal component of being Kahar, Ray rendered impotent the claims of elite society on Kahar labor as a matter of varna prerogative. Rather, Ray demanded that a hauler of water should be rewarded not with the satisfaction of knowing that he has lived up to his full potential in life as a Kahar, but with hard cash, and then should be left to pursue other callings. Ray added that many Kahars were cultivators, others had found employment in the military and in commerce, and those who were educated had attained high rank in civil and military service.[120] He encapsulated the Kahar struggle for noble kshatriya origins in an allegorical tale of a prince who, through a turn of fate, was raised in a poor family and unaware of his true origins. The prince grew up learning how to farm and do physical labor when, one day, his true identity was revealed to him. The prince's whole bearing immediately changed as he assumed the mantle of dignity; yet he remained a peasant, well-versed in the art of cultivation.[121]

If the twice-born held sway over shudra and untouchable by virtue of their greater control over the product of the land, the hierarchy such an ideology implied had long been reinforced by an ideology of physical work. Indeed, the stigma attached to labor was so powerful in Gangetic India that the very act of ploughing (*chasa*) constituted an important social delimiter, distinguishing the upper classes from the lower in the early nineteenth century.[122] The many descriptions in the district gazetteers of Gangetic Uttar Pradesh and Bihar make it abundantly clear that the elite prescription against ploughing held through the nineteenth century and into the twentieth. For example, in Ballia District in eastern Uttar Pradesh, H. R. Nevill noted that "high caste tenants seldom do the actual cultivation themselves, generally sub-letting their lands"; he added, however, that "they get less out of the soil, whether they sub-let it or cultivate it themselves or employ hired labour, than do the Koeris and Kurmis."[123]

Physical labor represented the point of convergence between social identity and economic exigency; as such, the simple act of cultivating a field—and the logic of agricultural production to which that act is inexorably tied—constituted the arena of historical possibilities for both economic and social change. It is not surprising, then, that the idea of labor was of such great importance to kshatriya reformers. As is evident in the leadership ranks of their various organizations, increasing numbers of first-line tenant cultivators were acquiring productive power and occasionally property rights over increasingly larger amounts of land. Now, in the early twentieth century, the physical boundary that upheld political, cultural, and social hierarchy was being questioned by reform-minded intellectuals. Indeed, some radicals went so far as to dispense with the boundaries entirely. Examples of the profound—and often violent—economic, political, and social consequences that would ensue are provided in the following chapter.

Conclusion

The profusion of jati reform movements in the late nineteenth and early twentieth centuries implies a changing universe of political and ethical concerns, expressed nevertheless in terms familiar to the Vaishnava religious milieu. The most explicit Vaishnava contour of kshatriya reform was the detailed cooptation of the dynastic genealogies of Ramchandra and Krishna, both as historical figures and as gods in their own right. But the articulation of kshatriya identity went beyond the reification of a specific Vaishnava historical framework. The very language, rhetoric, and texture of kshatriya reform reflected the institutionalization of Vaishnava belief, so much so that in some cases the kshatriya reformers themselves emerged from the universe of Vaishnava monasticism, in particular, from the monasticism centered on Ayodhya, the Ramanandi sampraday. This is not surprising: the Ramanandi sampraday was and is north India's largest Vaishnava monastic community, and Ramanandis had long been known for their open-mindedness on the question of caste. As we have seen, however, not all Ramanandis were inclined to lend their support to social movements whose ideologies, by implication, reinforced caste attitudes.

If the assertions of kshatriya identity, the claim to uniracial (Aryan) equality, and the insistence on the dignity of physical work (not to mention the recognition of the fundamental economic necessity of labor) cannot be understood independently of Vaishnava reform, neither can it be understood independently of the economic expansion of the nineteenth and early twentieth centuries. Many peasants and artisans appear to have been edged (if not catapulted) into positions of financial prosperity and were able thus to mount coordinated kshatriya identity campaigns. Ultimately, the dignity-of-labor rhetoric, grounded in a racial interpretation of varna, would constitute a significant challenge to the political economy of caste hierarchy. To many observers within and beyond kshatriya reform, the political economy of caste was predicated on a moral understanding of physical work—particularly the act of preparing a field by maneuvering a plow while walking behind a cow or bull—as personally degrading. However, an ideological redefinition of labor would eventually pose a philosophical dilemma for kshatriya reformers themselves (not to mention their communities), forcing a choice between kshatriya status (and the continued systemics of varna that such a status implied) and the Vaishnava assertions of the dignity of labor (which ultimately undermined the systemics of varna and rendered the need for a kshatriya identity obsolete). Such choices would be made in the context of dramatic political change, as nationalist and peasant politicians would look to the kshatriya organizations after 1920 in an effort to cultivate a rural base. The trajectories of such ideological and political movements and the manner in which they intersected are explored in the remainder of this study.

Finally, it is worth pointing out that as kshatriya identities centered on Ayodhya gained ideological and organizational strength in the early twentieth century, and particularly among the sizable Kurmi and Kushvaha peasant communities, Ayodhya also began to emerge on the north Indian political landscape as the place where God was born as Ramchandra. It has been argued recently that the current political turmoil over Ramchandra's birthplace (*Ramjanambhumi*) has its roots in a colonial historiography that was all too quick to perceive and assert an age-old enmity between Hindus and Muslims as the driving force of Indian history.[124] Overlooked in this argument are the social and religious contexts of the early twentieth century: the ideological need for a birthplace of Ramchandra can also be understood as symptomatic of the historiography of kshatriya ancestries grounded in a Vaishnava discourse. In other words, at some point claims of genealogical descent from God demand the physical presence of the remains of God. The recent controversy over a mosque built in Ayodhya in 1528 by the Mughal emperor Babar and the allegation that it not only occupies the site of Ramchandra's birth but was built with construction materials taken from the ruins of a temple marking that birth, demonstrates the extent to which the heightened communal consciousness of the twentieth century bleeds into debates over status in society, monastic or otherwise.

CHAPTER 4

Culture, Conflict, and
Violence in Gangetic India

Kshatriya reform represented an aggressive Gangetic populism in which a newly formed peasant and artisanal elite encouraged a
full-scale examination of the historical and mythological underpinnings
of their personal and jati identities. Among those engaged in this reform effort, Yadav, Kushvaha, and Kurmi kshatriyas were the most visible and numerically powerful. Strong in numbers and agrarian skill, many
were small landholders and powerful tenants, but their numbers included
a few large landowners as well as tenant-laborers. Most of them had toiled
for generations in the rich Gangetic alluvial soils and as a result of that
hard work and an intimate knowledge of local agricultural practice, had
amassed significant rural wealth and power. This newfound influence is
what enabled them, by the early 1900s, to mount the claim that they
were not shudra but kshatriya, descended from the proudest and oldest
families imaginable, the families of Ramchandra and Krishna, and to sustain that claim with annual meetings and colorful publications. Yet the
language of varna—in which brahmans were expert and upon which
British understanding of Indian society relied—continued to describe
these communities as *shudra,* or servile, by virtue of the physical labor
implicit in their professions.

But increasingly the voices of the peasants could be heard above the
din of imputed identities, voices asserting a new conception of themselves. By demanding a modicum of personal dignity and by claiming
and articulating a noble kshatriya past, the ideologues of these communities challenged both the political economy and political culture of
Gangetic India in a language that everyone was sure to understand. This
challenge was quick to draw immediate attention and equally quick at-

tempts at refutation from the social elite. Perhaps the first printed manifestation of this emergent antipathy was an anti–kshatriya reform booklet in both English and Hindi in 1907 authored by Kunvar Chheda Sinha,
published and widely circulated by the Rajput Anglo-Oriental Press. In
what must have seemed an infuriating manner to the new peasant kshatriyas, Sinha bemoaned the fact that "even after a century of English
rule and the spread of Western education the question of jati is still so
heavily debated, especially given the fact that modern education and
progress have given some jatis not only the opportunity but also the right
to better their lot."[1] Sinha ignored the cultural and economic transformations that had occurred to bring about social reform; rather, he tied
the rising concern with caste pedigree to policies of hierarchical ranking in the census office and to a desire on the part of jati activists to attain high posts in the colonial government. In so doing, he inverted the
arguments of the kshatriya reformers themselves, who cited military and
government service by leading community figures not only as a professional aspiration but as evidence of the distinct abilities of the jati as a
whole.[2]

Sinha's logic, which endowed the colonial, census-based discourse of
caste with historical agency in social and religious reform, has been employed in more recent analyses of caste movements in colonial India.
Most striking in this regard is the assertion that "the censuses themselves
instigated mobility aspirations and they do not necessarily reflect the actual processes taking place in society."[3] This general argument has been
widely circulated and characteristically describes the 1901 census as "a
powerful stimulus to the formation of modern, provincewide and even
countrywide caste associations and the development of broader solidarities."[4] The perception that the colonial fixation with status inspired
jati reform relies for the most part on an aggressive interpretation of census department records, particularly those sections of decennial reports
that detailed the very real concerns of jati activists with the official representation of regional caste hierarchy. Of particular importance are the
reflections of officials like L. S. S. O'Malley, director of the 1911 census in Bengal, Bihar, and Orissa, who noted that

there was a general idea in Bengal—that the object of the census was not
to show the number of persons belonging to each caste, but to fix the relative status of different castes and to deal with the question of social superiority. . . . The feeling on the subject was largely the result of castes having
been classified in the last census report in order of social precedence. . . .
Many castes were aggrieved at the position assigned them, and complained

that it lowered them in the public estimation. . . . Others thought it was a good opportunity to advance new claims.[5]

The question that must be raised, of course, is whether census classificatory practices actually *inspired* the campaigns for respectability and status or, conversely, whether such census practices merely attracted the attention of reformers, thus inspiring them to bury the responsible census officials in supplicatory memoranda. There is nothing in the observations of O'Malley to suggest the former case. The tendency was, rather, for colonial administrators to acknowledge that the hierarchical mindset of the census "greatly agitated" communities undergoing social and religious reform.[6]

The assessment of social and religious reform as a reaction to census whims does point, however, to the importance of official opinion for kshatriya publicists. Some kind of authoritative sanction was crucial for the assertion and maintenance of social status, and the frequency with which kshatriya-reform memoranda were dispatched to the census office reflects the ease with which elite representatives of peasant jatis could enter into a sensitive dialogue with British officialdom. Indeed, notwithstanding the sharp contrast between those who composed the "memorials" in a showy panegyric that bordered on sycophancy and those who received and read them with a highly skeptical eye, the correspondence over varna status in the census should be seen as part of a larger process of colonial culture in the making.[7] To argue that census opinion alone inspired and directed movements for social reform not only suggests that the reform ideologies implicit to the kshatriya movements were somehow inauthentic but ignores the religious dimensions of the history of social reform and the very real fact that a new elite had emerged among the peasantry that sought to avail itself of connections to the colonial political arena. As I have argued in the preceding chapters, social reform on behalf of shudras and untouchables in the Gangetic north was manifest in a semiorganized form at least since the early nineteenth century under the rubric of Vaishnava (and primarily Ramanandi) monasticism. In addition, sporadic peasant claims to kshatriya status had been articulated as early as the late eighteenth century in Awadh and the early nineteenth century in Bihar. The institutional heirs to such early reform efforts were the caste associations (*mahasabha*s) of the late nineteenth and early twentieth centuries, which combined the demand for high (usually kshatriya) status with a potent Vaishnava rhetorical content. *Kshatriyatva* (the essence of being kshatriya, or valor) constituted an important component of this new political framework for reform, in part because the martial element contained therein fit a colonial ideology that placed a premium on virility and power.[8]

In this light, the formulation that "the censuses themselves instigated mobility aspirations and they do not necessarily reflect the actual processes taking place in society" deserves closer scrutiny.[9] The profusion of census-directed jati memorials are depicted as false indicators of social change, and historians are therefore encouraged to ignore the wider cultural history that both occasioned and accompanied that change. The argumentation employed by Sinha in 1907 and refined by historians and sociologists in the 1970s and 1980s presents an image of entire caste mahasabha organizations involving countless thousands of members devoted only to garnering the crumbs of status and position from the British imperial table. There can be no doubt that kshatriya reformers were all too concerned with the political legitimization of their sociocultural identity, but this must be seen primarily as a symptomatic feature of the larger movement for respectability. The image of the scurrying, low-level *babu* (clerk) overlooks, consciously or unconsciously, the main agenda of these organizations: education, religious reform, economic frugality, physical integrity, and most important of all, personal dignity. These are goals that generally would not have been made explicit in petitions to census officials but which emerge clearly in the vernacular literature espousing both the religious and social reform movements of the late nineteenth and early twentieth centuries.

From Cowherd to Kshatriya

Despite the challenge to the social status quo implicit in kshatriya reform movements among groups heretofore accorded low status, kshatriya reformers saw themselves as an integral part of a larger Hindu universe. The rupturing of ties to superordinate groups was secondary to the object of community respect expressed in terms of kshatriya identity. Nevertheless, the increasing urgency of claims to kshatriya status served to offend many established high-status communities, primarily because of the social and cultural proximity such claims implied. Social reform would thus inevitably produce social strife. Strife, however, implies past cohesion. Such cohesion can be seen to have existed in the 1890s at certain levels, and was expressed in a particularly ardent manner by Goala peasant-pastoralists as a cultural solidarity with the landed, social elite during cow-protection agitation. Three decades later, that agrarian cohesion would be rendered obsolete by the strident call for Yadav-kshatriya identity.[10]

Organized primarily in opposition to the slaughter of cows and the consumption of beef during Muslim festivals and holidays, the cow-protection—or *gauraksha*—movement represented an important phase of a growing political and cultural activism in late nineteenth-century north India. This activism, the historian John McLane has suggested, was evident as well in the mobilizational systemics of the early Indian National Congress and in the increased competition between Hindu and Muslim elites for secular power.[11] National elite competition became intertwined with popular religious practice at the regional level, a combination that ultimately erupted in the Gangetic heartland over the issue of cow slaughter. This controversy peaked in 1893 as angry Hindus attacked entire Muslim village centers, assaulting butchers as well as low-status Hindus viewed as complicit in marketing beef. The cow-protection cause found enthusiastic support in cities and towns as well as villages, as agitators employed both local trade networks and powerful religious symbols to divide Hindus from Muslims as well as the British.[12] As *gau-mata* (mother cow) evolved into a unifying "Hindu" political symbol, the urban elites that peopled the Indian National Congress increasingly looked to it to develop a rural base, "despite the refusal of Congress leaders to allow the Congress to support cow protection."[13] McLane even suggests that it became "inevitable that the Congress, standing as it did for majority rule and parliamentary government, should have attracted advocates of restrictions upon cow slaughter."

The shifting agrarian tensions that accompanied the late nineteenth-century price rise in the Gangetic north, it has been argued, made cow protection an opportune issue for a kind of makeshift agrarian unity involving increasingly less powerful Hindu zamindars and increasingly more assertive Hindu tenants.[14] Gyanendra Pandey has investigated the nature of that agrarian unity from the perspective of the tenants and has argued that "the prevention of cow-slaughter became a major object of the *Ahirs* [generally synonymous with Goalas] as they advanced their bid for a higher social status." Pandey's data and observations concern the Bhojpuri region of eastern Uttar Pradesh and western Bihar where, he argues, "the agitation appears to have acquired its greatest social depth and an unexpected militancy." Citing official reports of the physical participation of Goalas in mob violence directed against Muslims and others involved in the sacrifice of cattle, as well as records of subsequent trials in which Goalas received sentencing, Pandey suggests "that we have evidence here of a relatively independent force that added a good deal of power to cow-protection activities in the Bhojpuri region—*marginally* 'clean' castes who aspired to full 'cleanness' by emphasizing the purity of their faith and the strictness of ritual adherence to it on the issue of cow-slaughter. In the case of the Ahirs this motive would certainly have been reinforced by their traditional and continued association with the business of tending cattle."[15] Pandey's observations reflect the importance of cow-protection violence to Goala/Ahir conceptions of status and identity, expressed here as a function of ritual cleanliness. His use of the term "marginal" highlights the notion that Goalas, like other peasants, straddled the fine line between shudra and elite in the political economy of the Gangetic heartland and were committed to the exploitation of that precarious stance to their fullest advantage.

Pandey makes brief reference to agitation in Patna and Gaya Districts and argues that these districts—adjacent to the eastern extension of Bhojpur into Gangetic south Bihar—experienced significant cow-protection activity in the early 1890s. The evidence of official reports bears out this assertion and, as in eastern Uttar Pradesh, Goalas played an important grassroots role in advancing the cause of gauraksha.[16] For instance, of the twelve cases of forcible seizure of cattle reported in the first five months of 1893 in Gaya District, six cited Goalas as the offending party (of the remaining six cases, four failed to identify the jati of the accused). Inasmuch as most of the twelve incidents occurred during or after the Bisua village cattle fair held that year on April 12, it is not unlikely that Goalas, as cowherds and dairy farmers, were involved in some of the other incidents as well. The following description of an incident at the mela, extracted from the judicial record, is typical of the activities of Goalas working for cow-protection:

In this case the complainant, who is a [Muslim] butcher, says he bought two cows at the Bisua *Mela* [fair] for Rs. 7–1 through one Dodal Chamar, because he was afraid that Hindus would not sell cattle to Muhammedans.

The first purchase was duly recorded by the owner of the Mela, and the usual receipt checcque was granted. But when the Chamar was going back along with both cows to have the second purchase recorded, he was suddenly stopped by the accused [Gopi Goala] and several others, and accused of buying cows for butchers. The cattle were snatched and carried off by the accused. Sub-Inspector Zahir Khan, of town Gaya, having received information that the accused and cattle were near the place where cattle sales were being recorded, went to the spot and managed to arrest accused Gopi Goala.

This description, and others like it, characterize Goalas as the shock troops of cow protection. The above case is of added interest because of the complicity of Dodal Chamar, an untouchable, in purchasing the cattle for the butcher Mangor Kassai, a Muslim. Such alliances were apparently not uncommon in the Gangetic core: in eastern Uttar Pradesh "the Chamar, far from being actively involved in the Cow-Protection movement, was in fact the target of a good deal of Gaurakshinist vilification and attack."[17] Consequently, a list of sixteen rules drawn up at a meeting of cow-protection activists in Gorakhpur District included the explicit message that "Chamars and others buy cows and sell them to butchers; and Musalmans and others are the very cause of the slaughter of cows. Cows shall not be sold into the hands of any such persons, and if any kind of cow die the owner shall sell its skin to a proper person, and apply the money to cow-protection."[18] Ironically, inasmuch as Chamars worked with leather, they would also be the "proper persons" to which the manifesto refers. By supporting the "Hindu establishment" in its cause célèbre, the protection of cows, Goalas symbolically allied themselves with the landed and powerful while distancing themselves from those socially and economically beneath them ("Chamars and others") in the Gangetic core. Goala aspirations in the 1890s drew on the cowherd ethos of Krishna's childhood milieu, albeit at the expense of Muslim religious custom. So long as Goala participation in cow-protection agitation remained devoid of any specific transformative, status-oriented rhetoric, the tenuous agrarian unity between landlord and tenant remained intact. However, a loosely expressed dedication to the Vaishnava world of Krishna would soon evolve by the early 1910s and 1920s into a commitment to a historical exegesis of that world in the form of Yadav-kshatriya identity, an identity that would serve to drive a wedge between Goalas and other cultivators on the margin of land control, on the one hand, and the landed elite on the other.

Conflict between the landed elite and marginal cultivators became manifest as physical confrontation in the teens and twenties of the present century. Official police reports of the 1920s describe in substantial detail the tensions and occasional violence between Goalas forwarding a Yadav-kshatriya identity and the landed elite who felt threatened by that new identity. This threat was perceived as economic as well as social, inasmuch as the systemics of varna provided the cultural justification for the agrarian perquisites demanded of cultivating tenants. While the Muslim elite also challenged the Yadav-kshatriya identity, they did so on purely economic and not religious grounds, and Yadav kshatriyas responded in kind. These tensions culminated with the threat of serious bloodletting on May 27, 1925, when a group of three thousand "Goalas" (Yadav kshatriyas) and an equal number of heavily armed "Babhans" (Bhumihar brahmans) faced each other at Lakho Chak village near Lakhisarai town, Monghyr District, in central Bihar.[19] Though official reports tended to employ the appellations Goala and Babhan, I have chosen to refer to the two parties in my description of this extended conflict simply as Yadavs and Bhumihars, terms that reflect both their own conception of themselves as well as the current usage. These and other reports make clear that the Lakho Chak showdown was only the most visible manifestation of a conflict that had been simmering for several years.[20]

The Lakho Chak riot itself was precipitated by the decision of local Bhumihar zamindars of Monghyr District to attack a *panchayat* (council meeting) of Yadavs that had convened in the village of Lakho Chak to discuss jati reform. The description of the riot in the official report indicates the formidable force brought to bear by the Bhumihars and that, if not for the timely intervention of local and district police to protect the peaceable Yadav meeting, serious violence would have been the likely result.

On the morning of the 27th, before the arrival of the armed police at Lakho Chak, a large body of rioters advanced upon the village. The local police intervened to expostulate and were at once surrounded, the Sub-Inspector and *Chaukidar* [village watchman] received grievous injuries and the other constables of the party were hurt. After ill-treating the local police, the rioters retired temporarily but returned to the attack soon after the arrival of the S.P. [Superintendent of Police] with his force. The Superintendent and S.D.O [Subdivisional District Officer] went out to meet the advancing rioters and attempted to parley with them. The attacking party, however, to the number of about 3000 armed with *lathis* [heavy, metal tipped bamboo truncheons], axes, and spears continued to advance and the police were forced to fire to protect themselves and the Goalas. Although temporarily checked by the fire, the Babhan party continued to advance as they outflanked the police on both sides, the police were forced to retire fighting to the village site three or four hundred yards to their rear. The retirement was effected in good order and after the defending party reached the village the rioters withdrew.[21]

The dramatic crisis that unfolded in 1925 under the hot May sun on the outskirts of Lakho Chak village was in fact the most recent and ex-

plosive act in the construction of a Yadav-kshatriya identity that had begun in the nineteenth century with claims of genealogical ties to Krishna. The movement took on a more urgent and organized form
throughout the Gangetic north in the early twentieth century with the
emergence of large-scale associations and active propaganda. In a lengthy
note to his superior Y. A. Godbole, the district officer of Purnea, S.D.O
Phanindra Nath Mukherji noted that he "first came across the Goala
movement in the Patna district in the year 1912."

The leader was Babu Damodar Prasad—a Goala landlord of Pachchimdar-
waza in Patna City. A huge meeting called the "Gope Jatiya Mahasabha"
was held in Kankarbagh and domestic service was eschewed except for tending cattle, sacred threads taken—and ceremonial purity was, I believe, put
down at 15 days. I have to depend on memory—other meetings were held
at Dinapur, Maner, and Mussorhi [Masaurhi]. I do not know if the movement had preceded elsewhere but I read in the papers of meetings in the
United Provinces of Agra and Oudh and elsewhere.[22]

Mukherji provided the above description by way of historical background. His subsequent portrayal of his own experiences in dealing with
the "Goala movement" in Purnea District in 1924 and 1925 demon-
strate both the importance of economic advancement to Yadavs as well
as the subtle techniques employed by them in mobilizing a kshatriya
identity.

The movement in this district has spread within the last year or so. The material condition of the Goalas in the western and southern portions of the
district is very prosperous. In fact in wealth measured in terms of cattle, land,
etc. they are in no way inferior to the average Bhumihars and Brahmins and
Chhatris [local variant of kshatriya, in reference to Rajputs]. The movement
in this district was I used to hear being fostered by Babu Swyambara Das,
late Deputy Inspector of schools in this district. He had lecturers brought
in from other districts and there were meetings held at Ghansurpur, Dhamdaha, Rupauli and several centres. The Goalas began to call themselves Ja-
davs, took sacred threads and gave out that they will do the ceremonial purification of Sradh after 13 days. The Bhumihars resented this as did the
Brahmins and Chhatris. An attempt was made to break up the meeting at
Ghansurpur but the police got timely notice and occurrence [*sic*] took place.
The Bhumihars later refused to allow the Goalas to draw water from the village wells and I had to go to Ghansurpur. I warned the leading Bhumihars
and with my privilege as a Brahmin I pointed out to them that the Bhumihars themselves had reduced the period of ceremonial purification from 15
to 13 days in several districts within living memory and that . . . their ancestors called themselves *Bavans* [variant of Babhans].[23]

Mukherji noted in addition that in many villages in Purnea District the dominant caste—whether Bhumihar brahman, Maithil brahman, or Rajput—organized a social boycott of Yadavs, with the object of making it extremely difficult for the latter to perform the rituals prescribed for kshatriya status. This obstacle was circumvented without much difficulty, as "the richer sections [of Yadavs] have come to the help of the poorer section and have either got Brahmins from Madhipura in Bhagalpur district where there are many Goala landlords or managed to win over opposition by making it worthwhile for the Brahmins and barbers to officiate."[24] It is clear from Mukherji's description, then, that pockets of Yadav economic power in Bihar played a large role not only in inspiring changing attitudes toward their sociocultural identity but in ensuring that the new identity being advanced stayed alive despite rural pressure to obliterate it. Nevertheless, economic contradictions internal to the Yadav community inevitably became manifest as, according to Mukherji, "The better off wanted to insist that the women-folk of the poor section will not sell Goetha (fuel cakes made from cowdung) or milk in the hats (weekly markets) and bazars. And that the women should follow in all respects the practices of the women of the higher castes. This gave rise to a few criminal cases but then the inexorable economic laws acted and the women folk of the poorer section are again selling cowdung cakes and milk."[25] The conclusion that must be reached, then, is that in the short term the consolidation of Yadav-kshatriya identity succeeded only to the extent that economic considerations allowed. Better-off Yadavs could not entirely subvent the incomes of their less-fortunate jati brothers and, importantly, sisters, but they certainly were able, as Mukherji's observations on ritual officiates indicate, to at least mobilize the wherewithal either to bring brahmans from a neighboring district or to increase the economic reward for local brahmans and hajjams (barbers) to perform the necessary ceremonial functions.

This glimpse into the household economics of Yadavs struggling to live up to a new Vaishnava and kshatriya ideal of dignity introduces an important element of caste reform, namely, a strictly circumscribed redefinition of acceptable female social, religious, and economic behavior. Such an imposition of male control over female lives is all the more striking given that many of the peasant families involved in the identity campaigns had benefited economically from the lack of any cultural proscription of women working in the field as well as in the home—in stark contrast to the mores of elite society. Hence the mid nineteenth-century adage, "A good caste is the Kunbin [Kurmi woman]; with hoe in hand, they weed the fields together with their husbands."[26] However, kshatriya reformers generally viewed the centrality of women in the economic success of the peasant family as an entrée to female independence and thus a serious threat to the integrity of not only the immediate household but the entire jati community. Baijnath Prasad Yadav of Banaras claimed, not atypically, that "the root cause of all the needless household expenses is the fickle greed of women" and urged "men to put a halt to the rule of women in the home." Yadav also argued against allowing women to sing in public, against permitting women to view the *barat* (the procession of the groom with his friends and male family members), and "against allowing women to attend the big festivals, where they would run the risk of being dishonored by one of the many low jatis that roam the crowds, which would thus bring dishonor upon our jati." Extending this particular line of reasoning, he vehemently criticized women who purchased glass bangles from "lascivious vendors, who are only too willing to grab our women's wrists and help them try on their wares."[27] Swami Abhayananda Saraswati, also of Banaras, cautioned Kurmis against educating their women, maintaining that such education could only have a negative effect on the children, on household work, and on the development of a loving relationship between a husband and wife.[28]

While women did take part in the reform movements, the greatest challenge they faced was to redress the growing male conceptualization of women as property to be manipulated and polished for the sake of a positive and powerful kshatriya image.[29] The participation of women in the organizational apparatus of kshatriya reform rhetoric was relegated, in the main, to the activities of *mahila sammelan*s (women's conferences), which usually occurred in conjunction with the regional and national meetings of the jati. These organizations pushed for government legislation against polygamy and for mahasabha resolutions providing for the education of boys *and* girls.[30] Nevertheless, it is doubtful that women involved in upgrading their gender status made much headway vis-à-vis the kshatriya-focused attitudes of their fathers, brothers, husbands, and sons.

That the control over the life and death of women was of paramount importance to the success of kshatriya identity can be seen in the boast by Nauvat Ray, the Kahar ideologue of Agra, that "many of our women even become *sati*," which can mean both becoming loyal wives and immolating themselves upon the husband's funeral pyre (the tone of the passage indicates that the latter meaning is intended).[31] This conceptualization of women as martyrs to the cause of community status extended as well into the nascent Hindi literary movement. An example is Gangaprasad, the Kushvaha-kshatriya historian cited in the previous chapter, who also published historical fiction under the name Gangaprasad Gupta. One of his novels, entitled *Vir Jaymal* (Valiant Defense), glorified the courage of Rajputs in battle against Muslims during the reign of Akbar. Of particular note, however, was his narrative of the death of Raja Prithviraj of Delhi and the self-immolation of his bereaved queen, Sanyogita, entitled *Vir Patni* (Brave Wife). Gangaprasad portrayed female martyrdom as an important embodiment of a kshatriya tradition that combined steadfast loyalty to husband with patriotic devotion to country, a evocation of the sacrificing female that he also perceived to be extant in Victorian literature of the previous century. Hence his translation of "The Young Fishermen," a story by the Victorian romance author George W. M. Reynolds (1814–1879), which Gangaprasad entitled *Kile ki Rani* (Queen of the Fort).[32]

While economic power enabled Yadavs to forge a kshatriya identity campaign, it is equally the case that a major aim of that campaign was an improvement of the economic position of Yadavs vis-à-vis superordinate landlords. This dilemma, in a sense, reflected the essence of the marginal status of Yadavs in society: having tasted some of the fruits of economic strength, they demanded more. The forced, unremunerative labor known as *begari* was the ground on which the battle for equal economic status was fought. The caste implications of begari were such that elite landlords expected it of nonelite (whether shudra or untouchable) fellow villagers. Labor in this context referred not only to agricultural work but, especially in the Yadav context, to nonremunerative efforts such as providing milk and *ghi* (clarified butter) at reduced rates or even free of charge. Thus, S. A. Khan, a district officer of Bhagalpur, noted in an official correspondence that "The low caste Hindus generally do some kind of 'begari' work for their landlords. A people wearing the sacred thread are taken as respectable and are exempt from gratis service of this type. They would also take it to be very much derogatory to work as daily labourers or even as hired ploughmen."[33]

The official record tells of an important meeting convened by Babu Shri Ballab Das in 1921 that was attended by approximately sixteen hundred Yadavs. Among the resolutions passed at this meeting was a plea to the government to take note of conflict "between the *zamindars* (landlords) and the *Gope Jotiya* having arisen over the begari question over which the latter have been oppressed by the zamindars, so much so that in several places several lives have been lost." This file also tells of a related incident several months earlier in which a rural council of Yadavs in Islampur Thana, Patna District, refused to allow members of the jati to provide ghi and goats to a Muslim landlord for a wedding feast. However, in contrast to the earlier cow-protection activity, anti-Muslim rhetoric was severely curtailed in the language of the resolution. The meeting specifically stated that "in the coming *Bakr-Id* this community will not create any disturbance in connection with the cow-killing and if, unfortunately, any engineered by other caste [*sic*] would happen, this community would have no hand in it."[34]

Two factors are important in understanding the Yadav disavowal of the anti-Muslim stance that they had so strongly advocated during the cow-protection agitation. First, and probably most importantly, the calculated and willful articulation of a kshatriya identity called for a refinement of the Yadav sociocultural position vis-à-vis superordinate and subordinate actors in the agrarian environment. No longer would it be sufficient to express vague designs for high status through open attacks on Muslims; a well-crafted kshatriya identity immediately placed Yadavs (and other cultivators) in social, economic, and cultural conflict with the twice-born elite, requiring a realigned, refined political program devoid of any content directed against a particular religious community. Naturally, those likely to be most offended by the culture of upward mobility implicit to Yadav identity would be the dominant Hindu groups. Second, and closely related, the characterization of the Yadav movement in positive class terms relative to zamindars was more likely to win the official support of the colonial administration, primarily because Yadavs could easily portray themselves as the victims of socioeconomic oppression rather than as perpetrators of anti-Muslim mob violence. The simple assumption of an aggressive kshatriya identity by Yadavs placed the onus upon superordinates to react violently, thereby casting the latter in the role of lawbreakers. This tactic had near-immediate results; according to the sociologist Hetukar Jha, "The reports [contained in file 171 of 1925] though written by government employees are not biased in favour of zamindars or in favour of government officers. The reporters did not hesitate to point out when they found that an officer of the rank of S.D.O. had sided with the zamindars at Samastipur (then a subdivision of Darbhanga) against peasants without conducting a proper enquiry."[35]

The essentially nonpartisan judgment of district officers in itself constituted a major victory for marginal peasants. Indeed, if anything, the reports expressed a significant degree of sympathy for the aims of the kshatriya reformers. It has already been noted that the local police force of Lakhisarai and the district police of Monghyr had come to the aid of the Yadav meeting being held in Lakho Chak village in 1925. In addi-

tion, Subdivisional District Officer Phanindra Nath Mukherji, cited at
length above, had gone to great pains to convince the Bhumihar landlords of Purnea District to refrain from harassing Yadav peasants; indeed,
he even lorded his own brahman status over the Bhumihars to remind
them of their own upward social mobility. Most reports described the
begari demanded by the landlords not as customary and benign agrarian perquisites but as oppressive "exactions."[36] Commenting on what
was perceived as an unjust economic arrangement, Commissioner J. A.
Hubback of Bhagalpur Division noted caustically that "the higher castes
(in that tract [South Monghyr] mainly Babhans) derive livelihood from
the land, and do as little as they can to earn it."[37] Hubback's phraseology indicates that he was not simply directing a pointed criticism at Bhumihars but was describing what he perceived as a nonproductive elite
class that survived off the sweat of "sturdy" peasants.

These official characterizations reflected the subtle alliance that was
being forged between the new kshatriya peasants on the one hand and
regional and local administrators (the former mostly British, the latter
mostly Indian) on the other. This alliance was spurred along by frequent
appeals to and representations of "*sarkar*" as a benevolent, caring government. The efforts by government as sarkar to protect the new kshatriyas from the abuses and threats of physical violence by the outraged
elite, and at the same time to mollify that outrage with reasoned pleas
for peaceful behavior, make clear that district officials and cultivators at
the productive core of Indian society were speaking to and regenerat-
ing each other in ideal terms. This emergent alliance extended as well
into the agrarian political context described above, as marginal peasants
reacted favorably to what they understood as the nonpartisan spirit of
British rule and the judicious exercise of administrative force. The most
telling example of this perception in the jati reform literature is without
question the contention of Gangaprasad, who wrote on behalf of Kushvaha kshatriyas, that "now this is the age of British rule. The lion and
the lamb can drink from the same pond and no one can say to another,
'thus a shudra is born.'"[38] Another example of this sentiment is found
in a pamphlet arguing kshatriya status for Kahars authored by Nauvat
Ray, who praised British rule as "an age of light from which darkness
can only flee."[39]

Notwithstanding what they perceived as the benevolence of British
officials, however, the new kshatriyas still had to contend with opposition to their social, cultural, and economic advancement organized by
the established landed elite. Perhaps the most galling element of this
form of resistance to Yadav-kshatriya identity were the "abuses, taunts

and jokes . . . hurled on the Goalas."[40] Particularly insulting, according to S. A. Khan (a district officer of Bhagalpur), were ten thousand printed copies of a leaflet of Bihari verse "sung by hired boys in the *mofussil* [countryside]," in which "Goalas are asked to stick to their old faith and customs."[41] The author of this leaflet gave his name as Bahuran of Ram Patti village north of Singheshwar *dham* [pilgrimage center] near Saharsa in northern Bhagalpur District and described himself as "a reputed Brahman." The distributor of the leaflet, however, was listed as one Raghunandan Jha (Jha is a well-known Maithil brahman surname) of the same address, suggesting Bahuran's likely identity.

Bahuran prefaced his verse with a short Sanskrit dedication to Radha and Krishna, which he concluded with the patronizing affront that he was merely "narrating the conduct of the Gopas to increase their knowledge." Indeed, throughout the leaflet Bahuran referred to Yadavs as *Gopa*s, the traditional term for the idealized, innocent cowherds of Krishna's mytho-historical boyhood in Mathura-Vrindaban. After dedicating several lines to descriptions of the eminence of Radha and Krishna and their exploits, Bahuran settled down to the serious business of persuading the Yadav community to renounce its upstart behavior. His efforts concentrated on several themes, the most important of which was the Yadav practice of donning the sacred thread and performing the shraddh funerary ceremony only thirteen days after the death of a family member:

> While you flaunt a sacred thread on your shoulders,
>> your women wake up to milk cows and herd calves.
> You work the plough while wearing the thread,
>> and force your women to labor in the fields.
> You've bought up all the weavers' cotton,[42]
>> and the scarcity has made cloth dear.
> *Gwalins* [Goala women] sell milk and curd all day long,
>> they wouldn't know how to spin thread.
>
> . . . .
>
> [How can] two opposing customs prevail in one family:
>> one-month shraddh and thirteen-day shraddh?
>
> . . . .
>
> Read the Laws of Manu wherein Gopas are said to be shudra,
>> and abandon shraddh after thirteen days.
> Be united and accept a one-month shraddh,
>> *this* should be the only reform of the Gopa jati.
>
> . . . .
>
> Your ancestors in Kashi, Vrindaban, Awadh, and Gokul,
>> have crammed full the stomachs of all the sadhus.

[This is how] they are allowed to wear the sacred thread
    and perform thirteen-day shraddh.
. . . .
Think for yourselves in groups of ten or twenty,
    and give up the spread of the sacred thread.

As a purposefully insulting document, Bahuran's verse reveals much
about the political economy of caste in the Gangetic north. His reference to Goalas ploughing, milking cows, and performing other menial
tasks while wearing the sacred thread reflects the profound socioeconomic challenge that the kshatriya (not to mention Vaishnava) reconsideration of dignified labor held for the social elite. His advice to gather
in "groups of ten or twenty" was surely calculated to foment divisiveness within the Yadav-kshatriya movement, the periodic meetings of
which were attended by Yadavs numbering in the thousands. The reference to "Gwalins" spending their entire days milking cows, chasing
cattle, and marketing their wares was surely meant to ridicule Yadav
women as immodest and Yadav men as lazy good-for-nothings who re-
lax while their wives do all the work. On this point, Bahuran chastised
Yadav men for letting their "mothers cut grass" and their "sisters sell
milk in the villages, towns, and markets." But he could not have been
more derisive than with the taunt that,

When your elder brother dies,
    you make his widow a happy bride.
Whenever the husbands of your daughters and sisters expire,
    you once again marry off their wives.

Another important theme in the text of the verse centered around
Bahuran's claim that the root cause of the Yadav-kshatriya campaign was
the work of Swami Dayanand and the Arya Samaj. However, while
Dayanand's ideas probably influenced kshatriya reform, there was a great
deal of institutional ambivalence regarding the role of Arya Samajis in
the reform movement itself.[43] It is in this context that Bahuran's comments should be understood. He pointedly accused Yadavs of having
"abandoned your family duties for the ideas of Dayanand and . . . thus
destroyed your good name," and he urged them in turn to "abandon
the ways of Dayanand, Gopas, for difficult times lie ahead." These verses
were intended as an affront to Yadav sensibilities, semantically calculated
to imply that support for kshatriya identity was synonymous with an affinity for the Arya Samaj.

Goala unity, which emerged in the political arena in 1893 as an amorphous dedication to Krishna and cows and expressed itself in anti-Muslim rioting, had become by 1925 a well-organized call for a Yadav-kshatriya identity that offended the twice-born sensibilities and socioeconomic power of village elites. As the new kshatriyas—Yadavs as well as Kurmis and Kushvahas—flexed their social, economic, and cultural muscles in the early twentieth century, they began to take a closer look at the political landscape around them. From their agrarian perspective, the most important political institutions were the Bihar Provincial *Kisan Sabha* (peasant association) and the Indian National Congress, especially insofar as each body developed an "agrarian program." That they responded to those dominant organizations by joining together to form their own political front, the *Triveni Sangh,* confirms the increasingly independent posture of kshatriya reformers in the early twentieth century.

Political Peasants

Mahatma Gandhi's great achievement was to revitalize the Indian National Congress in the late teens and twenties of this century by drawing in the support of what historians and political scientists—with some important, and relatively recent, exceptions—have called "the masses." Thus Lloyd and Suzanne Rudolph write that Gandhi transformed "the Indian National Congress from a body narrowly concerned with the interests of an anglicized elite to a socially concerned mass organization" by using "traditional symbols and language to convey new meanings and to reconstitute social action."[44] It cannot be denied that the rich cultural idiom that Gandhi drew upon throughout his political career proved profoundly effective in providing the Congress with a much broader base. Nevertheless, the "masses" that became involved in the Congress were far from undifferentiated. The aim of this section is to review the class dimensions of Indian nationalism and the caste dimensions of peasant radicalism, and to discern how both intersected with the sociocultural agenda of kshatriya reform.

Perhaps the best evidence of this fact in the Gangetic core is the growth in the 1920s and 1930s of the Kisan Sabha, which came to articulate a distinct peasant interest in contrast to the agrarian policies advanced by the Congress. An understanding of the political events of this period hinges to a great extent on the ideas and work of one remarkable man, Swami Sahajanand Saraswati. Born Navrang Ray in 1889, a *Jujhautia* brahman of Ghazipur District, Sahajanand Saraswati took the vows of sanyas at the age of eighteen (1907) and became a Dasnami sanyasi.[45] Sahajanand became involved in social reform activity when, in 1914 at the age of twenty-five, he was asked to address the annual conference of the Bhumihar Brahman Mahasabha held at Ballia in eastern Uttar Pradesh. After some determined reflection on his role as a sanyasi involved in social action, Sahajanand decided to devote himself fully to the cause of defining and maintaining a Bhumihar brahman identity for "Babhans." In response to the denigrations of Bhumihars by Maithil brahmans and others, Sahajanand cited a broad range of Sanskrit and orientalist authorities to argue that "the acceptance of charity and the discharge of priestly duties are not inevitably necessary for the brahmans." Rather, "even for the brahman, agriculture is preferable to the priesthood, and only in the absence of agriculture does the brahman have the right to perform the functions of the priest."[46] However, being brahman required a knowledge of Sanskrit and priestly ritual (*karmakand*), two assets in short supply among the Bhumihar community. Therefore, the founding of the Sitaram *Ashram* [sanctuary] to train students at Bihta, about sixteen miles west of Patna on the East India Railway line, signified the culminating achievement in Sahajanand's efforts to build a Bhumihar brahman identity.[47]

Sahajanand's role in the political history of Gangetic north India was, to a large extent, a reflection of his unsurpassed ability to bridge differences in sociocultural, religious, and economic background. And he was able to overcome those barriers in exciting ways, creating new patterns of social and political organization. For instance, even though Sahajanand was a Dasnami sanyasi, it is clear from his own work that he was heavily influenced by the Vaishnava discourse of reform. And it was precisely the social imperative of that Vaishnava discourse that pushed him increasingly toward political radicalism. According to the historian Walter Hauser, Sahajanand's reading of the *Bhagavat Purana*, a text central to Vaishnava bhakti, "made it explicit that to serve the people was like service and devotion to God."[48] Sahajanand also wrote a commentary on the *Bhagavad Gita*, published as *Gita Hriday* (The Heart of the Gita), which still stands as a remarkable personal testimony of socialist idealism founded on core Vaishnava tenets of correct social action.[49]

Sahajanand was influenced by Vaishnava belief in more mundane ways as well. The land and buildings that formed the original nucleus of the Sitaram Ashram Sahajanand received from a Bhumihar Ramanandi named Sitaram Das, whose wish in old age was to "create a *brahmacharya* [student] ashram where Bhumihar brahman boys can come to study the Vedas, Shastras, and other sacred texts."[50] However, the Swami's principled dedication to the common man and his keen commitment to social and economic justice no matter what the cost thrust him increasingly into a position contrary to that of the Bhumihar Brahman Mahasabha's image as an organization designed to represent the "aristocratic, powerful, landowning elite."[51] This emerges nowhere more clearly than in Sahajanand's own remarks describing the formative events of 1927:

The countless Bhumihar brahman benefactors, who in fact kept the ashram from closing with their total yearly subscriptions of thousands of rupees, nevertheless eventually became the sworn enemies of the ashram. Indeed, many of them lived near the ashram itself. This [their hatred] was due to the fact that I sided with the anguished Goalas and other *kisans* [peasants] who came to me, and raised a storm against their oppressive zamindars. If anyone goes to that area today to see for themselves the downtrodden people there, regardless of their jati or religion, he will be in total agreement with me and, therefore, the ashram. Indeed, there the question of jati does not arise.[52]

From this point on, Sahajanand would only perceive agrarian conflict as that between landlords and peasants: "Caste and class had merged into a single category of social and economic exploitation. The Sitaram Ashram had become in his words a 'symbol of revolution.'"[53] It will be remembered that the term "Sitaram" possessed symbolic power in nearby Awadh during the Baba Ramchandra–led peasant struggle of 1919–1921. The name of the ashram alone may well have played a significant role in convincing many local cultivators of western Patna District that, in fact, the Swami would lend a sympathetic ear to their complaints. That the buildings and land for the ashram had been donated by a Ramanandi sadhu could only have furthered this perception. To complete the image, the Swami had by this time already developed a begrudged reputation among his landlord critics of being "nothing if . . . not progressive."[54]

While it is exceedingly difficult to arrive at any clear sense of the socioeconomic composition of the Bihar Provincial Kisan Sabha, it is likely—especially given the willingness of local Yadav tenants to seek the aid of the Swami in the transformative year of 1927—that peasants on the tenancy/proprietorship margin became involved in one way or another through the late 1920s and 1930s. This impression is reinforced by Hauser's own earlier reading of the caste dimensions of the leader-

ship of the Kisan Sabha, which included a dominant group of Bhumihars in addition to Rajputs and Kayasths, "with occasional Muslims and
lower caste cultivating peasants, primarily Kurmis and Koeris."[55] Emphasizing the anti-landlord, pro-tenant stance of the organization,
Hauser points out that "While most Kisan Sabha leaders were Bhumihars, so were most of the major zamindars, including the ones who came
under sharpest attack by the Kisan Sabha. On the other hand, while there
are some Bhumihar tenants in Bihar it is estimated that upwards of 90
per cent are not, and of course many of the best peasant cultivators in
the province are Kurmis and Koeris."[56]

Nevertheless, while the Kisan Sabha may have satisfied temporarily
the political aspirations of many marginally elite cultivators, the rise of
the *Triveni Sangh* organization confirms that many Kurmi, Kushvaha,
and Yadav kshatriyas felt a growing need for distinct political representation.[57] Though the precise chronology of the emergence of the
Triveni Sangh is as yet unclear—one scholar placing its organizational
origins in the mid-1920s, other observers dating the formal naming of
the organization to 1934—early signs of political cohesion between Yadavs, Kurmis, and Kushvahas can be seen as early as 1930.[58] In that year
a district-level meeting of Kushvahas and Yadavs was held in the village
of Garve in central Shahabad District in southwest Bihar and was
presided over by Sheopujan Prasad Singh, a Kurmi-kshatriya leader. Individual Kushvahas (Tapsi Ram of Begampur, Raghu Vir Singh of
Dumraon) and Yadavs (Sheopujan Singh of Jitaura, Nandkishore Singh
of Tenuni) cooperated in contesting the local district board elections in
that and the following year, but fared badly. The Triveni Sangh was for-
mally constituted in 1934 at another Shahabad District conference. A
third district conference was held in 1936, when membership was estimated at approximately one million based on the number of Kushvahas, Yadavs, and Kurmis who had paid the four-anna (one-quarter of a
rupee) fee to join the organization.[59]

The movement expanded to the provincial level—partly in an effort
to court Congress support in the upcoming elections of 1937—under
the leadership of Guru Sahay Lal (who would later become a "backward
caste" leader and who, according to one account, had suffered severe
personal humiliation by the high-caste elite) and Dasu Singh (a Kurmi).[60]
Meanwhile, after 1935 the Congress was busy forming the Backward
Classes Federation to counter what they viewed as the dangerous class
features of the Triveni Sangh and Kisan Sabha movements. This federation groomed future "backward" leaders by co-opting men like Bir-

chand Patel (a Kurmi), Sheonandan Mandal, and later Ram Lakhan Singh Yadav. Having thus guaranteed its "backward class" "vote bank," the Congress subsequently refused to grant Triveni Sangh candidates tickets to contest the upcoming elections. Furious at what they could only perceive as the underhanded trickery of local Congress party bosses, the Triveni Sangh leaders pledged electoral war against the "cursed Congressites."[61] Following a hotly contested election in which two Triveni Sanghis emerged victorious in Shahabad District (Tapsi Mahto from Arrah constituency and Nandkishore Singh from Piro constituency), the war that had been waged with the ballot reverted to more violent means as high-status landlords reigned vengeful terror on whole Kurmi, Kushvaha, and Yadav villages. Conversely, in areas where the Triveni Sangh had not won, supporters consoled themselves with the ominous solace, "we lost by the vote, but we hadn't lost our *lathis*."[62]

The rift between Congress and the Triveni Sangh, while sizable, was not insurmountable, as the latter merged with the Congress-sponsored Backward Classes Federation in 1948. While this certainly signified the end of the Triveni Sangh as a distinct political entity, it should not be viewed as the decline of Kushvaha-Kurmi-Yadav political power. Triveni Sangh leaders were being given posts in the Bihar Congress as early as 1940, and Kurmis, Kushvahas, and Yadavs contested seats in the 1946 election on Congress tickets. Thus, what Triveni Sanghis lost in terms of the symbolic power inherent in their kshatriya identities they gained in terms of direct access to political power. And while Congress gained access to a formidable rural vote bank, the social and economic tensions they were able to contain during the heady days of the new republic would eventually rise to the surface to define the quality of Indian politics in the post-1947 era.[63]

Conversely, the failure to produce any sort of union between the Kisan Sabha and the Triveni Sangh in the 1930s, despite common economic interests, can only be explained by the historical antagonisms that existed between powerful Bhumihar landlords on the one hand and marginal Yadav, Kurmi, and Kushvaha peasants on the other. This basic enmity surfaces in a politically and socially charged description of the tenuous relationship between the Sangh and the Sabha:

The bridge between the Bhumihar messiah, Swami Sahajanand Saraswati, and [the] ideologues of the Triveni Sangh was never built. Despite the fact that members of the Sangh flocked to listen to the Swami's message of common struggle, the Bhumihar label stuck. When Kesari "Master" [a Triveni Sangh leader] visited the Swami's ashram at Bihta in Patna district, night had fallen. Looking around he saw that those who surrounded the Swami were all upper-caste Bhumihars. Horrified, the backward-caste leader crept away under the cover of darkness.[64]

This episode is recounted in a language and tone familiar to observers of late twentieth-century Bihar politics, but adjectives like "backward-caste" would have had little meaning in the 1920s and 1930s, when Sahajanand was making his overtures to the broad base of tenant-cultivators and the tenant-cultivators themselves—the new peasant kshatriyas—were joining to explore new modes of political expression. Master Keshari, the hardened Triveni Sangh orator, shrank from the overpowering Bhumihar presence in Sahajanand's Sitaram Ashram not because they were "upper-caste Bhumihars" and he was a "backward-caste leader," but because the memory of staunch Bhumihar opposition to peasant-kshatriya reform was too fresh in the minds of all Kurmis, Kushwahas, and Yadavs. Only in the 1940s and especially after Independence did such politically inspired labels as "backward" and "forward" become superimposed on the older and, by then, antiquated conflicts over varna.

Identity and Class

The 1890s began with the rise of anti-Muslim mob violence, perpetrated in large part by gangs of Goalas set on associating themselves with what they perceived as the respectable desire to prohibit the slaughter of cows. As such, this phenomenon constituted an expression, albeit vague, of Goala solidarity with the landed elite who led the *gauraksha* movement. This tenuous solidarity began to develop cracks by the beginning of the twentieth century, as marginal elites in general and Goalas in particular launched campaigns articulating kshatriya identities. At the core of the kshatriya reform movements resided a direct challenge to the social and economic supremacy of the twice-born elite, and as these movements progressed, cultural confrontation became physical conflict.

Importantly, however, as old solidarities grew obsolete, new cohesive forms began to emerge. The Triveni Sangh represented the political union of Bihar's three most populous peasant communities—Yadav, Kushwaha, and Kurmi kshatriyas. In addition to the fact that they possessed common economic interests, these three communities had exercised a common cultural logic to regenerate their identities. The electoral power of this union was clearly demonstrated in 1937, as was its potential for class formation. As we shall see in the next chapter, nationalist politicians, anxious to minimize the growth of class antagonisms that would not only threaten the fragile unified opposition to British rule but also their own superordinate status, worked successfully to co-opt Triveni Sanghis as part of an undifferentiated "backward class" component of the Indian National Congress.

But if it can be argued that the Congress benefited electorally from what those elite members of Congress saw as a broadly agrarian class element in its organizational structure, the counterargument can certainly be made that the new peasant kshatriyas gained in proportion access to power and policy formation. Indeed, the political power that ex-Triveni Sanghis wielded in the elite Congress ranks would have been understood reflexively as another example of the heights to which they themselves had successfully aspired in their programs for social reform. And when the limits of Congress's political vision (not to mention social semantics) could no longer accommodate the aspirations of its "backward" contingent, the latter would break away to create new political forms to articulate, once again, a distinct economic and social message. This is evident most recently in the emergence of the *Janata Dal* (People's Party) and in the increasingly independent political action of leaders like Ram Lakhan Singh Yadav, the late Karpoori Thakur, Mulayam Singh Yadav, and Laloo Yadav.[65] In a sense, and understandably given the urgency of the nationalist movement, Congress leaders sacrificed long-term political cohesiveness for the short-term goal of delaying political discontent among peasants.

Social and cultural conflict did not end, therefore, with independence in 1947. Kurmis, Kushvahas, and Yadavs first flexed their unfettered political muscle in the late 1970s with demands for greater representation in the state bureaucracy under the controversial extension of the "reservations" policy for a vaguely defined list of "other backward classes."[66] The reservation of political offices, administrative posts, and educational opportunities for "depressed communities" was enshrined in the Indian constitution, but only made explicit in state-by-state lists ("schedules") for untouchables and tribals; "other backward classes" would include a heavy preponderance of Kurmi, Yadav, and Kushvaha kshatriyas. Following the cessation of sporadic violence engendered by and in response to the backward classes movement, the 1980s would witness the emergence of overt, armed warfare over the control of land, spearheaded by the Communist Party of India (Marxist-Leninist).[67] Termed "Naxalite" after the initial experiments in militant landgrabbing conducted in the

Naxalbari area of west Bengal, the movement now features Kurmis, Ya-davs, and Kushvahas in Bihar as both victims and perpetrators of vio-lence (though, significantly, never in the same case) directed against the landed, and retaliatory attacks by the landed against the landless. His-torically, Kurmi, Yadav, and Kushvaha kshatriyas have been positioned on both sides of the margin of land tenancy and land ownership. This is a socioeconomic fact that, to a large extent, has hindered the forma-tion of subordinate and superordinate class groups purely on the basis of jati distinctions.

The Yadav move from cowherd to kshatriya from the 1890s to the 1920s and the politics of Kurmi, Kushvaha, and Yadav involvement in agrarian radicalism from the 1920s to the 1940s together reveal the shift-ing nature of the caste fissures that inform the history of Gangetic north India. Whether or not the "mobility aspirations" of low-status peasants and artisans reflected "actual processes taking place in society," kshatriya reform brought about real political and cultural change. And the degree to which kshatriya reformers were successful in creating an impression among those poised above them in the political and social economy of Gangetic north India can be measured by the willingness of agrarian elites to respond to their claims both with harsh words and violent deeds, and by the fact that the politics of kshatriya identity determined to a large extent the history of agrarian politics in the 1930s and 1940s.

Conclusions

This study has been concerned in particular with the ideological options that confronted those branded shudra, or servile, by the twice-born elite in the nineteenth and twentieth centuries. At this level of social-historical experience, the access to personal dignity afforded shudras by Ramanandis via the Vaishnava religious mainstream represented an important rupture in the culture of caste. Through the course of the nineteenth and twentieth centuries, and despite what were at times fractious internal differences of opinion, Ramanandi monks were not only willing to overlook social stigma in administering religious teachings and directing worship, but even welcomed shudras as equal members of the monastic community. This was particularly the case after 1918, when the Ramanandi sampraday would find itself embroiled in debates over the question of religious and social elitism in monastic society, eventually leaning toward a distinctively egalitarian stance. Given the increasingly high profile of Ramanandis in Gangetic society during this period, this constituted an important rejection of the boundary between twice-born and shudra.

For many ordinary people, however, the culture of caste remained too overpowering to be subverted by the weight of monastic opinion, however authoritative. This did not necessarily mean, however, that they succumbed to its epistemological weight. Rather, by the early twentieth century many former shudras (including, most importantly, millions of peasants) began to refashion themselves en masse as the kshatriya descendants of divine royal lineages and hence as equal members of the very elite that despised them. As part of that populist reform, and aimed directly at the caste systemics of agricultural and artisanal production, the new kshatriyas sought to transform the meaning of physical labor by questioning the social stigma attached to it. This would have dramatic—and often violent—repercussions in the countryside, as rural elites expressed resentment at the usurpation of their social and, hence, economic prerogatives. The history of kshatriya reform confirms, then, that as one descends to the perspective of those who suffer the brunt of social stigma, caste loses its epistemological force and is treated as ideology.

The variety of arguments put forward in peasant and monastic redefinitions hinged on the histories and hagiographies of important Vaishnava personages. Among monks, Ramanand and the chain of gurus that preceded and succeeded him assumed major importance; among peasants, Ram and Krishna and their genealogies became paramount. Not unexpectedly, there was significant overlap. On occasion, individual monks played a role in reformist campaigns for kshatriya identity, but their decision to do so depended on their perception of the relevance of caste in monastic life which, in turn, was a function of their specific sampraday identity. More importantly, becoming kshatriya was in large part predicated on being Vaishnava—in behavior, belief, language, and diet. This history should be understood, then, as two socioreligiously related but distinct cultural processes: For radical Ramanandis, Vaishnavism entailed a philosophical stance against all forms of elitism, social or religious; for Yadavs, Kurmis, Kushvahas and many other "reformed kshatriyas," Vaishnavism provided the discursive and historical frame for a new, elite status that drew on a hierarchical ideology to subvert a hierarchical world. In this sense, though the ideological poles of this study stand in rigid opposition, both represented reasonable and compelling options for the millions of ordinary people long stigmatized by the term shudra.

Print technology and the rise of local publishing houses played an important role in the articulation and evolution of both radical Ramanandi and kshatriya reform viewpoints. Indeed, I have suggested in chapter 2 that the increasing number of competing commentaries on a major hagiographical text, namely, the *Bhaktamal,* in the latter half of the nineteenth century served to quicken the pace and heighten the intensity of philosophical and theological disputes within the Ramanandi sampraday. There is no doubt that published religious tracts became a major means of expressing Ramanandi doctrinal opinion, superseding or working in tandem with such periodic assemblages as the kumbh. A similar argument can be made with reference to kshatriya reform, namely, that the ability to print several thousand inexpensive Yadav, Kurmi, or Kushvaha-kshatriya histories, along with guidebooks prescribing correct religious and ritual observances (complete with advertisements from shops in major towns willing to sell sacred thread to the aspiring kshatriya), contributed to the viability of the movement as a whole.[1]

The popularization of printing presses certainly allowed for one remarkable feature of kshatriya reform, namely, the ability of educated individuals in the stigmatized communities to usurp to some extent the role of monastic gurus as local spiritual guides, by disseminating reformist propaganda with high levels of religious content. Given the strong Vaishnava dimension of that religious content, it is easy to understand how Hindi-language publishing quickly became associated with what Christopher King has called the "Hindu heritage," and what that meant in more specific sectarian terms.[2] Prior to the rise of kshatriya reform, the publication of religious texts was directed for the most part to an expert readership which could then dispense religious teachings via oral disquisitions based on those texts. The best example of this is the *Bhaktamal,* which was written for a select class of religious and literary adepts in a restricted Vaishnava sampraday context. With the popularization of kshatriya reform, religious instruction was often boiled down to a few essentials—vegetarian diet, proper worship, appropriate behavior (particularly for women), the schedule and performance of life-cycle rituals—to serve the interests of social and political mobilization, and was transmitted directly to large social groups independently of any mediation by a local religious adept. Appropriately, therefore, the genealogical concerns of kshatriya reform were not with sampraday-related guru parampara (Ramanandi or otherwise), but with the royal lineages of Ramchandra and Krishna.

The vast scope of kshatriya-reform publishing also served to popularize a historical message that would have major political and religious implications in the decades to come, namely, that Muslim invaders over the previous millennium were responsible for destroying the same sacred royal lineages in which the new kshatriya readership was being persuaded to claim descent. Given the colonial historiography of religion, this would have constituted an eminently believable, not to mention politically acceptable, way of explaining the degraded state of once-proud kshatriya communities in the early twentieth century. The communalist potential of kshatriya reform literature shared as well a great deal with historiographical themes raised in radical Ramanandi writing in the early twentieth century. Perhaps this is one reason, long after the passing of kshatriya reform and the political culture that nurtured it (to which we will turn momentarily), this convenient history lesson, with Ayodhya and Mathura-Vrindaban as its geocultural epicenters, remains embedded in the mental world of ordinary north Indians.

Forward and Backward

In retrospect, it would appear that the populist, peasant-based call for a kshatriya past suddenly lost its voice after the 1940s. Certainly one hears little mention today of the kshatriya antecedents of Kurmi, Yadav, and Kushvaha political identity. In fact the shift from the cultural politics of the early twentieth century to the political culture of the 1990s is not one that occurred as a sharp break at Independence in 1947 but has been much more gradual, indeed, almost imperceptible. The implications of that shift are profound, however, signaling the demise of a political culture based on an ideology of martial power and the rise of politics based on democratic, demographic realities.

Of all the reformed kshatriyas, Yadavs maintained the highest political profile after 1940. The following decades saw the increasing political engagement of such organizations as the All-India Yadav Mahasabha, the All-India Yadav Youth League, and the Bharatiya Yadav Sangh. Despite this upsurge in Yadav political activity, however, the period witnessed increasingly fewer calls for a detailed investigation of the martial history of Yadavs. Indeed, even the brief but intense pressure by Yadav leaders in the 1960s for greater representation in the Indian armed forces and the creation of a Yadav regiment was supported not by a renewed elaboration of the ancient kshatriya glories of the community but by focusing on the participation of Ahirs in the 1857 rebellion (remembered now as the first war of Indian independence), the subsequent recruitment of Ahirs/Yadavs into the British-Indian army, and the valor of Yadav soldiers during the 1965 Indo-Pakistan war.[3] While Yadav organizations were becoming politically more active (if less avowedly kshatriya) after 1947, the analogous Kurmi bodies seemed to be in absolute decline. The All-India Kurmi Kshatriya Mahasabha, which had held twenty conferences between the years 1894 and 1933, held half as many conferences between 1934 and 1971, with a gap of over ten years between the twenty-fourth (1948) and twenty-fifth (1958) meetings. The 1971 meeting was of particular significance in that Dahya Bhai Patel, a so-cialist member of parliament who presided over the session, successfully advocated the deletion of the term 'kshatriya' from all conference an-nouncements—a decision which engendered substantial ill-will on the part of jati elders.[4] This same conference also saw increased ties between the Kurmi and Kushvaha communities, perhaps a spillover from the days of political cooperation in the 1930s; however, one hears almost no ref-erence at all to Kushvaha-kshatriya organizations.

What occasioned the decline of the kshatriya political idiom among Yadav, Kurmi, and Kushvaha peasants between 1940 and the present? While this question reaches beyond the scope of this study, the answer can be found in the changing politics of India or, more precisely, in the new politics of independent India. The previous chapter ended with the three main peasant movements for kshatriya identity co-opted by the late 1930s via the Triveni Sangh into the Backward Classes Federation of the Indian National Congress and, hence, into the struggle for independence from British rule. Triveni Sangh leaders no doubt based this strategic shift on the perception that the future of Indian political patronage was to be dictated by nationalist leaders dedicated to a quasi-socialist democ-racy and, in that context, committed to the amelioration of social and economic injustice. For Kurmi, Yadav, and Kushvaha leaders, this would represent a sea change in Indian political culture, since a kshatriya iden-tity only had meaning in the context of a colonial political system crafted around visions of martial grandeur. In independent India politics would be predicated instead on universal adult suffrage and a commitment to the welfare of the nation's citizenry and would be played out by Indian party politicians seeking Indian votes. The questions for the leaders of reformed kshatriya communities were, how to conceive of themselves in the new politics? how to relate to Indian social democracy?

In retrospect, the first indication that the prospect of an independent, social-democratic India would have a measurable effect on the Yadav, Kurmi, and Kushvaha identities could be seen in the nationalist con-ception of these peasant communities as components of a federation of "backward classes." This would lead to constitutional safeguards in the form of reserved legislative seats, administrative and educational ap-pointments, and other protective discriminations adopted by the first par-liament on behalf of untouchables ("scheduled castes"), tribals ("sched-uled tribes"), and "other depressed sections" of society.[5] Specific clauses in articles fifteen and sixteen (entitled "Prohibition of Discrimination on the Grounds of Religion, Race, Caste, Sex, or Place of Birth" and

"Equality of Opportunity in Matters of Public Employment," respectively) of the Constitution gave the government of India the power to legislate in favor of "the advancement of any socially and educationally backward classes of citizens or for the Scheduled Castes and the Scheduled Tribes." To throw moral and political weight behind these clauses, Prime Minister Nehru included in the "Objectives Resolution" (a memorandum outlining the philosophy behind the Constitution) the assurance that "adequate safeguards shall be provided for minorities, backward and tribal areas, and depressed and other backward classes."[6] But while the question of identifying scheduled castes and scheduled tribes was settled before 1947 (in large part due to the efforts of B. R. Ambedkar, the author of the constitution), exactly who composed the backward *classes*—or, as Nehru put it, the "other backward classes"—was a question left for subsequent generations.[7] This constitutional uncertainty, and the mixed record of government attempts to resolve it, would fuel the backward-classes movement after 1950.

The first attempt to identify the backward classes emerged in 1953, with the appointment of the Backward Classes Commission by the president of India. The commission, in a report submitted after two years of deliberation, indicated that caste was an important measure of "backwardness" and, as such, drew up a list of 2,399 castes they believed to be backward. However, five of the eleven members of the commission—including the head of the commission itself, the widely respected legal scholar Kakasaheb Kalelkar—voiced strong objections on philosophical grounds. In a dissent attached to the report, Kalelkar expressed his frustration that while "the caste system is the greatest hindrance in the way of our progress towards an egalitarian society, . . . the recognition of the specified castes as backward may serve to maintain and even perpetuate the existing distinctions on the basis of caste."[8] Thus, for many educated Indians, applying caste as a delimiting tool in the struggle to eradicate the inequalities of caste represented a philosophically self-defeating exercise. Their critics would charge that this philosophical dilemma was simply a convenient (and typically Gandhian) upper-caste ploy to delay indefinitely the pressing need to redress the millennia-old social injustices of caste. With this dilemma in mind, not to mention other more pressing political factors, the central government rejected the 1955 report on the grounds that the commission had not applied more objective criteria, such as income, education, and literacy, to determine backward status.

In the following decades, numerous state commissions were formed to devise methods of identifying "backward" on the basis of a regional caste list combined with a battery of social, educational, and economic litmus tests. In 1978 a new central government Backward Classes Commission was created, headed by B. P. Mandal. According to the Mandal Commission report, submitted at the end of 1980, fully 3,743 castes representing over 52 percent of the population of India were identified as "backward"; the commission therefore recommended additional reservations of 27 percent (so as to keep the combined total reservations for scheduled castes, scheduled tribes, and "other backward classes" under the constitutional limit of 50 percent).[9] The central and state governments would deal with the backward classes issue in a variety of ways, some more aggressive than others. Even the Congress Party, since the 1970s viewed as a bastion of brahman conservatism on the backward classes issue, would gradually inch toward a grudging recognition of the political necessity of granting reservations according to their own reading of the Mandal Commission recommendations. If a turning point can be discerned, it was the announcement in August 1990 by then Prime Minister V. P. Singh that his government would begin implementing the Mandal recommendations. This act set off a firestorm of vigorous "forward-caste" protests, including a rash of self-immolation attempts by university students, and even brought down V. P. Singh's National Front government. However, it effectively ensured that every major party would have to address the issue directly, not simply make gratuitous reference to it in campaign manifestos.

If reform on behalf of the backward classes posed a set of philosophical and logistical problems for the administrative and political elite, it posed an entirely different sort of dilemma for communities within the backward classes movement itself. The dominance of the "backward" rhetoric has meant, for members of many newly designated "backward" castes, that communities long engaged in sophisticated campaigns to garner self-respect as kshatriyas—reformed, educated, and socially advanced—had now to begin representing themselves as disadvantaged. While one object of jati mahasabha relations with government—whether British or Indian—remained the same, namely, the agitation for greater job opportunities, the entire tone of the relationship with government changed. No longer would caste leaders dispatch memorials to government bureaucracies elaborating the proud histories and extensive abilities of their communities as a justification for increased employment; the post-1947 leaders of the same communities have agitated for the passage of backward classes legislation—and hence symbolically impor-

tant reservations for jobs, university admissions, and seats in legislatures—
as a political and social obligation of government, so that the beneficiaries of that legislation, conceived as the downtrodden members of an
oppressive society, can lead their brothers and sisters out of the abyss of
institutionalized inequality.[10]

The demise of kshatriya reform politics does not mean, however, that
the religiously potent politics of *kshatriyatva* (martial valor) are no longer
to be seen in north India. That political idiom still survives, but has been
taken up by what is generally referred to as the "Hindu right," manifest
in Uttar Pradesh and Bihar as the *Sangh Parivar* (the family of the
Sangh): the Bharatiya Janata Party (BJP), the Vishwa Hindu Parishad,
and the Rashtriya Swayamsevak Sangh. Consequently, we still hear a great
deal about the martial qualities of Ramchandra and, increasingly, Krishna, though they are not articulated in terms of the genealogical antecedents of the communities that have come to be known as "backward," but as the basis for a new moral politics and a utopian social vision
centered in particular on the birthplaces of those divine personages.
Given the political topography of north India, it is generally assumed
that the "backwards" keep the Hindu right at arm's length. This is due
to the quasi-socialist leanings of most backward-class leaders as opposed
to the generally procapitalist leanings of the BJP (which has in the past,
collective wisdom tells us, relied upon the financial contributions of small
urban shopkeepers and the occasional major financial concern). It is also
often held that cadre support for the BJP is drawn largely from the upper castes who inhabit the burgeoning economic middle classes in the
cities, a social composition that would alienate the backwards. However,
BJP leaders make no secret of their desire to attract a greater peasant
following, and to do this they would naturally seek to exploit the by now
near-forgotten claims to kshatriya status by Yadavs, Kurmis, and Kushvahas of yesteryear. It is in this context that the Yadav identity of Bihar's
chief minister, Laloo Yadav, was called into question after his jailing of
the BJP leader Lal Kishan Advani, during the latter's "chariot ride"
through north India to "liberate" the birthplace of Ram (*Ramjanambhumi*) in 1989.[11] The implication is that if Laloo Yadav had been
true to the Vaishnava dimensions of his Yadav-*kshatriya* roots, he would
have supported the Ramjanambhumi movement and allowed Advani's
procession to make a grand entrance into eastern Uttar Pradesh from
Bihar. As yet it is unclear how "backwards" are responding to such
rhetoric, though the successes of the Hindu right at the polls in the past
decade and the support the Ramjanambhumi movement attracted in the

rural areas indicate that the new articulation of kshatriyatva is resonating with more than just the urban middle class and the rural elite.

The emergence of backward and kshatriyatva politics reflects not only the changing nature of politics but the changing political culture of India. In ideological terms 1947 represented a clear break with the past, a watershed in terms of how individuals perceived themselves as part of the Indian body politic. Fundamental to this ideological change is the fact—explicit in the constitution with reference to universal equalities and implicit in any political system organized around democratic processes—that from the point of view of government (as distinct from politicians, political parties, and voters themselves), caste no longer constituted the basis of an individual's political and legal being, as it had in British India. However, moving from a political culture based firmly on caste to one that repudiates casteism is easier said than done. Scholars will be left to speculate on the effect of such legal reorientations on mass politics and individual people; there can be no doubt, however, that the effects on both were interconnected and, as yet, are unresolved. The backward class movement was connected to the rise of a socialist-democratic state and reflected the popular perception that that state would respond to those who portrayed themselves as sufficiently needy. The new politics of kshatriyatva reflect, by contrast, a broad-based frustration with the nature of the moral order (or lack thereof) implicit to that state. The slow abandonment of the socialist components of the Indian state that now seems to be taking place is a process that of necessity reduces the extent to which the state can provide what it may have deemed in the past socially desirable employment, representation, and education. The issue that faces Yadavs, Kurmis, Kushvahas as the twentieth century draws to a close is whether they should relinquish the politics of "backwardness" altogether in favor of a return to their kshatriya reformist roots. If they were to do so, it would be natural for them to articulate kshatriya reform politically as kshatriyatva.

History and Consciousness

If I do not describe the history of kshatriya reform or Ramanandi radicalism in terms of subaltern consciousness, it is because to do so would be to understand the actors as perpetually put upon and to understand their ideologies in fundamentally negative terms—at best as forms of resistance destined to fall short of their utopian visions, at worst as predetermined national failures.[12] Kshatriya reform and radical Ramanandi ideologies were predicated on social change (whether real or imagined) and, as such, sought to inculcate new epistemologies, particularly at the level of popular religious consciousness. An understanding of political insurgency as the only worthwhile mode of peasant expression implies a theoretical frame that is impervious to such shifting social and mental worlds. This may appear as a critique of the subaltern studies project from the right.[13] In fact, it is not unlike a recent reflection from within.[14]

Fortunately, historical actors are not burdened by the theoretical paradigms and social categories that constrict social scientists, and social historians in particular. When we listen to what those historical actors have to say, we learn that significant, if commonplace, transformations took place on a regular basis throughout the nineteenth and twentieth centuries.[15] Perhaps these transformations are more easily discerned if we understand them as the crossing of boundaries. Such boundary crossings included the commonplace entry of shudras into north India's largest Vaishnava monastic order, the Ramanandi sampraday, and the radical (and largely successful) attempts by some in that sampraday to foster a more egalitarian monastic spirit. The crossing of boundaries also included the rejection by peasants and artisans of the shudra status that had for so long been ascribed to them, in favor of a kshatriya identity rich with Vaishnava meaning. Ramanandi and kshatriya reform each reflected a particular kind of consciousness predicated on the creation, maintenance, and definition of community, whether religious (sampraday) or social (jati). Both Ramanandi radicals and kshatriya reformers went about their programs by engaging in intellectual labor and propaganda and by articulating their views in popular presses throughout the Gangetic north. Their aggressive posture occasioned moments of conflict and sometimes even violence, but unlike subaltern consciousness, their voices did not require moments of conflict to be discernible. And though they lacked the glamour and grandeur of a rebellion or revolution, Vaishnava and kshatriya reform possessed their own kind of rebellious, revolutionary content, howsoever incremental and subtle it may have been.

The history of the Ramanandi sampraday and kshatriya reform in the nineteenth and twentieth centuries affords an insider's view of caste, an idea that has long been presumed to reside at the heart of India, rendering that place and its inhabitants unchanging, even timeless. Though caste may have become integral to British imaginings of India, the caste of varna remained politically real and culturally pervasive, if not religiously sacrosanct. Like race, varna did not exist beyond history but remained well within it, was not rigid and monolithic but flexible, indeed malleable. Because the social and cultural systemics of identity had long involved repeated reconciliations of varna and jati—the ideal and the real—the tools with which to manipulate caste were readily available. All that was required was a familiarity with royal or religious genealogies, the ability to apply them to present-day identities, and the wherewithal to present them in the language of history as an ancient present.

Social history, particularly peasant history, is too often written as if the actors do not think—or if they do think, that their thoughts and beliefs do not matter in the long run—and as if the only force that propels them through history is a concern with the contents of pocketbook and stomach. Basic common sense, however, tells us that historical change can on occasion be dependent upon moral principles and a sense of social justice. To write history, to engage opponents on the battleground of the past, to reform fundamental social groups, whether sampraday or jati, according to a new vision of the past—these were the accomplishments of thinking peasants and monks in Gangetic north India. For peasants history served identity, for monks history served hagiography. But for both, their discourses of history were rife with vital meaning. The constant, self-directed questioning of history by peasants and monks—

> Who were we, what has happened, and where are we going now?
> Gather round everyone and ponder these questions together.
> If we fail to appreciate the entirety of our past,
> we may never realize who we really are.[16]

or,

> Who could have exposed the fallacy of high and low
> if such a sadhu had not entered the world?
> Who else could have inspired the notion that no one is
> impure amid the tranquility of God's realm?[17]

—confirms that to write about the past, whether in terms of ancient kshatriya origins or in terms of the life of Ramanand, justified action in the present. The past was alive for peasants and monks in British India.

This was not disinterested history. Indeed, many times here I have referred to elements of it as polemic and propaganda. Yet it served an important historical purpose by allowing ordinary people to debate the merits of status and equality. Peasants ultimately wished for a society that did not deride individuals as shudra, and they therefore advocated reform. But they did this in what appears to have been a roundabout manner, namely, by asserting kshatriya origins in the ancient past and, hence, elite status in the present. This elitist strategy was remarkably effective, not to mention threatening, because of its epistemological implications. As one interested observer put it in 1925: "When everybody is somebody, then nobody is anybody."[18] Or, as a friend put it in 1987, "we used to be shudra, then we were kshatriya; now I'm not sure what we are."

Francis Buchanan

The survey work of Francis Buchanan (later Francis Hamilton) between 1809 and 1813 is one of the most detailed sources for the social and cultural history of Bihar and eastern Uttar Pradesh in the early nineteenth century. Inasmuch as portions of the present study, particularly chapter 1, rely on those surveys, and insofar as those surveys have been under-utilized as a source for religious and cultural history, it is appropriate to include a brief discussion of Buchanan's life and work. Buchanan has been dealt with in detail by historian Marika Vicziany, both with respect to the reliability of his numerical tabulations for economic history and as an example of the importance and evolution of the statistical method in imperial ideology. A surgeon by profession and a botanist by inclination, Buchanan first came to India in 1794, having joined the East India Company as a medical officer ten years earlier. Unhappy with tedious postings in rural Bengal, where the vegetation and wildlife failed to interest him, Buchanan sought through a variety of strategies to attain a more independent scientific position with the company. One such strategy involved becoming an expert on "native" society and culture. Buchanan soon developed a reputation as an irritant to the orientalist establishment, which was (in Vicziany's words) "inclined towards a Brahmanical interpretation of Indian society." By publishing an essay on Burmese Buddhism, Buchanan juxtaposed "the egalitarianism of Buddhism against the oppressive, hierarchical nature of Brahmanism. Buchanan's hatred of the entrenched Brahmin class in India, together with his critical reading of the religious scriptures, marked him out as a man ideally equipped to act as the Company's reporter on native affairs."

Buchanan did in fact receive a number of commissions, primarily from Governor-General Wellesley, to survey conquered, annexed, and neighboring regions of the subcontinent, including Burma, the defeated Tipu Sultan's Mysore in South India, Nepal, and, finally, Bengal.[1]

Notwithstanding his success as a collector of rare Indian botanical specimens and the posthumous recognition accorded him for his prodigious surveys, Buchanan's desire to attain an independent scientific posting was frustrated by political and administrative circumstances beyond his control.[2] Vicziany argues that Buchanan, driven by a desire to pursue his scientific interests despite (and perhaps because of) his unfortunate position, subordinated what we would today consider stringent statistical method to his botanical collections and research.[3] Her conclusion—namely, that Buchanan's Bengal accounts cannot be entirely relied upon for statistical data—is directed in particular at economic historian Amiya Kumar Bagchi's work on structural change in Bihar. Bagchi, who used Buchanan's tables as a statistical database, argued that Bihar experienced significant deindustrialization in the nineteenth century as a result of the colonial British presence; Bihar thus represented a microcosm of India itself, which was transformed during this century into a dependent economy on the periphery of Britain.[4] Vicziany disputes Bagchi's use of the statistical data, arguing that

Buchanan's evidence about the daily life of artisans is irritatingly incomplete. If there is good material here about wage rates, this is rarely accompanied by information about all the other, equally important aspects about artisan life. Some artisans owned or cultivated land, but Buchanan does not tell us how much land was involved or how much income was generated by doing this. It is the lack of detail in Buchanan's descriptive accounts which must alert us to the limitations of the statistical tables. . . . in Buchanan's day statistics meant something other than simple quantification of information.[5]

The information Buchanan provided about popular religion and culture, I would argue, is not subject to the same kinds of methodological pitfalls as his economic observations. Buchanan's abiding interest in non-brahmanical forms of social organization placed him, in fact, in a strong position to recognize and appreciate the significance of alternative religious and social identities. Vicziany notes that after Buchanan's first interest in natural history, much of his time "during the Bengal Survey was spent following up local legends, rumours and caste histories."[6] Based on my reading of the Buchanan manuscripts, this is clearly an understatement: the description of regional religious organization in these survey accounts, which I cite extensively, makes it abundantly clear in particular that Buchanan was fascinated by the many important institutional and ideological dimensions of Vaishnava, Shaiva, and Shakta belief.

The impulse for these accounts originated in 1807, when Buchanan was commissioned by the Court of Directors of the East India Company to survey, map, and report systematically on the territories of Bengal. Guided by a desire to seek out regions of botanical interest, his route did not follow the prescribed counter-clockwise direction recommended by his superiors at Fort William.[7] Rather, Buchanan began in Dinajpur and Rangpur (1807–1809), north of the Ganga in what is now Bengal proper; moved westward to Purnia (1809–1810) in north Bihar; then southwest through Bhagalpur (1810–1811); westward to Patna, Gaya, and Shahabad (1812–1813), all in south Bihar; and, finally, northeast to Gorakhpur (1813–1814) in what is now eastern Uttar Pradesh.[8] Buchanan produced detailed reports of Dinajpur, Rangpur, Purnia, Bhagalpur (which includes most of early twentieth-century Monghyr District), Bihar and Patna (the later Patna and Gaya Districts), Shahabad, and Gorakhpur (the later Gorakhpur and Basti Districts). The original manuscript copies of these accounts are housed in the Oriental and India Office Collection in the British Library, London.[9] Soon after Buchanan's death, these accounts, in addition to an account of Assam, were edited and published by R. Montgomery Martin as *The History, Antiquities, Topography, and Statistics of Eastern India*.[10] Martin has since been roundly criticized by students of the Buchanan manuscripts for his random editorial cuts of valuable material while preparing the volumes for publication (his blue pencil strokes through the text marking portions to be omitted are still discernible on the original manuscript folios), as well as for failing to give Buchanan enough explicit credit as the sole author of the work.[11] This was remedied to some extent by the publication of the original accounts of the Bihar districts by the Bihar and Orissa Research Society between 1928 and 1939; these editions (save that of Bhagalpur) were reissued in 1986 by a New Delhi publisher. The Dinajpur, Rangpur, and Gorakhpur accounts have never been published in their entirety.

Buchanan's interest in nonbrahmanical forms of religious and social organization extended as well to an exploration of kshatriya lineages. He included in his accounts a detailed description of local historical and dynastic knowledge (often in the form of legend or popular memory), together with his own information on kshatriya genealogy gleaned from the standard Indological texts and from his own interviews and translations. Buchanan maintained an interest in kshatriya lineages even after he returned to Scotland, where he produced an impressive compendium entitled *Genealogies of the Hindus, Extracted from Their Sacred Writings*.[12] This work, which consisted primarily of large, hand-drawn tables and charts, represented an early and significant expression of the British fascination with the culture of kshatriya history, a fascination that reached its peak with the work of James Tod.[13]

Buchanan's interest in kshatriya genealogy predated by nearly a century the huge body of Hindi pamphlet literature authored by popular intellectuals seeking a kshatriya past for peasants on the margin of land control (see chapters 3 and 4). Of course, the twentieth century does not mark the first time kshatriya genealogies were manipulated to buttress claims of high status. Historian Romila Thapar has suggested that royal genealogies were being fabricated by the brahmanical elite at the behest of "low-born" rulers in the ancient and medieval periods.[14] As the twentieth-century manifestation of kshatriya-lineage campaigns shows, the process of genealogy invention has continued into the present historical epoch, albeit at a much lower sociopolitical center of gravity. It can be argued that the historiographical significance of twentieth-century kshatriya reform lies in the fact that ever larger numbers of people at the most productive level of Gangetic society began to conceive of Ram and Krishna not only as gods but as ancestors, physically present in a historical past.

Hence, the genealogical representation (itself a form of historicization) of Vaishnava myth was not unique to the early twentieth century, nor were the kshatriya lineages a figment of Buchanan's early nineteenth-century colonial imagination writ large on Vaishnava culture a hundred years later. On the contrary, Buchanan recorded what he understood to be salient aspects of Gangetic belief, culture, and history. What he chose to record was colored by his own perceptions of what was important, but the phenomena he observed had to exist (or, at the very least, be claimed by his many and varied informants to exist) in order for him to observe them. Like the work of other servants of the company-*cum*-empire, Buchanan's work entered the arena of public dialogue. Like numerous other British interpretive compendia, Buchanan's accounts contributed to the direction and dimensions of political and cultural change; they did not, however, introduce wholly unfamiliar concepts.

APPENDIX 2

Dharnidharacharya and James Tod

In the late 1920s, when he was still a young Vaishnava intellectual of Ayodhya, Swami Dharnidharacharya was recruited to write the history of the wealthy subgrouping of "Awadhia" (or "Ayodhia") Kurmis concentrated in Patna, Gaya, and Saran Districts of Bihar. By 1930 he had published from Prayag (Allahabad) an important book on the history of the community, entitled *Shri Awadhvamshiya Kshatriya Martandah* (roughly translatable as "Honourable Awadh-Lineage Kshatriyas of the Sun").[1] The arguments and organizational layout of this book offer a glimpse of the mechanics of asserting a kshatriya identity, especially insofar as it relied on British Indological literature, and James Tod's *Annals and Antiquities of Rajast'han* in particular. Dharnidharacharya addressed two areas of overwhelming concern: his personal religious identity and his community identity as a kshatriya descended from the region of Awadh surrounding the town of Ayodhya. In terms of relative space devoted to each subject, the latter took marked precedence over the former. The two strands of identity were nevertheless fundamentally intertwined: Dharnidharacharya claimed preceptor (*guru*) descent and Awadh-centered kshatriyas claimed genealogical (*vamshiya*) descent from the same divine source, Ramchandra of Ayodhya, the earthly manifestation of God. Dharnidharacharya's discussion of his religious identity fills the last forty-five pages (116–61) of the book and speaks to such issues as philosophy of religion, the Vaishnava avatars, the correctness of image worship and performance of funerary rites as prescribed in the Vedas, and sampraday history, including in particular his own tale of the vagaries of becoming a Ramanuji in the midst of an increasingly Ramanandi Ayodhya.

Dharnidharacharya's life, and in particular recollections of the Ramanuji-Ramanandi crisis of 1918–21, which filled the formative years of his religious development, are recounted in chapter 3 (see the section entitled "Kshatriya Reform and Ramanandis"). It is significant, however, that the narrative of this conflict makes up the final nineteen pages of Dharnidharacharya's book. The first three pages of the main body of the book, moreover, are a blessing to Ramchandra and Ramanuja, the two central components of Dharnidharacharya's religious personality, and a brief discussion of his own name and village. The remainder of the book (pp. 4–115), recalling the kshatriya past of his community, was thus framed between introductory and concluding text that reflected the core concerns of the author's religious identity. This framework is symbolically appropriate, I would argue, inasmuch as the kshatriya past depended on the details of Vaishnava memory and identity, firmly rooted in the present.

The central part of his text begins with a brief recounting of the main kshatriya branches descending from the sun and moon in a primeval age. The discussion then turns to a more lengthy narrative of the evolution of those lines into "historical" time, with special focus on the descent of the solar lineage in Ayodhya as continued through Ramchandra's sons, Lav and Kush. This is followed by a brief outline of the main clan lines said to descend from Kush. Concluding this portion of the book is a lengthy delineation of correct ritual and commensal observances for orthodox, elite Hindus. As evidence for this reconstellated kshatriya past, Dharnidharacharya cited an immense range of information and interpretation, in both Sanskrit and vernaculars—including six Vedas, fifteen Upanishads, seven *darshan* (philosophy), four *sutra* (aphorisms), three *vyakarana* (grammars), sixteen *dharmashastra* (moral treatises), seven *samhita* (pilgrimage codes), nine *itihas* (histories), thirteen *puran* (mythologies), one *kavya* (poetry), six *kosh* (lexicons), two *jyotish* (astrologies) and three *niti shastra* (ethical treatises).[2] This material provides the basis for the wealth of detail provided in Dharnidharacharya's account. However, a critical component of the argument is the transition from cosmological time to historical time, and for this the author relies on the interpretation found in Lieutenant-Colonel James Tod's massive contribution to Indological scholarship, *The Annals and Antiquities of Rajast'han, the Central and Western Rajpoot States of India*, compiled in the early nineteenth century.[3]

The intellectual challenge that confronted Dharnidharacharya was to confirm in scholarly terms the link between the extant Awadh-kshatriya identity of Kurmis in the central Gangetic tract and the remembered kshatriya heartland of *Aryavarta*, the region "conquered" by Aryas in north India. Doing so required the historical extrapolation of mythological meaning detailing the lineage of Ramchandra of Ayodhya. Such an extrapolation was readily available in Tod's *Annals*, which Dharnidharacharya cited to the following effect:

> The offspring of the sun-born [*surya-putra*] Vaivashwata arrived at the banks of the *Sindhu* [Indus] and *Ganga* [Ganges], and established his capital at Ayodhya, which was in fact the first settlement of Koshala. Tod then writes . . . that "two branches (Suryavamshiya) emigrated from Koshala, [one of which] established Rohtas on the banks of the *Son* river, east of *Ara* [Arrah] and west of Patna." *(At this time Suryavamshiya kshatriyas in the vicinity of Patna came to be well known as Awadhvamshiya kshatriyas.)* And the other branch settled in the Kohari country in the vicinity of *Lahaur* [Lahore].[4]

This is not an exact translation of Tod's prose but a fairly accurate paraphrase.[5] Moreover, the portion I have italicized is not to be found in Tod but is consciously inserted by Dharnidharacharya himself—hence his use of parentheses. Further, Dharnidharacharya presents no evidence to support the claim that the emigrant Suryavamshiya branch that settled in Patna eventually became known as "Awadhvamshiya," or belonging to the lineage (*vamsh*) of Awadh. It is this lack of evidence, one presumes, that opponents of kshatriya identity movements would have highlighted in an effort to undercut the status claims of cultivators.[6] Dharnidharacharya's assertion of identity between Awadhvamshiya and Suryavamshiya kshatriyas can of course be understood as a dexterous manipulation of Tod's work; it also represents the point of convergence between history, identity, and belief. In other words, transposing an allegiance to the great progenitor Ramchandra onto an Awadh-oriented kshatriya identity was a perfectly natural Vaishnava intellectual move. Dharnidharacharya would assert that no supporting evidence is necessary: the geographic roots of Awadh-kshatriya identity would be patently obvious to him and his audience, with or without Tod's account.

But the fact that Dharnidharacharya chose to rely on Tod for what is the pivot between his mythological and historical exegesis is in and of itself important and speaks to the magnitude of Tod's *Annals* (and related orientalist literature) in the evolution of kshatriya reform. Tod's work was and is widely read by Indologists and, consequently, has experienced numerous reprintings in England.[7] It represented for the colonial reader a well-known and readily accessible description of the "traditional" nobility of north India. Less well known is the fact that eight chapters of volume one of Tod's *Annals*, made up of approximately eighty-nine pages under the title "History of the Rajpoot Tribes," were translated into Hindi by Pandit Ramgarib Chaube and published by Khadgavilas Press in 1913; earlier translations had been published in Bengal in the 1890s.[8] The Khadgavilas (or "lusty sword") Press was an important early publishing house in Bankipur, the civil lines of Patna where much of the business of empire took place in Bihar. Its translation of Tod's *Annals* was cited by Dharnidharacharya in his retelling of the Awadhvamshiya-kshatriya past.

The eight chapters in question represent Tod's attempt at piecing together a "history" of the Rajput (kshatriya) clans of Rajasthan from Puranic sources and at relating that mytho-historical body of knowledge to classical European and Old Testament lore. Thus some of Tod's chapter subheadings read as follows (the relevant chapter numbers are in parentheses):

Genealogies of the Rajpoot princes (1)

Connection of the Rajpoots with the Scythic tribes (1)

Legends of the Poorans confirmed by the Greek historians (2)

Synchronisms (3)

The dynasties which succeeded Rama and Crishna (5)

Analogies between the Scythians, the Rajpoots, and the tribes of Scandinavia (6)

Tod's romantic fascination for the misty links between European and Indian antiquity reflected the broader orientalist musings of the period, an analysis of which can be found in S. N. Mukherjee's study of the life of Sir William Jones.[9] Among the many parallels of legend drawn by Tod, one of the most singular is his speculation regarding the lineages of Kush (Ramchandra's son) and Cush (the son of Ham, whose progeny were allegedly cursed by Noah to eternal servitude). In a footnote to his discussion of the suryavamshiya Kushvaha descendants of Ramchandra, Tod remarked that

the resemblance between the Cushite Ramesa [Ramchandra's Kushvaha] and the Rameses of Egypt [Noah's lineage through Ham] is strong. Each was attended by his army of satyrs, Anubis and Cynolcephalus, which last is a Greek misnomer, for the animal bearing this title is of the Simian family, as his images (in the Turin museum) disclose, and the brother of the faithful Hanooman. The comparison between the deities within the Indus (called

Nil-áb, 'blue waters') and those of the Nile in Egypt, is a point well worth discussion.

Of course, for Tod the beginning and end of all these speculations was the neverending search for a trace of the memory—in the form of myth—of human origins: "The *Genesis* of India commences with an event described in the history of almost all nations, the deluge, which, though treated with the fancy peculiar to the orientals, is not the less entitled to attention." And, more to the point: "These [Greek, Roman, pagan, and Indian] traditions appear to point to one spot, and to one individual, in the early history of mankind, when the Hindu and the Greek approach a common focus; for there is little doubt that Adnat'h, Adiswára, Osiris, Bághés, Bacchus, Menu, Menes, designate the patriarch of mankind, Noah."[10] Indeed, the desire to reconnect the remembered yet fragmented past of mankind permeated the European orientalist imagination in the eighteenth and nineteenth centuries, exemplified best in Max Müller's famous advice to young Indian Civil Service candidates over five decades later (1882) "that his heart should not sink when approaching the shores of India, for he was 'going to his "old home", full of memories, if only he can read them.'"[11]

If Tod's overriding concern was his desire to reach back into the recesses of human memory to arrive at some protohistorical truth about the nature of the human species, his more immediate object in these eight chapters was to present the patterned meaning of Indian mythology in a way that European readers could both understand and appreciate. And fortunately for the historian of British-Indian ideas, Tod is completely candid about the sources for his account:

Being desirous of epitomising the chronicles of the martial races of Central and Western India, it was essential to ascertain the sources whence they draw, or claim to draw, their lineage. For this purpose I obtained from the library of the Rana of Oodipoor [Udaipur] their sacred volumes, the *Pooráns,* and laid them before a body of pundhits, over whom presided the learned Jetty Gyanchandra. From these extracts were made of all the genealogies of the great races of Soorya and Chandra, and of facts historical and geographical.[12]

Here Tod adds that of this large body of literature, the most useful for writing Rajput history were the *Bhagavat, Skanda, Agni,* and *Bhavishya* Puranas. It should not be concluded, however, that Tod or any other British orientalist was the first to apply Puranic literature to a reconstruction of the past and that this application was simply imitated by later

Indian intellectuals. Quite the reverse is true: Tod, and orientalists generally, looked to this and other literature primarily because it presented an image of the past with valuable information for the present.[13] Certainly the historical format in which they rendered the material was markedly difference from Indian renderings; nevertheless, the purpose of that rendering was familiar: a description of the past to explain the present. What is remarkable is that Dharnidharacharya, thoroughly ensconced in the social and religious upheaval of the early twentieth century, deemed Tod's rendition of the Puranic past useful in his own reclamation of genealogical origins. Part of the reason was that Tod's *Annals* were perceived as a politically sanctioned body of knowledge; after all, James Tod was not only a lieutenant-colonel in the British army, he was the political agent of the Honorable Company to the powerful western Rajput states, symbolic to many—both British and Indian—of martial valor. The two texts under consideration, *Annals and Antiquities of Rajast'han* and *Shri Awadhvamshiya Kshatriya Martandah,* though different in outlook and scope, bear one striking similarity: an overriding concern for origins. Tod expressed it in terms of Noah and the flood; Dharnidharacharya in terms of Ramchandra and the sun. But they spoke directly to each other across the nineteenth century in a language both could understand.

APPENDIX 3

Gopa Charitam

The following verse, which was composed by one "Bahuran," a brahman of northern Bhagalpur District in the early 1920s, urged Goalas to give up their claims to high status as Yadav kshatriyas. According to S. A. Khan, a district officer in Bhagalpur at the time, the verse was reproduced in large quantities in leaflet form and "sung by hired boys in the *mofussil* [countryside]."[1] I have cited this verse extensively in chapter 4 and provide a full translation here as an example of the language employed by those who stood in radical opposition to kshatriya reform.[2] Bahuran's taunting jibes represent a complex and integrated poetic expression that combines pointed references to religious ideas, economic roles, and social status. The verse begins in a religious context, moves to a mytho-historical past, enters the economic, religious, and social immediacy of the present, and concludes with a call for a return to an idyllic past when brahmans were brahmans, shudras were shudras, and hierarchical prerogative went unquestioned. As a brahman appropriation of the Vaishnava past that Goalas had worked to conceive, a past based on genealogical ties to Krishna and Radha, *Gopa Charitam* most certainly constituted a serious affront to Yadav kshatriya sensibilities. Adding insult to injury, the author tried to turn that appropriated history against its original purpose: the redefinition of Goala identity as Yadav kshatriyas.

Gopa Charitam:

Shloka:
In supplication to Radha, the auspicious daughter of Brishbhanu,

Who is the presiding mistress of the *ras*[3] and who dwells in Krishna's
 heart.
In supplication to Krishna, who steals the hearts and clothes of the
 women of Braj,[4]
Who has two arms, carries the flute in his hand, has a deep complexion,
 and wears a garland of wild flowers.
I, Bahuran by name, a reputed brahman, relate the conduct of the *Gopas*[5]
 to educate them,
Gopas who are the followers of Dayanand.[6]

Doha:

In heartfelt remembrance of the couple that lives at Vrindaban,
I describe the behavior of the gopas, without any pretence of being a
 guru, and with out any sinister motive.

Campfire Tale
(told in the manner of the wayfarer)

Oh Gopa *jatiyo*,[7] you understand the austere virtues of Krishna
 of *Golok*,[8] who took his birth as an avatar in Mathura.
Born a member of the Yadu lineage in the sacred home of
 Basudev, he lifted the weight of Earth.   1[9]
Afraid of Kans,[10] Basudev carried the boy Krishna on his own
 head to Gokul,
To the home of his friend, Nand Ray, the headman of Braj and
 the husband of Yashomati.   2
Dronabasu[11] and *Dhara*[12] performed austerities, and to reward
 them Krishna took human form.
Knowing their pure hearts, he assumed an image of unparalleled
 beauty.   3
The boy Krishna would playfully steal milk, curd, and butter
 from the milkmaids to tease them,
And would accompany the cowherd boys to tend their cattle in
 the jungle.   4
He danced ras with all the *Gopis*,[13] filled his mind with wisdom,
 and created a heavenly life for all.
So renowned is the auspicious vaishya lineage of Braj, worthy
 recipients of all India's adoration.   5
In the company of Shri Krishna, the Gopas delivered themselves
 of wordly sin and took god into their hearts.
Chanting "hare Krishna, hare Krishna," they worshipped *Govinda
 Gopal*[14] and led successful lives.   6
Devotees like Ajamil, Swapach, Sajan Kasai, Mira Bai sang the
 praises of god,
Performed unparalleled devotions, and finally submerged
 themselves in the godhead.   7

The many sins of scavengers, hunters, and savages were cleansed,
even Ravidas found refuge in Krishna.

Through bhakti and *bhajan*[15] all of them went to heaven, but
you Gopas have pinned your hopes to the sacred thread.[16]   8

Oh Gopa jatiya, read the Bhaktmal, think only of god and reform
your lives.

God will surely abandon you if you forget your dharma and
oppose brahmans.   9

Remember the *dvaparyug*,[17] have faith in the Vedas and the
Puranas, maintain family rituals, and god will sustain you.

Abandon the ways of Dayanand, Gopas, difficult times lie ahead
in the Kaliyug.   10

Hay, Hay, Hay, words fail me, you Gopas have fallen far from the
path of virtue.

Your mothers cut grass, your sisters sell milk in the villages, towns,
and markets.   11

You wear the sacred thread on your shoulders while your women
wake up to milk your cows and round up your calves.

You work the plough with your sacred threads on, and make your
women labor in the fields.   12

You've used up all the weavers' cloth, and the scarcity of cotton
makes thread expensive.

Gwalins[18] sell milk and curd all day long, they would not know
how to spin sacred thread.   13

When your elder brother dies, you transform his widow into a
happy bride.

Whenever the husbands of your daughters and sisters die you
marry off their wives afresh.   14

Born into the Gopa vamsh, you shamelessly claim to be of the
kshatriya vamsh.

You ignore the Vedas and Puranas and become two jatis in one:
you call yourselves *kulin*.[19]   15

Even though you work to be a noble jati, no one accepts tobacco
that you've touched.

Two opposing customs prevail in one family: one-month shradh
and thirteen-day shradh.   16

[You can only] thank yourselves, your wisdom, and the tempera-
ment of your jati,

[You can only] thank your marriage brokers and your priests, for
all your ancestors have been sent to heaven.[20]   17

Read the Laws of Manu wherein Gopas are given as shudras, and
abandon shradh after thirteen days.

Be united and accept a one-month shradh, this should be the
reform of the Gopa jati.   18

If shudras perform the fire sacrifice, worship *shalgram*,[21] and
offer cooked food to Vishnu,

The sage Yagyavalkya decrees that they will be destroyed and sent
    to hell.   19

Your ancestors in Kashi, Vrindaban, Awadh, and Gokul, have
    filled the stomachs of all the sadhus.[22]

[This is why] they can wear the sacred thread and perform
    thirteen-day shradh.   20

Without asking the permission of lord Krishna, you have assumed
    the sacred names of Gurudatta, Gauridatta, Raj, Ratinath,
    Shrikant, Ayodhyanath, Govind Lal, Kalanath, and Kantalal.[23]   21

Badrinath, Yadunath, Parmanand, Sada Shiva—kiss their pictures
    and cling tight to them.

You have taken it upon yourselves to propitiate the gods and your
    ancestors, and have fulfilled all your desires.[24]   22

You have abandoned your family duties for the ideas of Dayanand,
    and have thus destroyed your good name.

You have even forsaken the praises that hundreds of virtuous men
    sang on your behalf.   23

I ask god with folded palms, why has the wisdom of the Gopas
    been destroyed?

Think for yourselves in groups of ten or twenty, and give up the
    spread of the sacred thread.   24

Do not be offended by me, think only of the common good for
    all.

You were the mainstay of our lives and this dispute has caused us
    great pain.   25

My name is Bahuran and I live in Ram Patti village north of the
    pilgrimage center of Singheshwar in Bhagalpur District.

Follow this good advice and avoid improper behavior.   26

If you Gopas take exception to my faults, then grant me respect-
    ful pardon.   27

Notes

Introduction

1. For definitions of peasant society, see Daniel Thorner, "Peasantry," in David Sills, ed., *International Encyclopedia of the Social Sciences* (New York: Macmillan, 1968), 11:508; Teodor Shanin, "Peasantry: Delineation of a Sociological Concept and a Field of Study," *European Journal of Sociology* 12 (1971): 289–300; and Sidney Mintz, "A Note on the Definition of Peasants," *Journal of Peasant Studies* 1, no. 1 (1973): 91–106. Also useful are the historiographical discussion in David Ludden, *Peasant History in South India* (Princeton: Princeton University Press, 1985), 3–14, and the contradictions of community and class inherent in peasant society noted by Victor V. Magagna, *Communities of Grain: Rural Rebellion in Comparative Perspective* (Ithaca: Cornell University Press, 1991), 2–21.

2. Richard B. Barnett, "Images of India from Alexander to Attenborough," Jefferson Society lecture, University of Virginia, 16 September 1983.

3. For an introduction to the complexity of Hindu monasticism, see G. S. Ghurye, *Indian Sadhus* (1953; 2d ed., Bombay: Popular Prakashan, 1964); and Parshuram Chaturvedi, *Uttari Bharat ki Sant-Parampara* [The North Indian Sant Tradition], 3d ed. (Allahabad: Leader Press, 1972).

4. All three monastic lifestyles—itineracy, spiritual study, and soldiering—can be contained within one order; see Peter van der Veer, *Gods on Earth: The Management of Religious Experience and Identity in a North Indian Pilgrimage Centre* (London: Althone, 1988).

5. An important study in this field is Kenneth G. Zysk, *Asceticism and Healing in Ancient India: Medicine in the Buddhist Monastery* (New York: Oxford University Press, 1991).

6. Hence, implicit to this study are questions not unlike those that concerned A. Appadurai in *Worship and Conflict under Colonial Rule: A South Indian Case* (Cambridge: Cambridge University Press, 1981), 6–7: What are the relation-

ships between the religious, the political, the economic, and the social in colonial India? What underpins hierarchy in the social order? And how do we define and measure change in the caste system?

7. See, for example, János M. Bak and Gerhard Beneke, eds., *Religion and Rural Revolt* (Manchester: Manchester University Press, 1984).

8. The role of Saya San (1930s) in lower Burma and Swami Sahajanand Saraswati (1920s to 1940s) in north India are but two examples; on the former, see James Scott, *The Moral Economy of the Peasant: Rebellion and Subsistence in Southeast Asia* (New Haven: Yale University Press, 1976); on the latter, see Walter Hauser, *The Politics of Peasant Activism in Twentieth-Century India* (Delhi: Oxford University Press, forthcoming), and Hauser, ed., *Sahajanand on Agricultural Labor and the Rural Poor* (New Delhi: Manohar, 1994).

9. Peter Brown, "The Rise and Function of the Holy Man in Late Antiquity," in *Society and the Holy in Late Antiquity* (Berkeley and Los Angeles: University of California Press, 1982), 105–6.

10. Hence this history should be understood as an important part of the process of ideological change described by Peter van der Veer in *Religious Nationalism: Hindus and Muslims in India* (Berkeley and Los Angeles: University of California Press, 1994).

11. The material for such an inquiry must be based largely on vernacular sources that reflect the conscious ideologies of peasants and monks and reveal the unconscious discourses in which they participate. In saying this, however, I do not wish to suggest that vernacular sources are somehow more "authentic" than official or nonofficial (i.e., nationalist) English-language sources; both must be approached with the utmost caution so as to "distinguish what they *describe* from what they attempt to *explain*" (Sandria Freitag, *Collective Action and Community: Public Arenas and the Emergence of Communalism in North India* [Berkeley and Los Angeles: University of California Press, 1989], 16). In English-language documents this entails peeling away the layers of colonial or nationalist apprehensions; vernacular sources may also contain some of these apprehensions, but with a strong overlay of religious and social polemic.

12. Ronald Inden, *Imagining India* (Oxford: Basil Blackwell, 1990), particularly chapters 3 and 4.

13. See Lewis Wurgaft, *The Imperial Imagination: Magic and Myth in Kipling's India* (Middletown: Wesleyan University Press, 1983), for an engaging venture into the psychohistorical and literary dimensions of this idealization.

14. Shahid Amin, "Gandhi as Mahatma: Gorakhpur District, Eastern UP, 1921–22," in Ranajit Guha, ed., *Subaltern Studies: Writings on South Asian History and Society*, vol. 3 (Delhi: Oxford University Press, 1984), 1–61.

15. Government of Bihar and Orissa (GOBO), Political Department, Special Section, file no. 80 of 1921, "Report of Sadhus taking part in non-cooperation," part 2, 3, Bihar State Archives, Patna. The observer was Krishna Ram Bhatt, an employee of the Tata Iron and Steel Company at Jamshedpur in Bihar; his observations are taken from paragraph 73 of the Bihar and Orissa Police Abstract of Intelligence in the above-mentioned file. See the following chapter for a discussion of soldier monasticism.

16. GOBO, Political Department, Special Section, file no. 80 of 1921, part

2, 3. One crore, or *kror,* is equal to ten million; hence Bhatt is referring to the entire population of India.

17. GOBO, *Index to the Proceedings of the Political Department, Special Section,* in the Bihar State Archives, indicates numerous reports compiled on the subject of "political sadhus," especially between the years 1920–35, when Gandhi dictated the terms of Indian politics. As I note below, this represented a renewed interest in the politics of monasticism on the part of colonial officials.

18. *Anandamatha,* trans. Basanta Koomar Roy (1941; reprint, New Delhi: Orient Paperbacks, 1992); Jawaharlal Nehru, *The Discovery of India* (New York: John Day, 1946), 44. *Anandamatha* was originally published in 1882 in *Bangadarshan,* Bankim's literary monthly, and subsequently translated into English as *The Abbey of Bliss* by Nares Chandra Sen-Gupta (Calcutta: M. Neogi, 1906). On the circumstances of Bankim's authorship, see Tapan Raychaudhuri, *Europe Reconsidered: Perceptions of the West in Nineteenth-Century Bengal* (Delhi: Oxford University Press, 1988), 117 and passim.

19. See the reflections of van der Veer, *Religious Nationalism,* on the constituent elements of nation implicit to the Indian context.

20. See Gyanendra Pandey, *The Construction of Communalism in Colonial North India* (Delhi: Oxford University Press, 1990), esp. 23–65, "The Colonial Construction of the Indian Past."

21. Romila Thapar, "Interpretations of Ancient Indian History," *History and Theory* 7, no. 3 (1968): 318–35; and "Religion, Communalism, and the Interpretation of Indian History," public lecture, Wesleyan University, 18 November 1992. See also K. N. Panikkar, "A Historical Overview," in S. Gopal, ed., *Anatomy of a Confrontation: The Babari Masjid-Ramjanmabhumi Issue* (New Delhi: Penguin, 1990), 22–37.

22. Sleeman, *A Report on the System of* Megpunnaism *or, The Murder of Indigent Parents for their Young Children (who are sold as Slaves) as it prevails in the Delhi Territories, and the Native States of Rajpootana, Ulwar, and Bhurtpore* (Calcutta: Serampore, 1839), 11.

23. This recommendation was not acted upon by the government. Sleeman's opinions were part of the ever-widening scope of colonial police power in the early nineteenth century, and the bandits and thugs that he sought to supress were holdovers of institutionalized violence from an era when the reach of the state was not nearly so total. See Stewart Gordon, "Scarf and Sword: Thugs, Marauders, and State-Formation in Eighteenth-Century Malwa," *Indian Economic and Social History Review* 6, no. 4 (1969): 403–29.

24. See Disraeli's speech to Parliament, 27 July 1857, partially reproduced in Ainslee T. Embree, ed., *1857 in India: Mutiny or War of Independence?* (Boston: D. C. Heath, 1963), 11–12.

25. Freitag, *Collective Action and Community,* 161–62. Note in particular the activities of Sriman Swami and Khaki Baba (also known as Khaki Das).

26. Saiyyid Muhammad Tassaduq Hussain, *Kitab-i Sadhu* [The Book of Sadhus] (Sadhaura, Umballa District: n.p., 1913). The author is described as "Head Constable, Saharanpur Police Lines"; the book is dedicated to P. B. Bramley, then Deputy Inspector General of Police, and on p. 5 it is noted that the work was sanctioned by Government Order no. 3232 of 1913.

27. These individuals were described in history sheets sent from R. S. F. Macrae, of the Bihar police, to E. L. L. Howard, chief secretary to the Government of Bihar and Orissa, 3 November 1921, and included as appendices in GOBO, Political Department, Special Section, file no. 80 of 1921, part 2, 8–20.

28. See Ranajit Guha, *Elementary Aspects of Peasant Insurgency in Colonial India* (Delhi: Oxford University Press, 1983), 106–8, on the postcolonial historiography of rebellion and the unfortunate tendency of the historian's voice "to merge with that of the local sub-divisional officer as he speaks of the 'bad characters' and 'the criminal sections'" (107).

29. See C. A. Bayly, *The Local Roots of Indian Politics: Allahabad, 1880–1920* (Oxford: Clarendon Press, 1975); and John R. McLane, *Indian Nationalism and the Early Congress* (Princeton: Princeton University Press, 1977), part 4.

30. Walter Hauser, "Swami Sahajanand and the Politics of Social Reform," presented at the annual meeting of the Association for Asian Studies, Washington, D.C., 4 April 1992. Hauser quotes Swami Sahajanand Saraswati's autobiography, *Mera Jivan Sangharsh* [My Life Struggle] (Bihta, Patna: Shri Sitaram Ashram, 1952), 185 and (on Saraswati's relations with Gandhi more generally) 212–13. Hauser's essay is forthcoming in the *Indian Historical Review* 18, no. 2 (January 1992), which is now over two years behind schedule; I am grateful to the author for allowing me to cite the original.

31. On this historiographic problem, see Freitag, *Collective Action and Community*, 8–12.

32. Bayly, *Local Roots of Indian Politics*, exemplifies this approach.

33. Ranajit Guha, "On Some Aspects of the Historiography of Colonial India," in Guha, ed., *Subaltern Studies: Writings on South Asian History and Society*, vol. 1 (Delhi: Oxford University Press, 1982), 1–8; for the quote below, 3.

34. Gyanendra Pandey, "Peasant Revolt and Indian Nationalism: The Peasant Movement in Awadh, 1919–22," in Guha, ed., *Subaltern Studies*, 1:147–48, 168–71. The subaltern approach, grounded in a Marxist-Gramscian historical framework, can obscure the sampraday that is implicit to most sadhus and therefore overlook the subtle yet important religious and political meanings in the history of Indian political consciousness. Here, for example, Pandey tantalizes the reader with fragments of information regarding the religious context out of which Baba Ramchandra emerged, and then dismisses that context as "the hold of religious symbols on the mind of the peasant" (171) before returning to the more urgent questions of agrarian exploitation, peasant violence, Congress elitism, and colonial manipulation. A similar approach can be discerned in Guha, *Elementary Aspects of Peasant Insurgency*, 18, who sees religion as an ideological force that sustains the negative self-image of the peasant "by extolling the virtues of loyalty and devotion, so that he could be induced to look upon his subservience not only as tolerable but almost covetable." See also Guha's discussion of the springtime festival of *Holi*, 33–36 and passim.

35. This has been elaborated by Philip Lutgendorf, *The Life of a Text: Performing the Ramcaritmanas of Tulsidas* (Berkeley and Los Angeles: University of California Press, 1991), 374–78. In a rich discussion of peasant mobilization in Awadh that in many ways presaged Pandey's work, Majid Siddiqi, *Agrarian Unrest in Northern India* (New Delhi: Vikas, 1978), 113, observed that Baba

Ramchandra's popular appeal was derived in large part from the fact that he carried a copy of the Tulsidas Ramayana on his back and was able to recite from it with considerable force; this point is pursued in greater detail in Kapil Kumar, "The Ramacharitamanas as a Radical Text: Baba Ram Chandra in Oudh, 1920–1950," in Sudhir Chandra, ed., *Social Transformation and Creative Imagination* (New Delhi: Allied, 1984).

36. Noted in Pandey, "Peasant Revolt and Indian Nationalism," 167–68. See also Siddiqi, *Agrarian Unrest*, 110, 117.

37. *Collective Action and Community.* Freitag argues that communalism is the result of a combination of historical developments, beginning in the nineteenth century with a gradual state withdrawal from involvement in important urban public occasions, such as religious festivals, in favor of a new brand of imperial assemblage wherein large landholders—deemed the "natural" leaders of British India—ritually subordinated themselves to the British monarch. This colonial withdrawal from the popular stage afforded local urban notables, themselves prohibited from participation in imperial politics, a public arena in which status could be expressed and confirmed. With the rise of nationalist sentiment in late nineteenth and early twentieth-century India, the same local notables would gradually reshape the public arena to accommodate an Indian version of nation. As the public arena became nationalized, the national need for an "other" against which to measure itself was projected onto the public arena as communal antagonism. Communalism represented, then, a necessary evil that colonial, nationalist India had to internalize as part of the process of becoming an independent nation-state.

38. Ibid., 16. A danger of the focus on crowd behavior as text (an approach that the subaltern collective shares) is that people are defined not by what they believe, think, say, and write, nor by the alliegances they claim, but solely by what they do. In order to exist for the historian they must act collectively against an other; when they are quiescent, or even when they work toward a goal that engages no immediate and vociferous opposition, they escape notice. When they riot, they accommodate themselves to the logistical needs of a public arena that make no room for complex identities. See Freitag, *Collective Action and Community,* 239–41; and Sumit Sarkar, "The Conditions and Nature of Subaltern Militancy: Bengal from Swadeshi to Non-Co-operation, *c.* 1905–22," *Subaltern Studies,* 3:273–74.

39. Freitag, *Collective Action and Community,* 199–209.

40. Ibid., 28–31; and Richard Schechner and Linda Hess, "The Ramlila of Ramnagar," *Drama Review* 21, no. 3 (1977).

41. See also in this context Lutgendorf, *The Life of a Text,* chapters 5 and 6.

42. Ashis Nandy, *The Intimate Enemy: Loss and Recovery of Self under Colonialism* (Delhi: Oxford University Press, 1983), 7. The ramifications of the colonial kshatriya ideal included the ideological evolution of an Indian *Homo militaris,* bred to serve in the ranks of the British Indian army. See Richard Fox, *Lions of the Punjab: Culture in the Making* (Berkeley and Los Angeles: University of California Press, 1985), esp. 27–51, 140–59. The "search for martial Indianness" also bred anti-imperial ideologies, such as the "immensely courageous but ineffective terrorism of Bengal, Maharashtra and Panjab led by semi-Westernized, middle-class, urban youth" (Nandy, *The Intimate Enemy,* 7).

43. A. Appadurai, "Is *Homo Hierarchicus?*" *American Ethnologist* 13, no. 4 (November 1986): 748–49. See also Nandy, *Intimate Enemy*, 31–32.

44. Imtiaz Ahmad, "Caste Mobility Movements in North India," *Indian Economic and Social History Review* 7, no. 2 (1971): 164–91; and Lucy Carroll, "Colonial Perceptions of Indian Society and the Emergence of Caste Associations," *Journal of Asian Studies* 37, no. 2 (1978): 233–50. These studies are not concerned with monastic society, as such. See chapter 4 for a lengthier discussion of the arguments forwarded in these essays.

45. See Nicholas B. Dirks, "Castes of Mind," *Representations* 37 (Winter 1992): 56–78; and Bernard Cohn, "The Census, Social Structure and Objectification in South Asia," in *An Anthropologist among the Historians and Other Essays* (Delhi: Oxford University Press, 1990), 224–54. Both Dirks and Cohn note the distinction between a colonial discourse of caste and Indian conceptions of social relations. For useful clues to the social and ethnohistorical ramifications of both, see Christopher A. Bayly, "Peasant and Brahmin: Consolidating Traditional Society," chapter 5 of *Indian Society and the Making of the British Empire* (Cambridge: Cambridge University Press, 1988), esp. 155–68; and Dirk H. A. Kolff, *Naukar, Rajput and Sepoy: The Ethnohistory of the Military Labour Market in Hindustan, 1450–1850* (Cambridge: Cambridge University Press, 1990).

46. For an introduction to these disagreements, see Louis Dumont, *Homo Hierarchicus: The Caste System and Its Implications,* trans. Mark Sainsbury, Louis Dumont, and Basia Gulati (Chicago: University of Chicago Press, 1980); and Appadurai, "Is *Homo Hierarchicus?*"

47. See *The Laws of Manu,* introduction and notes by Wendy Doniger, trans. Doniger and Brian K. Smith (New York: Penguin, 1991), 6 (*Manusmriti* I.31). According to Doniger, this myth appears in the much earlier *Ṛg Veda* 10.90. As for structural interpretations of this hierarchy, see Dumont, *Homo Hierarchicus,* 67–68, and on caste and varna, 72–75; and Edmund Leach, "Caste, Class and Slavery: The Taxonomic Problem," in Anthony de Reuck and Julie Knight, eds., *Caste and Race: Comparative Approaches* (Boston: Little, Brown, 1967), 10–11.

48. This is evident in the fact that shudras have aspired successfully to kingship and have manipulated genealogies to provide themselves with "acceptable" kshatriya antecedents. See Romila Thapar, "Genealogy as a Source of Social History," *Indian Historical Review* 2, no. 2 (January 1976): 259–81; and "Society and Historical Consciousness: The *Itihasa-Purana* Tradition," in S. Bhattacharya and R. Thapar, eds., *Situating Indian History for Sarvepalli Gopal* (Delhi: Oxford University Press, 1986), 353–83. The fabrication of kshatriya genealogies is not a universal impulse throughout the subcontinent, however; of particular note are the Nayaka kings of Tamilnadu who were said to have glorified their shudra origins. See V. Narayana Rao, D. Shulman, and S. Subrahmanyam, *Symbols of Substance: Court and State in Nayaka Period Tamilnadu* (Delhi: Oxford University Press, 1992). I am grateful to Dr. Sandria Freitag for bringing this reference to my attention.

49. Marc Galanter has argued that the term "untouchability" was first used by the Maharaja of Baroda in 1909. See his "The Abolition of Disabilities—

Untouchability and the Law," in J. Michael Mahar, ed., *The Untouchables in Contemporary India* (Tucson: University of Arizona Press, 1972), 243, 298. On "dasyu" and "dasa," see Romila Thapar, "The Image of the Barbarian in Early India," *Comparative Studies in Society and History* 13, no. 4 (1971): 408–36; reprinted in Thapar, *Ancient Indian Social History*, 2d ed. (New Delhi: Orient Longman, 1984), 152–92. On the problem of nonpejorative terms, see R. S. Khare, *The Untouchable as Himself: Ideology, Identity, and Pragmatism among the Lucknow Chamars* (Cambridge: Cambridge University Press, 1984), esp. 154; for the definition of "achhut" as contrived by an untouchable ascetic, see 83–84.

50. See R. S. Khare, "The One and the Many: Varna and Jati as a Symbolic Classification," in Sylvia Vatuk, ed., *American Studies in the Anthropology of India* (New Delhi: Manohar, 1978), 35–61; and S. J. Tambiah, "From Varna to Caste through Mixed Unions," in Jack Goody, ed., *The Character of Kinship* (Cambridge: Cambridge University Press, 1973), 191–229.

51. Dirks's history of the colonial sociology of knowledge in "Castes of Mind" is of particular value here.

52. Edward Said, *Orientalism* (New York: Pantheon, 1978). Said was less concerned with India than with the Middle East and paid less attention to history than hermeneutics. See David Kopf, "Hermeneutics versus History," *Journal of Asian Studies* 39, no. 3 (May 1980): 495–506.

53. Nandy, *The Intimate Enemy*, xii.

54. Dirks, "Castes of Mind," 74.

55. See Heinrich von Stietencron, "Hinduism: On the Proper Use of a Deceptive Term," in Gunther D. Sontheimer and Hermann Kulke, eds., *Hinduism Reconsidered* (New Delhi: Manohar, 1989), 11–13.

Chapter 1

1. See Bernard Cohn, "The Role of the Gosains in the Economy of Eighteenth and Nineteenth-Century Upper India," *Indian Economic and Social History Review* 1, no. 4 (1964): 175–82; Dirk Kolff, "Sanyasi Trader-Soldiers," *Indian Economic and Social History Review* 8 (1971): 213–20; and Christopher Bayly, *Rulers, Townsmen and Bazaars: North Indian Society in the Age of British Expansion, 1770–1870* (Cambridge: Cambridge University Press, 1983), esp. 125–44.

2. Bayly, *Rulers, Townsmen and Bazaars*, 242.

3. Sushobhan C. Sarkar, "A Note on Puran Giri Gosain," *Bengal Past & Present* 43 (April-June 1932): 83–87; see also Jonathan Duncan, "An Account of Two Fakeers, with their Portraits," *Asiatic Researches* 5 (1808): 45–46.

4. See Suranjan Chatterjee, "New Reflections on the Sannyasi, Fakir and Peasants' War," *Economic and Political Weekly* 19, no. 4 (28 January 1984); and Atis K. Dasgupta, *The Fakir and Sannyasi Uprisings* (Calcutta: K. P. Bagchi, 1992), 34–40.

5. See David Lorenzen, "Warrior Ascetics in Indian History," *Journal of the American Oriental Society* 98, no. 1 (1978): 72–75, who examines briefly the underlying causes of the conflict. Jamini Mohan Ghosh, *Sanyasi and Fakir*

Raiders in Bengal (Calcutta: Bengal Secretariat Book Depot, 1930), provides a narrative of the skirmishes primarily from the imperial military perspective.

6. Ms. letter from then Captain James Rennell, dated 30 August 1766, in possession of his grandson Major Rodd, cited in Col. Henry Yule and A. C. Burnell, *Hobson-Jobson: A Glossary of Colloquial Anglo-Indian Words and Phrases, and of Kindred Terms, Etymological, Historical, Geographical and Discursive* (London, 1903), s.v. "Sunyasee" (p. 872).

7. Of course, the late nineteenth-century novelist Bankim Chandra Chattopadhyay took a keen interest in the conflict as a Bengali nationalist, the result of which was the novel *Anandamatha* (1882; first translated into English as *The Abbey of Bliss* by Nares Chandra Sen-Gupta [Calcutta: P. M. Neogi, 1906]), a portrayal of sanyasi soldiers as prototypical Indian freedom fighters. On "rebellion" as a misnomer, see Lorenzen, "Warrior Ascetics in Indian History," 72–75.

8. Hence the term *naga* (Sanskrit *nagna* and Hindi *nanga*, meaning "naked") by which they are generally known. However, nakedness was and continues to be a bone of contention between Shaiva and Vaishnava nagas at the kumbh and elsewhere. See Surajit Sinha and Baidyanath Saraswati, *Ascetics of Kashi: An Anthropological Exploration* (Varanasi: N. K. Bose Memorial Foundation, 1978), 121–22. There are also indications that the term is related to *nag*, or snake, especially given the symbolic importance of the snake to both Shaiva and Vaishnava arms.

9. Government of India, Foreign Department, Secret Branch proceedings, nos. 5 and 6 of 21 January 1773, National Archives of India, New Delhi.

10. W. H. McLeod, *The Evolution of the Sikh Community: Five Essays* (Delhi: Oxford University Press, 1975), 1–19. McLeod argues that the arming of Sikhs was not a consequence of unilateral directives by the high-caste *Khatri* leadership (particularly the tenth guru, Govind Singh) in response to Mughal persecutions in the seventeenth and early eighteenth centuries, but occurred over a much longer period and was the result of social and not political change. By deemphasizing the political context, however, McLeod fails to explain why Jat peasants were armed in the first place; instead he assumes the a priori existence of a proud martial tradition and vigorous physical culture among early medieval Jats prior to their attraction to Sikhism. (Here McLeod relies on Irfan Habib, "Presidential Address," *Proceedings of the Punjab History Conference 1971* [Patiala: Punjabi University, 1972], 49–54.) McLeod thus asserts that "we may be sure that the Jats did not enter the Panth empty-handed. They would have been bearing arms many years before Guru Arjan died in Lahore [in Mughal captivity under mysterious circumstances, in 1606]" (12). This argument has received as well some criticism from within the Sikh community, since it runs counter to the accepted hagiography of the gurus, particularly that of the tenth guru, Govind Singh. On his critics, see McLeod, *The Sikhs: History, Religion, and Society* (New York: Columbia University Press, 1989), 40, 126.

11. J. N. Farquhar, "The Fighting Ascetics of India," *The Bulletin of the John Rylands Library* 9 (1925): 444; and "The Organization of the Sannyasis of the Vedanta," *Journal of the Royal Asiatic Society*, July 1925, 483 n. 1. Ghurye, *Indian Sadhus*, 92, 101, agrees that shudras provided the main breeding ground for warrior sanyasis. This continues to be the general perception among sanya-

sis, as indicated by Ramchandra Giri, mahant of Damami math near Sitamarhi in north Bihar, in conversation with the author, 25 November 1994. For challenges to the communal basis of the arming of Shaivas, see Ghurye, *Indian Sadhus*, 108–9; cf. also the version given in Sinha and Saraswati, *Ascetics of Kashi*, 94–95. The Dasnami order is said to have been founded by the ninth-century south Indian philosopher-theologian Shankaracharya.

12. For example, even though Swami Sadananda Giri, *Society and Sannyasin [A History of the Dasnami Sannyasins]* (Rishikesh: Swami Sadananda Giri, 1976), 26, disputes the assertion that shudras were recruited into the order as warriors, he admits nonetheless a distinct scorn on the part of orthodox Dasnamis for the extant akharas of soldier sadhus (37).

13. Ramanand's status as a follower of Ramanujacharya became a contentious issue in the early twentieth century, at which time a radical faction succeeded in transforming the hagiography of the order by removing Ramanujacharya from the preceptor genealogy, or *guru-parampara*. See chapter 2 for an extended discussion of the debate surrounding this ideological change and its social and cultural dimensions.

14. For the Galta tradition, I rely on Richard Burghart, "The Founding of the Ramanandi Sect," *Ethnohistory* 25, no. 2 (Spring 1978): 129–31.

15. Cf. Burghart, "Founding of the Ramanandi Sect," 131. Two of the banned disciples of Ramanand, namely, Kabir and Ravidas (and particularly the former), are known for their pointed critiques of caste hierarchy.

16. Van der Veer, *Gods on Earth*, 139; B. P. Sinha, *Ram Bhakti men Rasika Sampraday* [The Rasika sampraday in Ram worship] (Balrampur: Avadh Sahitya Mandir, 1957), 119–21.

17. On the social dimensions of nonmonastic military recruitment during this period, see Kolff, *Naukar, Rajput and Sepoy*.

18. Van der Veer, *Gods on Earth*, 88.

19. See Monika Thiel-Horstmann, "Warrior Ascetics in Eighteenth-Century Rajasthan and the Religious Policy of Jai Singh II" (unpublished essay, no date). I am grateful to the author for providing me a copy of this essay.

20. In addition to Thiel-Horstmann, see Gopal Narayan Bahura and Chandramani Singh, *Catalogue of Historical Documents in the Kapad Dwara [royal warehouse], Jaipur* (Amber-Jaipur: Jaigarh Public Charitable Trust, 1988), v–vii, on Jai Singh II's growing attraction—which, in part, accounts for his interest in Vaishnava affairs—to the Bengali Vaishnavism of Chaitanya and the Gauriya Vaishnava Goswamis of Vrindaban.

21. Documents nos. 1176 (undated, from the nine Ramanandi mahants), 1483 (also undated), 1277 (referring to bairagis, dated 29 April 1733), and 1275 (dated 28 March 1736), listed in Bahura and Singh, *Catalogue of Historical Documents in the Kapad Dwara, Jaipur.*

22. See nos. 1506, 1507, 1518, and 1520 (all undated), ibid. The last of these, in which several Ramanandi mahants make a series of specific pledges to Jai Singh II, is reproduced as well in A. K. Roy, *History of the Jaipur City* (New Delhi: Manohar, 1978), 26, and is discussed in Thiel-Horstmann, "Warrior Ascetics in Eighteenth-Century Rajasthan."

23. In this argument, soldier monasticism and the entry of the lowly into

the monastic orders would have been joined in the institutional memory of the monastic orders at some later date. Pursuing this line of reasoning would require great care in amassing, and dating, oral tradition, since such tradition would be held to reveal more about the contemporary constitution of the orders than about recruitment alleged to have occurred in the distant past. I should note that I am raising all these questions in current research on the history and historiography of armed monks in northern India.

24. Perhaps the strongest indication of their continued relevance in the religious life of northern India is the central ritual role played by the military akharas during the main bathing days of the *kumbh mela*, India's premier pilgrimage festival, which lasts a month and takes place every three years, alternating between Hardwar, Prayag (Allahabad), Ujjain, and Nasik. During the last *maha* (great) kumbh at Prayag (in early 1989), the main day for immersion in the *triveni* (the confluence of the Ganga, Yamuna, and subterranean Saraswati) fell on 6 February: approximately five million people, including most importantly tens of thousands of naga sadhus whose akhara processions are the centerpiece of the event, immersed themselves in the sacred water on that day alone; the total festival population was over ten million. See "Pilgrims Pouring in for Holy Dip," *Hindustan Times,* 6 February 1989, 10; and "Over a Crore for Kumbh," *Hindustan Times,* 13 January 1989, 9, for details of important bathing dates and astrological calculations.

25. For a discussion of this typology, see Peter van der Veer, "Taming the Ascetic: Devotionalism in a Hindu Monastic Order," *Man,* n.s., 22, no. 4 (December 1987): 680–95.

26. W. G. Orr, "Armed Religious Ascetics in Northern India," *Bulletin of the John Rylands Library* 25 (1940): 96. This adage appears in slightly different form in a collection of proverbs by C. E. Luard, compiled around 1900. Luard, "Central Indian Proverbs," Mss.Eur.E.139, Oriental and India Office Collection, British Library, London, ff. 381–82.

27. This is not to say that such documents do not exist. To the contrary, substantial records are housed in monastic institutions throughout the north; the issue is primarily one of access, particularly to records held by the military akharas. For example, van der Veer, *Gods on Earth,* 154, reports that he was refused access to the papers in the *Hanuman Garhi,* the main naga institution in Ayodhya.

28. Francis Buchanan, *An Account of the District of Purnea in 1809–1810* (Patna: Bihar and Orissa Research Society, 1928; reprint, New Delhi: Usha Jain, 1986); *An Account of the District of Bhagalpur in 1810–1811* (Patna: Bihar and Orissa Research Society, 1939); *An Account of the Districts of Bihar and Patna in 1811–1812,* 2 vols. (Patna: Bihar and Orissa Research Society, 1934; reprint, New Delhi: Usha Jain, 1986); *An Account of the District of Shahabad in 1812–1813* (Patna: Bihar and Orissa Research Society, 1934; reprint, New Delhi: Usha Jain, 1986); and "An Account of the Northern Part of the District of Gorakhpur, 1812," Buchanan-Hamilton Papers, Mss.Eur.D.91–92, Oriental and India Office Collection, British Library, London. Given the dates for the Shahabad account, the true dates for Gorakhpur are probably 1813–14. See Appendix 1 for a discussion of Buchanan's life and work. The accounts of the Ben-

gal (proper) and Gorakhpur districts have never been published in their entirety, though substantial extracts were published in Robert Montgomery Martin, *The History, Antiquities, Topography, and Statistics of Eastern India. . . .*, vol. 1: *Behar and Shahabad*; vol. 2: *Bhagulpoor, Goruckpoor, and Dinajapoor*; vol. 3: *Puraniya, Rongopoor, and Assam* (London: Wm. H. Allen, 1838). I refer to this work below as *Eastern India*.

29. See, for example, Buchanan, *Bihar and Patna, 1811–1812*, 1:57–262 ("Topography of the Division"), and 313–85 ("Of the Hindus"); and *Shahabad, 1812–1813*, 38–151 ("Topography of the Division"), and 182–226 ("Of the Hindus"). In each work, the sections entitled "Of the Hindus" include the discussions of both caste and sect. It should also be noted that Buchanan's interest in the religious dimensions of north Indian life seemed to increase as he progressed from Bengal into Bihar and eastern Uttar Pradesh. As evidence one need only peruse his *Purnea, 1809–1810*, which offers comparatively less detail on sects, gurus, and belief; in the subsequent accounts westward, Buchanan devoted much greater attention to such matters and even provided detailed numerical data, which I discuss below. Buchanan's seeming lack of interest in such matters in his accounts of Purnea and of districts in Bengal proper may have been due to the Bengali pandits who accompanied him, who would have seen no reason to comment on religious details familiar to them in Bengal; once they entered Bihar and eastern Uttar Pradesh they may have had occasion to remark on the dramatic differences in monastic tradition and forms of worship.

30. Buchanan, *Bihar and Patna, 1811–1812*, 1:375. Dasnamis also sought service outside British territory after 1800, as was clear by the brief visit of Kamptagiri's force of fifteen hundred mounted soldiers to the encampment of the Maratha Mahadji Scindia in Malwa in 1809. See Thomas D. Broughton, *Letters Written in a Maratha Camp in 1809* (London: J. Murray, 1813), 129. Kamptagiri was a disciple of Kanchangiri, himself a disciple of the celebrated gosain commander Anupgiri who served the nawabs of Awadh and others in the latter half of the eighteenth century.

31. H. H. Wilson, *Sketch of the Religious Sects of the Hindus* (Calcutta: Bishop's College Press, 1846; reprint, New Delhi: Cosmo, 1977; first published 1828–31), 53. He added, however, that "there are, it is true, exceptions to this innocuous character, and robberies, and murders have been traced to these religious establishments" (53–54).

32. On rasiks as part of a threefold typology of Ramanandi asceticism (along with naga and tyagi), see van der Veer, *Gods on Earth*, 159–72; on rasiks as practitioners of Vaishnava devotion and performance, see Lutgendorf, *The Life of a Text*, 309–21. Both Lutgendorf and van der Veer rely in large part on the detailed study of Bhagwati Prasad Sinha, *Ram Bhakti men Rasika Sampraday*.

33. This theorization of the ascetic is from Khare, *The Untouchable as Himself*, 25.

34. Buchanan, *Account of Shahabad, 1812–1813*, 63–64.

35. Shankaracharya, according to his *advaita* (or nondualist) philosophical vision, posited plural reality to be a product of delusion and argued that cognitive unity could only be achieved through the exploration and perfection of knowledge. Ramanujacharya responded to this strict monism by positing that

while final and unequivocal truth is to be found in the divine, the divine expresses itself in the multiplicity of the material world; therefore, to seek to discern the falseness of plural reality is a singularly misguided endeavor. Ramanuja favored bhakti as the best and highest way of reconciling the contradictions of existence, perceiving divinity, and achieving supreme bliss.

36. See McLeod, *Evolution of the Sikh Community,* 6–7, on the several religious strands in Guru Nanak's teachings.

37. Buchanan, *Bihar and Patna, 1811–1812,* 1:67–68. In the published version of this passage, kholesah is spelled *khalesah,* an error that would have rendered Buchanan's observation devoid of meaning were it not for his qualifier ("or original Sikhs") and his use of the term *kholesah* elsewhere (see, for instance, the description on p. 368).

38. Many Dasnamis sanyasis today contend that Shri Chand was saddened (*udas*) at being passed over by his father for leadership of the religious community, and hence his followers have since borne the appellation "*Udasin,*" or full of sorrow (see Ghurye, *Indian Sadhus,* 141–43). Ghurye views this etymological explanation with skepticism, noting that "even the sectarian Udasins themselves are hard put to it to provide a rational explanation of the term."

39. Ved Parkash, *The Sikhs in Bihar* (Patna: Janaki Prakashan, 1981), 152: "Amar excommunicated the *Udasins,* lest the new Sikh religion should meet the same fate as the other mendicant orders of the country." Parkash does not elaborate on the nature of that fate.

40. H. A. Rose, "Udasis," in James Hastings, ed., *Encyclopedia of Religion and Ethics* (New York: Charles Scribner and Sons, 1921), 504. Rose notes that one of these subsects, *Bhagat Bhagwan,* claims a large following among Udasins in eastern India. This statement is corroborated by Ghurye, *Indian Sadhus,* 145, who, however, notes a comparatively small following in western Bihar. Though Buchanan refers to the prevailing Nanakpanthis in Bihar only as Kholesah Sikhs and Nanakshahis, it seems probable that they belonged to the Bhagat Bhagwan subsect of Udasins.

41. On the nineteenth and twentieth centuries, see Rajiv A. Kapur, *Sikh Separatism: The Politics of Faith* (London: Allen and Unwin, 1986); and Fox, *Lions of the Punjab.* Sachchidanand Sharma, *Udasi Sampraday aur Kavi Sant Rena* [The Udasi Sampraday and the Poet-Saint Rena] (Dehradun: Sahitya Sadan, 1967), 22–23, argues that many Udasins no longer wish to acknowledge their historical connection to Guru Nanak and the Sikhs because the Akali-led Gurudvara reclamation movement of 1921 displaced Udasin control of many Sikh shrines in the Punjab.

42. On this point, see H. H. Wilson's observations with respect to brahman versus ascetic gurus in his *Sketch of the Religious Sects of the Hindus,* 30–31.

43. It is entirely possible, however, that tensions within the Ramanandi sampraday over the question of status and attitudes toward caste may have had a role in the distinctions being posited between brahman and nonbrahman Ramanandis. See the following chapter on these tensions, which erupted into a full-blown dispute in 1918 and remain unresolved today.

44. Buchanan, *Shahabad, 1812–1813,* 219–20. Elsewhere (*Bihar and Patna,*

1811–182, 1:374), Buchanan noted that "The term Vaishnav is not considered as disgraceful for a Brahman, as is the case in Bengal and in the south."

45. Buchanan, *Bihar and Patna, 1811–1812*, 1:369.

46. Buchanan, "Account of Gorakhpur, 1812," 139–345.

47. Buchanan, *Bihar and Patna, 1811–1812*, 1:68. Followers of Vaishnava gurus in Patna city itself were divided almost equally, according to Buchanan, between "Ramawats" (Ramanandis) and Radhaballabhis. However, outside of Patna Radhaballabhis were notable for their relative scarcity. Later, Buchanan noted (1:374) that

> The Ramanandis indeed will instruct their followers in the worship of any god of the side of Vishnu, such as Rama, Krishna, Nrisingha, and Bamana among the Avatars, or Narayan, and Vishnu among his heavenly forms. Although all these are considered as various forms of the same god, yet the mode of worshipping each is different; Vasudeva is considered as the same with Krishna. No separate worship is by this sect offered to the spouses of these gods; but their worship is always conjoined with that of the male, so that Krishna is never worshipped without Radha, nor Rama without Sita. Rama and Sita are, however, considered as the proper deities of this sect; and the Ramanandas have not the presumption to consider themselves as above the worship of the gods.

The importance of this devotional flexibility on the part of Ramanandis will become clearer in subsequent chapters.

48. Buchanan, *Purnea, 1809–1810*, 274. However, an inkling of the social inequities that would come to divide the Ramanandi sampraday a century later can be discerned here. Buchanan noted that "Part [of the Ramanandis] are *descended of Brahmans*, have images, and bestow instruction on the followers of Vishnu, who worship that god under the form of Ram. There are also some Ramayits who are Sudras, and serve the others in bringing water and other such occupations, but are not allowed to eat in company" (my emphasis). The phrase "descended of Brahmans" points to the fact that whether or not the individual guru was himself a brahman, his guru genealogy (or guru *parampara*) could often reveal the individual's predilections regarding caste commensality. I take up this point in detail in the following chapter.

49. Buchanan, *Bihar and Patna, 1811–1812*, 1:357.

50. Ibid., 1:352. Buchanan's observations on the stringent gastronomy of Vaishnavas are repeated in *Shahabad, 1812–1813*, 220.

51. Buchanan, *Bihar and Patna, 1811–1812*, 1:376.

52. Ibid., 1:358, 369.

53. Ibid., 1:369. See also *Purnea, 1809–1810*, 269. Further, a perusal of the caste enumerations in any of the Bihar accounts (e.g., *Bihar and Patna, 1811–1812*, 1:330–50; *Shahabad, 1812–1813*, 195–211) will reveal many communities classified as shudra and lower who looked to Dasnamis as spiritual guides in the early nineteenth century.

54. Buchanan, *Bihar and Patna, 1811–1812*, 1:387–89; see also 358. Parshuram Chaturvedi, an encyclopaedic source on medieval saints and bhakti literature, has noted more recently that Udasins have assumed many of the superficial traits of Hindu sadhus, and have assimilated many standard Hindu customs; see *Uttari Bharat ki Sant-Parampara*, 425.

55. Indeed, Buchanan mentioned one wealthy Dasnami near Patna who transferred his monastic allegiances to the Nanakpanthi order (*Bihar and Patna, 1811–1812,* 1:81). Buchanan noted as well that the individual in question was known for his eccentricity and occasional bouts of violent behavior, brought on in part by his disappointment at the loss of followers subsequent to his conversion. "Being a violent man, this disappointment, it is said, has made him outrageous and fearless, and it is alleged that he attacks all traders passing his house with loaded cattle, and partly by importunity, partly by force compels each to give him a trifle, and they do not think it worthwhile to complain." It should be noted, however, that there were exceptions to the Nanakpanthi-Dasnami affinities. For example, Buchanan mentioned elsewhere (*Purnea, 1809–1810,* 272) that about seventy akharas of Bengali Vaishnavas (followers of Chaitanya) had been Udasins, or Nanakpanthis.

56. Ghurye, *Indian Sadhus,* 142–43. "Vaishnava ascetics" for Ghurye meant primarily those sadhus associated with the Ramanandi sampraday, while "Saiva sadhus" meant those attached to Shankaracharya's Dasnami organization. "Vedanta" refers to the "the end of the *Vedas,*" signifying the philosophical discourses based on Vedic texts that led to the resurgence of Hindu thought with Shankaracharya and, hence, monist.

57. Sinha and Saraswati, *Ascetics of Kashi,* 138. Nevertheless, it would also seem that at least some Udasins joined ranks with Ramanandis, a point I return to in chapter 2.

58. Amardas Udasi, *Udasi Mat Darpan* (no bibliographic information provided), 491–92, cited in Sharma, *Udasin Sampraday,* 23.

59. Government of India (hereafter GOI), *Census of India, 1891,* vol. 5: *The Lower Provinces of Bengal and Their Feudatories* (Calcutta: Bengal Secretariat Press, 1893), table 16, 76; GOI, *Census of India, 1901,* vol. 6-A: *The Lower Provinces of Bengal and Their Feudatories,* part 2 (Calcutta: Bengal Secretariat Press, 1902), table 13-A, 194–256. As I note below, however, terminological imprecision with regard to religious identity rendered much of the census data on monasticism of little value.

60. See Richard Eaton, "Approaches to the Study of Conversion to Islam in India," in R. C. Martin, ed., *Approaches to Islam: Religious Studies* (Tucson: University of Arizona Press, 1985), 107–23. A more elaborated consideration of the process, termed "inclusion, identification, and displacement," can be found in Eaton's more recent work, *The Rise of Islam and the Bengal Frontier, 1204–1760* (Berkeley and Los Angeles: University of California Press, 1993), 268–90 and passim.

61. Sinha and Saraswati, *Ascetics of Kashi,* 49–52, 115.

62. Van der Veer, *Gods on Earth,* 37 (for the quote) and 143–46. On Shuja ud-daula's patronage of the sampraday, see Buchanan in Martin, *Eastern India,* 2:485.

63. Wilson, *Sketch of the Religious Sects of the Hindus,* 67–68.

64. Herbert Hope Risley, *The Tribes and Castes of Bengal* (Calcutta: Bengal Secretariat Press, 1891; reprint, Calcutta: Firma Mukhopadhyay, 1981), 1:533–34; Buchanan, *Bihar and Patna, 1811–1812,* 1:334; *Shahabad, 1812–1813,* 198. Unfortunately, Risley's survey was organized strictly accord-

ing to caste, listed in alphabetical order by jati nomenclature (cf. the method-
ology employed by Buchanan, described above); Risley paid little direct attention to religious communities that appealed to supracaste loyalties, in part because the existence of such loyalties undermined the supposed impermeability
of caste boundaries on which his racial theories were grounded. (On these theories, and the anthropometry and nasal indeces that sustained them, see Risley,
The People of India [Calcutta: Thacker, Spink, 1915] and Christopher Pinney,
"Colonial Anthropology in the 'Laboratory of Mankind,'" in C. A. Bayly, ed.,
An Illustrated History of Modern India, 1600–1947 [London: National Portrait
Gallery, 1990], 252–63.) As a result, even though the information under each
of Risley's jati headings contained potentially valuable descriptions of the culture, religion, and mythology of the eastern Gangetic Plain, it is more difficult
to elicit religious trends for the population as a whole. In addition, Risley referred not to specific monastic communities, such as Ramanandis and Dasnamis,
but to the broad sectarian components of modern Hinduism, namely Vaishnava,
Shaiva, and Shakta belief. Nevertheless, if the peasants of Gangetic India found
Vaishnava belief and institutions increasingly relevant to their lives, it is certain
that this boded well for the Ramanandi sampraday.

65. Jogendra Nath Bhattacharya, *Hindu Castes and Sects: An Exposition of
the Origin of the Hindu Caste System and the Bearing of the Sects toward Each
Other and toward Other Religious Systems* (Calcutta: Thacker, Spink, 1896), 29.
Bhattacharya's observation is particularly revealing. First, it implies that many
"low" people (no doubt a reference to shudra and untouchable peasants and artisans) had advanced economically in the preceding century, and that they were
directing their newfound wealth toward the articulation of a new religious and
social ideology. Second, it captures the sensitivity of monks to both prevailing
public opinion and hard economic realities. In other words, notwithstanding the
fact that Bhattacharya—an elite, educated Bengali pandit—took a dim view of
the process (he decried the spread of Vaishnavism as little more than the constant, mindless repetition of *Hari,* or Vishnu), he saw it as entirely natural and
appropriate that sadhus would desire to attract followers, for whatever motives,
be they material or spiritual.

66. Buchanan, "Account of Gorakhpur, 1812," 336. This observation occurs in Haripur town, Nichlaul thana.

67. Of course, the term possessed a strong Vaishnava connotation in Bengal and western Uttar Pradesh. Bengali Vaishnavas were followers of the ecsta-
tic bhakti of Chaitanya; see Sushil Kumar De, *Vaishnava Faith and Movement
in Bengal* (1942; 2d ed., Calcutta: K. L. Mukhopadhyaya, 1961). An account
of the Vaishnava gosains who worship Krishna and Radha in and around
Mathura and Vrindaban in the nineteenth century can be found in F. S. Growse,
Mathura: A District Memoir (1880; 3d ed., revised and enlarged, Allahabad:
Northwest Provinces and Oudh Government Press, 1883), 192–98.

68. Buchanan, *Bihar and Patna, 1811–1812,* 1:374; *Shahabad, 1812–1813,*
53 (Buchanan spells the name Arah; later British-Indian maps refer to Arrah);
Buchanan in Martin, *Eastern India,* 2:483; Risley, *The Tribes and Castes of Bengal,* 1:300.

69. For instance, in Bhagwanpur, a large village three miles north of Nawada

town in Gaya District, the assistant subdivisional officer observed that "there is . . . an old Thakurbari which is erected by Gosain-ji, which is taken care of by the residents." Village Notes (hereafter VN), Gaya District, Thana Nawada, no. 400, Gaya Collectorate Record Room, 1909–14, Bihar. Other similar instances of gosains associated with Vaishnava temples are described in VN, Patna District, Thana Barh, no. 254, Patna Collectorate Record Room, 1909–14, Bihar; VN, Gaya District, Thana Mufassil Gaya, no. 35, Gaya Collectorate Record Room. The "Village Note" surveys were carried out to facilitate land settlement operations in Bihar in the early 1900s. Each village note was a four-page form upon which an assistant subdivisional officer recorded his observations and interviews in an ordered sequence of fifteen categories. The social and cultural complexion of a village was captured at the end of every village note in section 15, entitled "General Notes." For a discussion of some research implications of the village notes, see James R. Hagen and Anand A. Yang, "Local Sources for the Study of Rural India: The 'Village Notes' of Bihar," *Indian Economic and Social History Review* 13, no. 1 (January-March 1976): 75–84.

70. VN, Gaya District, Thana Aurangabad, no. 934, Gaya Collectorate Record Room. The subdivisional officer added, "There is a pucca *Samadhi* [burial site for a gosain] near it also built by him. The gosain Bisunpur is a very old and respected man. People go to him and give him money as offering. He has many chelas." Additional instances of Shaiva gosains can be found in VN, Gaya District, Thana Nawada, no. 445, Gaya Collectorate Record Room; VN, Patna District, Thana Hilsa, no. 78, Patna Collectorate Record Room; VN, Shahabad District, Thana Piro, no. 189, and Thana Mohania, no. 663, Arrah Collectorate Record Room, 1909–14, Bihar.

71. It has been suggested as well that the monastic distinctions evident today among Ramanandis—namely, between nagas, *tyagi*s (or austere ascetics), and *rasika*s or (aesthetes)—enabled them to absorb all manner of Shaiva ideas and practices and relate them to the worship of Ramchandra; while such structural looseness certainly would have contributed to the increasing strength of the Ramanandi sampraday, I am wary of relying on a modeling of the Ramanandi present to explain the Ramanandi past. It is possible, for example, that the absorption of Shaiva ideas and practices produced, or at least further accentuated, some of the present-day typological distinctions between Ramanandis. On the structure of the present-day Ramanandi sampraday, see van der Veer, *Gods on Earth*; the general point was raised in a reader's report on the present work, received in January 1994.

72. Buchanan in Martin, *Eastern India*, 2:483; Wilson, *Sketch of the Religious Sects of the Hindus*, 204.

73. See Risley, *The Tribes and Castes of Bengal*, 1:26; and William Crooke, *The Popular Religion and Folklore of Northern India*, 2d ed. (London: A. Constable, 1896; reprint, New Delhi: Munshiram Manoharlal, 1978), 1:86.

74. Ghurye, *Indian Sadhus*, 79.

75. GOI, *Census of India, 1891*, vol. 5, table XVI, 76; GOI, *Census of India, 1901*, vol. 6-A, part 2, table XIII-A, 194–256; GOI, *Census of India, 1911*, vol. 5: *Bihar and Orissa*, part 3: "Imperial Tables" (Calcutta: Bengal Secretariat Book Depot, 1913), table 13-A, 97–119.

76. GOI, *Report on the Census of Bengal, 1872* (Calcutta: Bengal Secretariat Press, 1872), 136.

77. GOI, *Census of India, 1911,* vol. 5: *Bihar and Orissa,* part 1: "Report" by E. A. Gait (Calcutta: Bengal Secretariat Book Depot, 1913), 239 (remarks by L. S. S. O'Malley).

78. The subjective nature of the census interview as a methodological failure of previous censuses is raised by E. A. H. Blunt, director of the 1911 census for Uttar Pradesh, in vol. 15: *United Provinces of Agra and Oudh,* part 1: "Report" (Allahabad: Government Press, 1912), 131.

79. Ibid., subsidiary table 8-A, 156–57. Even in the eastern Uttar Pradesh districts, Vaishnavas had the edge on Shaivas and far outnumbered Shaktas.

80. At the risk of jumping ahead to the last decade of this century, it can be suggested that the successful (if short-lived) recruitment of many—but by no means all—sadhus into the political campaigns of the essentially middle-class Hindu right (particularly as spearheaded by the *Vishwa Hindu Parishad* and organized around the reclamation of the birthplace of Ramchandra) is an attempt by some sadhus to reoccupy a position of political and social centrality in modern Indian life.

Chapter 2

1. Richard Burghart interpreted Nabhadas's Bhaktamal as evidence of "the broadening of the criteria for recruitment into a Vaishnavite sect[,] thereby enabling the sect to compete more effectively for devotees and disciples" in the seventeenth century; see "The Founding of the Ramanandi Sect," 133. Burghart cites a 1903 commentary on the Bhaktamal, authored by Sitaramsharan Bhagvan Prasad and recently republished by the Tejkumar Press in Lucknow. I discuss an earlier edition of this commentary and the author himself, Sitaramsharan Bhagvan Prasad, in the pages below.

2. Similar ideological tensions between ortodox and nonorthodox were present in other monastic communities, most notably the Dasnami order at the beginning of the twentieth century, though those tensions were not expressed in terms of the hagiography of Shankaracharya. For an example, see Sinha and Saraswati, *Ascetics of Kashi,* 96–97.

3. While *sant* has often been translated as "saint," the two words are distinct in both etymology and meaning; sant is derived from the Sanskrit *sat,* or "truth," whereas saint is derived from the Latin *sanctus,* meaning sacred. Hence a more accurate, though cumbersome, translation for sant would be "truth-exemplar." For differing interpretations of what constitutes inclusion in the sant genre, see John Stratton Hawley and Mark Juergensmeyer, eds. and trans., *Songs of the Saints of India* (New York: Oxford University Press, 1988), 3–7; and Karine Schomer, "The Sant Tradition in Perspective," in Schomer and W. H. McLeod, eds., *The Sants: Studies in a Devotional Tradition of India* (Delhi: Motilal Banarsidas, 1987), esp. 1–9.

4. Thus van der Veer's main criticism of Daniel Gold, *The Lord as Guru: Hindi Sants in the Northern Indian Tradition* (New York: Oxford University

Press, 1987), in the *Journal of Asian Studies* 47, no. 3 (August 1988): 678–79: "Although the name of Ram is central to *sant* tradition and Ramanand is often said to be the guru of Kabir, there is no mention of the most important 'Vaishnava' ascetic tradition of North India, that of the Ramanandis."

5. See, for instance, Linda Hess's introduction to *The Bijak of Kabir*, ed. and trans. Hess and Shukdev Singh (Delhi: Motilal Banarsidass, 1986).

6. See Schomer, "The Sant Tradition in Perspective," 8; and Charlotte Vaudeville, "*Sant Mat*: Santism as the Universal Path to Sanctity," in Schomer and McLeod, eds., *The Sants*, 21.

7. Charlotte Vaudeville, *Kabir* (Oxford: Oxford University Press, 1974), 1:36 n. 3 (see also 113–14).

8. Richard Burghart, "The Founding of the Ramanandi Sect," 121–39. Burghart approached the life of Ramanand not from the perspective of sant literature, but as an anthropologist interested in Indian monastic communities in general and in the Ramanandi sampraday in particular.

9. This characterization of Ramanand is drawn from John Stratton Hawley, "The Sant in Sur Das," in Schomer and McLeod, eds., *The Sants*, 192 and n. 1.

10. Hawley and Juergensmeyer, eds., *Songs of the Saints of India*, 17.

11. Shabda 41, *The Bijak of Kabir*, trans. Hess and Singh, 55. *Shabda*, or "word," refers to the organizational sequence of Kabir's verse.

12. See Hess, Introduction to *The Bijak of Kabir*, 9–13.

13. *Darshan* 127, cited and translated in K. N. Upadhyaya, *Guru Ravidas: Life and Teachings* (Dera Baba Jaimal Singh, Punjab: Radha Soami Satsang Beas, 1982), 208.

14. *Adi Granth* 29, cited in Hawley and Jurgensmeyer, eds., *Songs of the Saints of India*, 17.

15. David Lorenzen, "Traditions of Non-Caste Hinduism: The Kabir Panth," *Contributions to Indian Sociology*, n.s., 21, no. 2 (1987): 267. Lorenzen adds here that subsequently "Kabir Panth sadhus have very gradually moved toward caste Hinduism [although] the traditions of the Panth retain a quite separate 'non-caste' character."

16. Ibid., 280. The notion of non-caste Hinduism is in part the result of a long-standing debate between those who view the "Great Tradition" of "caste" Hinduism as the dominant cultural monolith that encompasses all of Hindu society—twice-born, shudra, and untouchable—and those (including Lorenzen) who have attempted to forward an understanding of shudra and untouchable religious experience as the basis for separate and competing ideologies. See also 263–64.

17. This and other kshatriya campaigns are considered in chapters 3 and 4, below.

18. Quoted in R. S. Khare, *The Untouchable as Himself*, 48. Khare cites Chandrika Prasad Jigyasu, *Santapravara Ravidas Saheb* [Eminent Saint Ravi Das Sahib], 2 vols. (Lucknow: "Janata's Welfare Publications" [a pseudonym provided by Khare to shield the identity of the publisher; see 174], 1968).

19. Hawley and Juergensmeyer, eds., *Songs of the Saints of India*, 9. Hawley cites Julie Womack, "Ravidas and the Chamars of Banaras," an essay written for the Junior Year Abroad Program of the University of Wisconsin in Benares, 1983.

20. Before the twentieth century, it was generally thought that Ramanand produced little in the way of written or verse compositions from which his life could be reconstructed. After 1921, Swami Bhagavadacharya decided to devote his life to the compilation of traditions regarding the life and work of Ramanand. Bhagavadacharya and the controversies surrounding his efforts are discussed below.

21. The description of the Galta tradition relies on Burghart, "The Founding of the Ramanandi Sect," esp. 129–31. Galta, it should be noted, figured in the history of Vaishnava soldiering described in the previous chapter.

22. A total of fifty-two gateways were designated at the Galta gathering. Besides the thirty-six originating with Ramanand, twelve emanated from Nimbarka, and the remaining four derived from Madhvacharya and Vishnuswami.

23. Burghart, "The Founding of the Ramanandi Sect," argues that four from that circle—namely, Kabir, Ravidas, Dhanna, and Sen—had in the meantime gained independent followings, and that this may have contributed to the exclusion of their Ramanandi followers from the sampraday in the early 1700s. See also Parshuram Chaturvedi, *Uttari Bharat ki Sant Parampara* [The North Indian Sant Tradition], 218–252.

24. Richard Burghart, "Renunciation in the Religious Traditions of South Asia," *Man*, n.s., 18, no. 4 (December 1983): 641.

25. Considering his importance, remarkably little is known of Priyadas save that he was a resident of Vrindaban, a disciple of one Manohardas (a follower of the Bengali Chaitanya) and famed for his public narrations of the Nabhadas Bhaktamal. See R. D. Gupta, "Priya Dasa, Author of the *Bhaktirasabodhini*," *Bulletin of the School of Oriental and African Studies* 32, no. 1 (1969): 57–70.

26. See R. D. Gupta, "The *Bhaktirasabodhini* of Priya Dasa," *Le Muséon* 81, no. 3–4 (1968): 554.

27. For some of those stories, see Hawley and Juergensmeyer, eds., *Songs of the Saints of India.*

28. For an overview of the religious-historical significance of printing presses in the nineteenth and twentieth centuries, see Kenneth W. Jones, *Socio-Religious Reform Movements in British India* (Cambridge: Cambridge University Press, 1989), 213–15.

29. A similar intellectual reflexivity resulting from the use of print is evident in the performance, recitation, and commentary of Tulsidas's *Ramcharitmanas* in cities and towns throughout north India. See Philip Lutgendorf, "Ram's Story in Shiva's City: Public Arenas and Private Patronage," in Sandria Freitag, ed., *Culture and Power in Banaras: Community, Performance, and Environment, 1800–1980* (Berkeley and Los Angeles: University of California Press, 1989), 45–49. For a juxtaposition of oral versus print transmission of meaning across generations in the European context, see Roger Chartier, *The Cultural Uses of Print in Early Modern France*, trans. Lydia G. Cochrane (Princeton: Princeton University Press, 1987).

30. According to J. F. Blumhardt, *Catalogue of the Library of the India Office Library*, vol. 2, part 3: *Hindi, Panjabi, Pashtu, and Sindhi Books* (London: India Office Library, 1902), this edition was "translated by Hari Bakhsh Raya from a Hindustani version by Lala Tulsi Ram of the Braj original."

31. J. F. Blumhardt, *Catalogue of the Hindi, Panjabi and Hindustani Man-*

uscripts in the Library of the British Museum (London: British Museum, 1899), 67, referred to the third edition, noting that this commentary was authored by Pratap Sinha, Maharaja of Sidhua (near village Pararona, Muzaffarpur District), and translated into Hindi at the request of his son, Madan Gopal Lal, by one Pandit Kalicharana. In his more detailed consideration, Kailash Chandra Sharma, *Bhaktamal aur Hindi Kavya mem Uski Parampara* [The Bhaktamal and Its Tradition in Hindi Poetry] (Rohtak: Manthan Publications, 1983), 136, makes note of both the original publication date and that of the twelfth edition, and observes (136–37) that the original author of the commentary was Tulsiram, the translator Pratap Sinha. Sharma makes no reference to Pandit Kalicharana.

32. "The Bhaktamal: text, commentary, and list of names." The bibliographic details of Bhagvan Prasad's commentary are less than clear: According to Sharma, *Bhaktamal aur Hindi Kavya mem Uski Parampara,* 141, the commentary was first published in 1903 in six parts as *Bhaktisudhasvadtilak* [The Sweet Nectar of Bhakti] by Babu Baldev Narayan, *vakil* (or pleader) of Kashi. This would appear to be the edition referred to by George Grierson, "Gleanings from the Bhakta-Mala," *Journal of the Royal Asiatic Society,* 1909, 608–9, who notes in 1909, however, that it was "in course of publication." The edition I have used here was also issued in six parts, in two volumes of three parts each, by the Chandraprabha Press in Kashi, between the years 1903 and 1909. On the inside title page one Baldev Narayan Sinha (described here as *vakil* of Gaya District) is credited for having arranged the publication of the earlier imprint. R. D. Gupta, "The *Bhaktirasabodhini* of Priya Dasa," 552 n. 22, maintains that "this is the oldest printed edition." Later editions were published by the Naval Kishore Press (1913, 1925) and the Tejkumar Press (1962), both in Lucknow. On the high scholarly regard for the Sitaramsharan Bhagvan Prasad, see Sharma, *Bhaktamal aur Hindi Kavya,* 142–43, and Grierson, "Gleanings," 609, 623.

33. *Shri Bhaktamal,* 2:420 and 432, respectively. Bhagvan Prasad pointed out that the nineteenth-century Indologist Horace Hayman Wilson and other English scholars mistakenly placed Ramanand fifth in descent from Ramanuja, whereas according to the Bhaktamal he was twentieth (see also 414). Grierson includes this correction in his article "Ramanandis, Ramawats," in Hastings, ed., *Encyclopaedia of Religion and Ethics;* see esp. 571.

34. Bhagvan Prasad cites Tapasviram, along with other bibliographic sources, in *Shri Bhaktamal,* 2:426.

35. For more on Tapasviram's scholarship and poetry, see Shivpujan Sahay, *Hindi Sahitya aur Bihar* [Hindi Literature and Bihar] (Patna: Bihar Rashtrabhasha Parishad, 1963), 2:5–7, esp. n. 3. Sahay (6 n. 3) renders the title of the work in question *Rumaze Mehovafa.* Tulsiram, as noted above, was the author of *Bhaktamalpradipan.*

36. *Shri Ramanand Yashavali* was published in 1879 by the Suryya Prabhakar Press, Kashi. There is a great deal of mytho-geographic symmetry here that should not pass unremarked. The *Agastyasamhita* (or hymns of Agastya) was of central importance in the early development of the "Rama cult" and, consequently, of Ayodhya as a pilgrimage center; see Hans Bakker, *Ayodhya* (Groningen: Egbert Forsten, 1986). Agastya himself is thought to have been a

Vedic sage who figured in both the *Ramayana* and *Mahabharata* and, according to a strict reading of those and other Sanskrit texts, to have been responsible for rendering the southern peninsula hospitable for Arya religion and culture; see, e.g., K. A. Nilakanta Sastri, *A History of South India from Prehistoric Times to the Fall of Vijayanagar,* 3d ed. (Madras: Oxford University Press, 1966), 68–81. The Ramanandi controversy of 1918–21, which originated in Ayodhya, concerned the question of whether Ramanand should be regarded as the sole originator of bhakti in the north or continue to be regarded as merely the northern, Gangetic transmitter of southern bhakti and all that it implied. The former, Ramanand-centered position could be read as the expression of northern dissatisfaction with the important fact that the two theologians thought to have straddled the horizon of religious thought in post-Vedic India were Shankara and Ramanuja, products of the culture and civilization of the southern peninsula. That the final debate over the question of Ramanand took place in 1921 in Ujjain, on the edge of the south, further adds to the subcontinental scope of the controversy.

37. Reprint, New Delhi: Asian Educational Services, 1983, 1987. See pp. 94–95.

38. *Shri Bhaktamal,* 2:414–32.

39. "Shri" is an honorific that precedes the name; 108 is an auspicious number that indicates the number of times the prefix "shri" occurs before the name, or, in other words, the extent of veneration due the individual.

40. This point has also been noted by Baldev Upadhyay, in *Vaishnava Sampradayom ka Sahitya aur Siddhant* [The Literature and Philosophy of the Vaishnava Sampraday] (Varanasi: Chaukhamba Amarbharati Prakashan, 1978), 247.

41. Bhagvan Prasad, *Shri Bhaktamal,* 2:415. Bhagvan Prasad's phrasing echoes the early seventeenth-century verse of Nabhadas:

> After him [Ramanuja] came Ramanand in whom every blessing took form.   (6)
> The splendor of Ramanuja's doctrine spread like nectar all over the world.   (7)

See Gilbert Pollet, "Studies in the Bhakta Mala of Nabha Dass" (Ph.D. diss., School of Oriental and African Studies, University of London, 1963), 174.

42. Of or having to do with *smriti,* remembered knowledge (that contained in the *dharmashastra* texts), which is based on *sruti,* revealed knowledge (that contained in the Vedic texts).

43. This mantra was either *om ramaya nama* (in the name of Ram) or *om namo narayanaya* (in the name of Narayan). After 1918, the former would indicate allegiance to the radical Ramanandi faction, the latter to the Ramanuji faction.

44. Bhagvan Prasad, *Shri Bhaktamal,* 2:421–22.

45. To describe Ramanand's codisciples, Bhagvan Prasad employed the term *achari guru-bhai,* which can be translated as "virtuous (or overly virtuous) gurubrothers." More importantly, the term "achari" is quite close to "acharya," a designation that prior to 1921 referred to a class of powerful Ramanandis who claimed high status and special privileges within the sampraday and, consequently, maintained strict commensal separations from the rank and file. They would be

the target of prolonged criticism by a radical wing of the sampraday after 1921 and would be referred to as "Ramanujis." See the section in this chapter entitled "The Rise of Radical Ramanandis."

46. On the significance of commemoration as a way of extending the past into the future, see Edward S. Casey, *Remembering: A Phenomonological Study* (Bloomington: Indiana University Press, 1987), 216–57 and passim. I am grateful to my colleague Vera Schwarcz for this reference.

47. See Shivnandan Sahay, *Shri Sitaramsharan Bhagvan Prasad-ji ki Sachitra Jivani* [An Illustrated Biography of Shri Sitaramsharan Bhagvan Prasad] (Patna: Khadgavilas Press, 1908), 5–6. This differs only slightly from a guru parampara given in Bhagvan Prasad's *Shri Bhaktamal*, 2:414, which places Ramanand twenty-first in descent from Ramanuja, who is described here as "Shri 108 Swami-ji". That Bhagvan Prasad was referring to Ramanuja is confirmed in a passage on the following page (415) in which Ramanand is described as a vehicle for the continued spread of "the glory of the auspicious path of Shri 108 Ramanuja."

48. Buchanan, *Bihar and Patna, 1811–1812*, 1:373. Jagannath Das's remarks should be contrasted with a version Buchanan recorded further east in Purnia District that described Ramanand as a brahman from Ayodhya who traveled south to study under Ramanuja. See *Purnea, 1809–1810*, 274.

49. J. N. Farquhar, "The Historical Position of Ramanand," *Journal of the Royal Asiatic Society*, April 1920, 185–92.

50. Farquhar's view reflects the difficulty scholars have had in trying to date Ramanand. He also advances the interesting hypothesis that Ramanand was in fact a member of a now extinct Ramchandra-worshipping order of South India. This argument has been rejected by a number of scholars, most notably perhaps by Shrikrishan Lal, "Swami Ramanand ka Jivan Charitra" [A Biography of Swami Ramanand], in Pitambar Datt Barthwal, ed., *Ramanand ki Hindi Rachnaen* [The Hindi Works of Ramanand] (Kashi: Nagari Pracharani Sabha, 1955), 40–42.

51. See Farquhar's clarification of "The Historical Position of Ramanand" and his response to critics in the *Journal of the Royal Asiatic Society*, July 1922, 373–80.

52. See the Grierson collection at the Oriental and India Office Collection, British Library, London. The letters are catalogued under Mss.Eur.E.223.XI.93: "Correspondence with Sita Ram." *Rai Bahadur* and *Lala* are prefixes connoting a respected status in society.

53. Sitaram (Lala), *Ayodhya ka Itihas* [History of Ayodhya] (Prayag [Allahabad]: Hindustani Academy, 1932).

54. Sita Ram to George Grierson, 29 June 1920, Grierson Papers. The substance of this letter was eventually published in the "miscellaneous communications" portion of the April 1921 issue of the *Journal of the Royal Asiatic Society*.

55. Grierson, "Ramanandis, Ramawats," 570, was of the opinion, however, that the "shri mantra" of the sampraday was "*om ramaya nama*."

56. Farquhar, "The Historical Position of Ramanand," 191.

57. Grierson was also intimate with Indian Sankritists, particularly in Bihar: a full quarter century after his departure from the subcontinent and retirement

to England, the Bihar and Orissa Sanskrit Association conferred upon him the title of *"vagisha,"* or savant. See Grierson to Dr. Bari Chand Shastri (acknowledging the honor), 30 September 1921, Grierson Papers.

58. I utilize the term *Shri Vaishnava* to refer to Ramanuja-oriented Vaishnavas; however, many who were to be distinguished after 1921 as either Ramanandis or Ramanujis would claim the title. Likewise, prior to 1918–21 the term *Ramanandi* would have indicated individuals who would later be distinguished as either Ramanuji or Ramanandi. *Shri,* incidentally, is an honorific, akin to "revered."

59. Sahay, *Shri Sitaramsharan Bhagvan Prasad-ji ki Sachitra Jivani,* 35.

60. Buchanan, *Bihar and Patna, 1811–1812,* 1:373–74.

61. Burton Stein, "Social Mobility and Medieval South Indian Sects," in J. Silverberg, ed., *Social Mobility in the Caste System in India* (The Hague: Mouton, 1968), 92.

62. GOI, *Census of India, 1911,* vol. XV: *United Provinces of Agra and Oudh,* part 1: "Report," subsidiary table 8-A.

63. van der Veer, *Gods on Earth,* 102–3; my account of the controversy relies in part on van der Veer's description (101–7), though I disagree on some minor points of interpretation. Additional details come from Swami Jayramdas, "Shrisampraday ke Sajag Prahari Anantshrivibhushit JagadguruRamanandacharya Shriswami Bhagavadacharya ji Maharaj" [The Vigilant Protector of the Shri Sampraday, the Forever-shri-adorned (i.e., infinite shri) JagadguruRamanandacharya Shriswami Bhagavadacharya Ji Maharaj], in Swami Hariacharya, ed., *Shrisampraday Manthan* [The Stirrings of the Shrisampraday] (Varanasi: Swami Hariacharya Prakashan, 1991), part 2, 120–25.

64. Swami Dharnidharacharya, *Shri Awadhvamshiya Kshatriya Martandah* [Honorable Awadh-lineage Kshatriyas of the Sun] (1930; 2d ed., Chapra: Awadhvamshi Kshatriya Sabha, 1936), 143–44. This is a "caste-history" pamphlet, a fact of no small importance given the religious identity of the author. I return to a consideration of this remarkable individual in chapter 3.

65. "Shri Ramanand Sampraday ke Vartman-Vidvan" [Contemporary Scholars of the Ramanandi Sampraday], in Avadh Kishor Das, ed., *Ramanand-Granth-Mala ka Shri Ramanandank* [Special Issue of the Ramanand Book Series dedicated to Ramanand] 1, no. 5–6 (Ayodhya: Shri Ramanand-Granthmala Prakashan Samiti, 1935–36), 62. This publication contains numerous essays, poems, and prose tributes by various authors to Ramanand and the Ramanandi sampraday, and will be referred to hereafter simply as *Ramanandank.*

66. Jayramdas, "Shrisampraday ke Sajag Prahari," 122. Van der Veer, *Gods on Earth,* 104, notes that Bhagavadacharya changed the suffix of his name from "das" to "acharya" as an affront to the Ramanujis. Van der Veer also observes that he was from Bihar; however, a sectarian account describes him as a Kanyakubja Brahman from Sialkot, Punjab, born in September-October 1880, and that he traveled widely throughout north India before coming to Ayodhya. See Vijay Raghav Prapann, "Acharya-Parampara ke Apratiya Purush: Swami Bhagavadacharya" [The Skeptic of the Acharya Parampara: Swami Bhagavadacharya], in *ShriMath Smarika* [A Memorial of the ShriMath] (Varanasi: ShriMath, Panchganga Ghat, 1989), 251. Both van der Veer and Prapann note

that Bhagavadacharya was briefly attracted to the Arya Samaj; the latter holds that it was only a passing phase.

67. Jayramdas, "Shrisampraday ke Sajag Prahari," 122, asserts that both committees were founded by Bhagavadacharya. According to "Shri Ramanand Sampraday ke Vartman-Vidvan," 62, the latter committee was formed in 1918 at the urging of Sitaramiya Mathuradas, another leading Ramanandi of Ayodhya. In any case, both committees reflected the strong imprint of Bhagavadacharya.

68. Jayramdas, "Shrisampraday ke Sajag Prahari," 122; Prapann, "Acharya-Parampara ke Apratiya Purush," 253.

69. Jayramdas, "Shrisampraday ke Sajag Prahari," 123. According to Vijay Raghav Prapann, "Ramanand Sampraday men Ujjain Kumbh—Ek Adhyayan" [The Ramanandi Sampraday at the Ujjain Kumbh—an Investigation], in *Amrit Kalash* [The Nectar Jar] (Varanasi: Shri Math, 1992), 15, the Ramanuji side was defended by two scholars, Swami Ramprapann and Swami Ramanujadas.

70. B. P. Sinha, *Rama Bhakti men Rasika Sampraday,* 320–22, cited in Burghart, "The Founding of the Ramanandi Sect," 131–32.

71. Jayramdas, "Shrisampraday ke Sajag Prahari," 122.

72. Three of the four judges were naga mahants, according to Prapann, "Ramanand Sampraday men Ujjain Kumbh," 15. In addition, van der Veer, *Gods on Earth,* 103–4, cites a 1958 autobiography—*Swami Bhagavadacharya* (Alvar, Rajasthan: Shri Ramanand Sahitya Mandir, 1958)—in which the fraud is said to be readily admitted.

73. Shyamsundar Das, "Ramavat Sampraday," *Nagaripracharani Patrika,* n.s., 4, no. 3 (1924): 329.

74. *ShrimadRamanand-digvijayah* [The World-Conquest of Shri Ramanand] (Abu: Shri Ramshobhadas Vaishnaven, 1927), 18. Since reissued as *ShriRamanand-digvijayah* (Ahmedabad: Adhyapika Shrichandandevi, 1967), but without the lengthy preface. See also Lal, "Swami Ramanand ka Jivan Charitra" 43; and Burghart, "The Founding of the Ramanandi Sect," 133.

75. Jayramdas, "Shrisampraday ke Sajag Prahari," 123.

76. Ghurye, *Indian Sadhus,* 152.

77. Avadh Kishor Das, "*Yogank* aur Shri Ramanandacharya" [*Yogank* and Shri Ramanandacharya], *Ramanandank,* 75–76.

78. Sahay, *Shri Sitaramsharan Bhagvan Prasad-ji ki Sachitra Jivani,* 5–6.

79. Brajendraprasad, *Shri Rupkala Vak Sudha* [The Essence of Shri Rupkala's Sayings] (New Delhi: Dr. Saryu Prasad [the author's son], 1970), 14. *Rupkala* was Bhagvan Prasad's rasik name.

80. Bhagvan Prasad, *Shri Bhaktamal* (Lucknow: Tejkumar Press, 1962), 283.

81. Dharnidharacharya, *Shri Awadhvamshi Kshatriya Martandah,* 148. For Ramanujis in present-day Ayodhya, see van der Veer, *Gods on Earth,* 104–6. Mention of the dispute continues to evoke an spirited response all over north India.

82. Van der Veer, *Gods on Earth,* 104; Jayramdas, "Shrisampraday ke Sajag Prahari," 122.

83. It is said that prior to 1921, Raghuvaracharya and Bhagavadacharya were close friends, the former having prevailed upon his own guru, Rammanoharprasad, to initiate the latter as a rasik Ramanandi (Jayramdas, "Shrisampraday ke Sajag Prahari," 122). Raghuvaracharya's authorship of such a text is appropriate, inasmuch as the eighteenth-century founder of the Bara Asthan,

Swami Ramaprasad, was said to have authored the commentary of the sampraday's main doctrinal text, entitled *Janakibhashya* (The Discourses of Sita), and introduced a tilak known as "Bindu Shri"—the bindu representing Sita. See Ghurye, *Indian Sadhus*, 167.

84. Jayramdas, "Shrisampraday ke Sajag Prahari," 123, implies that his decision to shift to Ahmedabad was not unconnected to the financial assistance offered him from a prominent *seth*, or banker-businessman.

85. Bhagavadacharya, *ShriJanakikripabhashyasya* [The Discourses of Shri Janaki, or Sita] (Ahmedabad: Swami ShriRamcharitracharya Vyakaranacharya, 1958). The contentious circumstances surrounding this work are recounted by Bhagavadacharya in the introduction, 1–42 (and esp. 1–7). The similarity of the title to Ramaprasad's eighteenth-century discourse, *Janakibhashya*, should be noted.

86. Bhagavadacharya, *ShriRamanandabhashyam* [The Discourses of Shriramanand] (Ayodhya: Swami Shribhagavadacharya-Smaraksadan, [1963?]). Though the publication gives no date, the year is taken from Bhagavadacharya's preface (pp. 5–18) which is dated August 26, 1963. The text purports to be Ramanand's commentary of Badarayana's *Brahmasutra*, describing thereby Ramanandi dualist doctrine. See the postscript, 201–6, for sampraday reactions to the impending publication of this volume.

87. Ghurye, *Indian Sadhus*, 168.

88. The proceedings of this festival were published as *SwamiBhagavadacharyaShatabdiSmritiGranth* [A Book Commemorating a Century of Swami Bhagavadacharya] (Ahmedabad: Shrichandanbahin "Sanskritibhushana," 1971).

89. Jayramdas, "Shrisampraday ke Sajag Prahari," 124. It should be noted that according to a 1987 publication, Raghuvaracharya's disciple Ramprapannacharya was declared jagadguru Ramanandacharya in 1974 by scholars and students connected to the Shri Ramanand Sanskrit Mahavidyalay in Varanasi. However, this declaration does not seem to have gained wide acceptance in the sampraday. It may have provided the stimulus, however, for the decision on the part of sampraday leaders to declare Bhagavadacharya jagadguru Ramanandacharya at the 1977 Prayag kumbh. See Swami Rameshwaranandacharya, *Vedarthchandrika* [Illuminations on the Vedas] (Porbandar, Gujarat: ShriRamanandacharyaPith, 1987), 15–16. The author, Rameshwaranandacharya, is Ramprapannacharya's disciple and currently aspires to the seat of jagadguru Ramanandacharya; the other main claimant, who seems to have stronger institutional support, is Swami Haryacharya, a second-generation disciple of Bhagavadacharya.

90. I would therefore disagree also with Burghart's conclusion ("The Founding of the Ramanandi Sect," 134) that 1921 constituted a final act of exclusion. The radical faction certainly sought the religious exclusion of the acharyas, labelled Ramanuji, but the greater social inclusion of heretofore stigmatized groups in the sampraday.

91. van der Veer, *Gods on Earth*, 106.

92. See chapters 3 and 4 for a discussion of these movements. A significant contribution was made by Swami Dharnidharacharya (after 1921 a Ramanuji), in his *Shri Awadhvamshiya Kshatriya Martandah*, a Kurmi tract.

93. Cf. Bernard Lewis's reflection that a "new future required a different past." See his *History—remembered, recovered, invented* (Princeton: Princeton University Press, 1975), 11. The newly interpreted life of Ramanand, in this sense, can be understood as a charter for future action.

94. In Hindi, *Shri Ramanand-Granthmala Prakashan Samiti*. Responsible as well for the publication of the *Ramanandank*, as noted on the inside cover page.

95. This could be a veiled reference to the alleged expulsion from the company of Raghavanand and his codisciples, as remembered by the Ramanuji faction.

96. Bhagavadacharya, "Shri Ramanandacharya aur Shri Vaishnava Dharma" [Ramanand and Vaishnava Belief], in *Ramanandank*, 12.

97. Sitaramiya Mathuradas, "Hinduon ka Gaurav arthat Shri Shri Ramanandacharya" [The Savior of the Hindus, or Shri Shri Ramanandacharya], in *Ramanandank*, 5.

98. Shyamsundar Das, "Ramavat Sampraday," 340. This is an oblique reference to the famous couplet attributed to Ramanand.

99. Buchanan in Martin, *Eastern India*, 2:485.

100. Bhagavadacharya, "Shri Ramanandacharya aur Shri Vaishnava Dharma" 10, 12.

101. The biographical information for Bhagvan Prasad is drawn from Shivnandan Sahay, *Shri Sitaramsharan Bhagvan Prasad-ji ki Sachitra Jivani*; Brajendraprasad, *Shri Rupkala Vak Sudha*, 16–17; and Shivpujan Sahay, *Hindi Sahitya aur Bihar*, 2:57–61.

102. Bhagvan Prasad's father (Tapasviram) and paternal uncle (Tulsiram) were regionally famous as Bhaktamal exegetes and had retired to lives of spiritual devotion in Ayodhya. For more on Tapasviram and his rasik poetry, see Shivpujan Sahay, *Hindi Sahitya aur Bihar*, 2:6; and Shivnandan Sahay, *Shri Sitaramsharan Bhagvan Prasad-ji ki Sachitra Jivani*, 4–10.

103. Sahay, *Shri Sitaramsharan Bhagvan Prasad-ji ki Sachitra Jivani*, 17–18.

104. Many rasik Ramanandis append the suffix *sharan* to their names as the final aspect of a five-staged initiation sequence. B. P. Sinha, *Ram Bhakti men Rasika Sampraday*, 180–86, cited in Lutgendorf, *The Life of a Text*, 317.

105. Sahay, *Shri Sitaramsharan Bhagvan Prasad-ji ki Sachitra Jivani*, 37–38.

106. Along the lines of a Chamar convert to Christianity who reportedly refused to perform a menial task by responding, "I have become a christian and am one of the the Sahibs; I shall do no more *bigar* [forced labor]." Russel and Lal, *Tribes and Castes of the Central Provinces*, 1:316, cited in Pandey, *Construction of Communalism*, 90.

107. Sahay, *Shri Sitaramsharan Bhagvan Prasad-ji ki Sachitra Jivani*, 35.

108. Buchanan, *Bihar and Patna, 1811–1812*, 1:329–39; Martin, *Eastern India*, 2:466–70. Buchanan notes that in Gorakhpur both Halwais and Kandus were included as Vaishyas and thus considered twice-born (Martin, *Eastern India*, 2:465).

109. These movements are explored in the following chapters.

110. Lala Sitaram, *Ayodhya ka Itihas* [History of Ayodhya] (Prayag: Hindustani Academy, 1932), 46.

111. This point emerged repeatedly, and without any prompting on my part, in discussions with Ramanandis, most recently with Mahant Lakshmananan-dacharya of the Balanand Math (Jaipur, 15 December 1994), and Baba Gyan Das, a mahant of Hanuman Garhi in Ayodhya (Delhi, 14 November 1994).

112. Burghart, "Renunciation in the Religious Traditions of South Asia," 644. It should be noted that Burghart referred to the monks he studied as Ra-manandis, even though the prevailing opinion in Janakpur was Ramanuji. See also his "The History of Janakpurdham: A Study of Asceticism and the Hindu Polity" (Ph.D. diss., School of Oriental and African Studies, University of London, 1978), 105–9. Note, however, the criticism of Burghart in van der Veer, *Gods on Earth*, 68–69.

113. Sitaram to Sir George Grierson, 29 June 1920. Grierson Papers (Correspondence), folio 2.

114. Das, "Ramavat Sampraday," 337 (emphasis is mine).

115. The dispute over varna in the Ramanandi sampraday is described in "Shri Ramanand Sampraday ke Vartman-Vidvan," 74, from which the quotes in this paragraph are taken.

116. By mention of this viewpoint, the author implies that Udasins represented an integral yet distinct Ramanandi subgrouping. This would seem to indicate that a portion of the Nanakshahi community was absorbed into the Ramanandi sampraday during the nineteenth century.

117. Members of each faction, in order to substantiate their positions on the issue, referred repeatedly to such ancient textual authorities as *Manu Smriti, Bhagavad Gita,* not to mention a host of Vedic texts. The anonymous author of "Shri Ramanand Sampraday ke Vartman-Vidvan," cynically compared these texts to *Kamdhenu,* a mythical cow that gives an endless supply of milk, and noted with disdain that "whatever proof you want, you will find it in the *shastras* [law codes]" (74).

118. Ghurye, *Indian Sadhus,* 168.

119. The current disagreements over caste in the sampraday are reflected in the contradictory interpretations of van der Veer and Burghart. See *Gods on Earth,* 172–82, and "Renunciation in the Religious Traditions of South Asia," 641–44. Their renderings have much to do with their respective geographic orientations: Van der Veer worked and lived in Ayodhya, now dominated by "pure" Ramanandis; Burghart's earliest research was in Janakpur (in Nepal), and he later worked in Galta near Jaipur as well, dominated by "pure" Ramanujis. Indeed, Burghart's greater familiarity with Ramanuji views sheds light on his decision to argue (in "Founding of the Ramanandi Sect") that Ramanand did not in fact establish the Ramanandi sampraday.

120. Based on discussions with Ramanandis at the 1995 *ardh* or "half" kumbh recently held in Allahabad, Haryacharya of the Shri Math Acharya Pith, Rajghat, Varanasi, is generally regarded as the dominant claimant to the position of jagadguru Ramanandacharya. His guru was Shivramacharya, whose guru was Bhagavadacharya. However, Rameshwaranandacharya, a highly regarded scholar of Kosalendra Math, Ahmedabad, also claims the honor. Despite his guru parampara descent from Raghuvaracharya, who befriended Bhagavadacharya in 1918–19 and later became a main Ramanuji opponent, Rameshwaranandacharya

is universally regarded as an important contributor to the compilation of Ramanandi tradition and scholarship, even by Ramanandis who regard Haryacharya as the jagadguru Ramanandacharya. A third claimant to the title is Ramnareshacharya of Shri Math, Panchganga Ghat, Varanasi, who, it would appear, regards Bhagavadacharya as his immediate predecessor in the position. An important fact in his favor is his possession of the site regarded by Ramanandis as the original residence of Ramanand in the fourteenth century.

121. On ambiguity and social discourse, see Khare, *The Untouchable as Himself,* esp. 8, 35–36, 46–48, and 171 n. 3.

Chapter 3

1. H. H. Risley, "Ethnographic Appendices," in GOI, *Census of India, 1901,* vol. 1: *India* (Calcutta: Office of the Superintendent of Government Printing, 1903), 55–57. Shudras and untouchables were listed under "Hindus"; the analagous terms for Muslims, according to Risley, were "*ajlaf*" and "*arzal,*" respectively, which together made up approximately 56 percent of the Muslim population—itself 15 percent of the total population. The numbers I have given in the text are for Hindus only; if we include ajlaf and arzal jatis, the actual size of the stigmatized population in Uttar Pradesh and Bihar would be much greater.

2. See James Hagen, "Indigenous Society, the Political Economy, and Colonial Education in Patna District: A History of Social Change from 1811 to 1951 in Gangetic North India" (Ph.D. diss., University of Virginia, 1981), on the increasing levels of education and literacy among peasants in Bihar.

3. As a general rule, I employ the jati nomenclature prescribed in the reform literature itself; often, as is the case here, I simplify the jati names by dropping the term, "kshatriya." Kurmi, Yadav, and Kushvaha should thus be read as Kurmi kshatriya, Yadav kshatriya, and Kushvaha kshatriya; together, they accounted for nearly half of the "shudra" population listed in the 1901 census.

4. This theme is touched upon in virtually every jati reform pamphlet of the period.

5. And mostly by way of sociology and anthropology: the organizational history of the Kurmi-kshatriya movement has been presented in K. K. Verma, *Changing Role of Caste Associations* (New Delhi: National Publishing House, 1979), esp. chapter 2, "The All-India Kurmi Sabha: Historical Perspective," 13–35. On Yadav kshatriyas, see M. S. A. Rao, "Yadava Movement," in his *Social Movements and Social Transformation* (New Delhi: Manohar, 1987), esp. part I (chapter 4), 123–48. More recently, reference to these movements appears in Pandey, *The Construction of Communalism in Colonial North India,* 90–94.

6. The Kayasths were among the first to organize publicly for social and educational reform. See the work of Lucy Carroll, especially "Caste, Community and Caste(s) Association: A Note on the Organization of the Kayastha Conference and the Definition of a Kayastha Community," *Contributions to Asian Studies* 10 (1977): 3–24; for an early consideration of Kayasth identity, see R. M. Shastri, "A Comprehensive Study into the Origins and Status of the Kayasthas," *Man in India* 2 (1931): 116–59. See Karen Leonard, *The Social History of an*

Indian Caste: The Kayasths of Hyderabad (Berkeley and Los Angeles: University of California Press, 1978), on Kayasths in the Mughal and post-Mughal period.

7. See M. N. Srinivas, *Religion and Society among the Coorgs of South India* (Oxford: Oxford University Press, 1952). For a theorization of Sanskritization as a historical process, see Srinivas, "Mobility in the Caste System," in Milton Singer and Bernard Cohn, eds., *Structure and Change in Indian Society* (Chicago: Aldine, 1968), 189–200.

8. There are, in addition, a host of other, primarily semantic, objections to the idea of Sanskritization. Some have questioned the appropriateness of a term associated with brahmanical elitism to describe what was, in many cases, a radically anti-Brahman phenomenon; see, for instance, Gail Omvedt, *Cultural Revolt in a Colonial Society: The Non-Brahman Movement in Western India, 1873 to 1930* (Bombay: Scientific Socialist Education Trust, 1976). Others have objected to the epistemological misappropriation of the term Sanskrit; see J. F. Stahl, "Sanskrit and Sanskritization," *Journal of Asian Studies* 22, no. 3 (May 1963): 261–75. As Stahl notes (p. 275), Srinivas himself was the first to encourage a move away from the oversimplified notion of Sankritization and toward a more culturally relevant terminology. On the inappropriate general usage of the term, see Lucy Carroll, "The Temperance Movement in India: Politics and Social Reform," *Modern Asian Studies* 10, no. 3 (1976): 419.

9. E. A. Gait, "Report," in GOI, *Census of India, 1901*, vol. 6: *The Lower Provinces of Bengal and Their Feudatories*, part 1 (Calcutta: Bengal Secretariat Press, 1902), 379.

10. Buchanan, *Bihar and Patna, 1811–1812*, 1:325. Buchanan's remark implies that they thought of themselves as brahmans.

11. GOI, *Census of India, 1901*, vol. 6, part 1, 379.

12. Buchanan, *Bihar and Patna, 1811–1812*, 1:329. Notwithstanding his categorization, Buchanan noted (p. 329) that Kayasths in Bhagalpur District professed high status on the basis of their claim to descend from the holy dust that covered the body of *Brahma*.

13. Risley, "Ethnographic Appendices," 56.

14. Risley, *The Tribes and Castes of Bengal*, 1:452.

15. Risley, "Ethnographic Appendices," 55–56.

16. Risley's Bihar hierarchy comprised "Brahmans, Other castes of twice-born rank, Clean Sudras, Inferior Sudras, Unclean castes, Scavengers and filth eaters"; "Ethnographic Appendices," 56–57.

17. Buchanan, *Bihar and Patna, 1811–1812*, 1:326–27 (my emphasis).

18. Ibid., 337.

19. Buchanan, *Shahabad, 1812–1813*, 198–99. Buchanan (in Martin, *Eastern India*, 2:468–69) describes these Kurmis as *saithawar* and equates them directly with Ayodhya Kurmis of Bihar, noting that they constitute fully 52 percent of the Kurmis in Gorakhpur District. The exact meaning of the term *saithawar* is unclear: *saita* translates as auspicious moment, *sai* meaning prosperity; in Urdu *sa'i* describes one who is hard-working. The common Persian suffix, *war*, denotes having or possessing, suggesting that saithawar is more of a positive adjectival term describing one who is prosperous, diligent, or auspiciously born.

20. Buchanan in Martin, *Eastern India*, 2:468. The less-detailed observa-

tions of Henry Miers Elliot in the mid-nineteenth century resemble those of Buchanan three decades earlier. In his *Memoirs of the History, Folklore, and Distribution of the Races of the North Western Provinces of India* (London: Trubner, 1869), Elliot notes (1:157) that among the several Kurmi geocultural subidentities "in Oudh [a corruption of Awadh] . . . , the notorious Darshan Singh has ennobled his tribe by the designation of Raja."

21. Richard Barnett, *North India between Empires: Awadh, the Mughals, and the British, 1720–1801* (Berkeley and Los Angeles: University of California Press, 1980), 135–36. The more recent arguments of Dirk Kolff, *Naukar, Rajput and Sepoy*, are of relevance here as well.

22. Buchanan in Martin, *Eastern India*, 2:468–69. Similarly, of the Kurmi population in Shahabad District, Buchanan, *Shahabad, 1812–1813*, 198–99, commented that "200 families perhaps can read and write, and 150 of them do not cultivate with their own hand, being descended of persons, who with the title of Chaudhuri managed the divisions into which the immense barony (Pergunah) of Chayanpur [in the southwest of the district] was divided." Unfortunately, Buchanan failed to specify here the Kurmi subgroups from which this heightened concern with identity emerged. By the early twentieth century, kshatriya reformers would recognize and emphasize the dignity of labor and plowing, in contrast to this early rejection of shudra status.

23. VN, Patna District, Thana Barh, no. 200 (village Berhua). A general sense of the local political and economic influence of awadhia Kurmis in this region can be gleaned from village nos. 200–20.

24. Anand A. Yang, *The Limited Raj: Agrarian Relations in Colonial India, Saran District, 1793–1920* (Berkeley and Los Angeles: University of California Press, 1989), 47.

25. Buchanan, *Bihar and Patna, 1811–1812*, 1:310–11.

26. Buchanan, *Purnea, 1809–1810*, 196–97.

27. Elliot was secretary to the Sudder Board of Revenue, in what was then the North Western Provinces, and compiled a "supplemental glossary" designed for incorporation into a larger glossary of judicial and revenue terms then being assembled by Horace Hayman Wilson, entitled *A Glossary of Judicial and Revenue Terms, and of Useful Words Occurring in Offical Documents Relating to the Administration of the Government of British India* (London: Wm. H. Allen, 1855; reprint, Delhi: Munshiram Manoharlal, 1968).

28. Elliot, *Memoirs of the History, Folklore, and Distribution of the Races of the North Western Provinces of India* (reprinted under the unfortunate title, *Encyclopaedia of Caste, Customs, Rites and Superstitions of the Races of Northern India* [New Delhi: Sumit Publications, 1985]), 1:185.

29. Ibid., 187

30. M. N. Srinivas, *Caste in Modern India and Other Essays,* (Bombay: Asia Publishing House, 1962), 66.

31. See Christopher Pinney, "Colonial Anthropology in the 'Laboratory of Mankind,'" 252–63.

32. On Awadh, see Barnett, *North India between Empires,* 135–36; on the bestowal of kshatriya status by the Mughal emperor on "a spurious Rajput clan," see Kolff, *Naukar, Rajput and Sepoy,* chapter 4.

33. See Dirks, "Castes of Mind."

34. Dilip Sinha Yadav, *Ahir Itihas ki Jhalak* [A Glimpse of the History of the Ahirs] (Lucknow, Allahabad, and Etawah: Krishna Press, 1914–15), 1. A sense of the overwhelming atmosphere of social and economic change is reflected in this phrase, *yeh samsar parivartanshil hai,* which was employed repeatedly by jati reformers throughout the early twentieth century.

35. See Verma, *Changing Role of Caste Associations,* 13–14; and Swami Abhayananda Saraswati, *Kurmi Kshatriya Itihas* [The History of the Kurmi Kshatriyas] (Banaras: Shivaramsinha, 1927), 114–17.

36. Government Order No. 251/VIII-186A-6, dated 21 March 1896, to the Inspector General of Police, Northwest Provinces and Oudh. Cited in Swami Abhayananda Saraswati, *Kurmi Kshatriya Itihas,* 117.

37. Devi Prasad Sinha Chaudhari, *Kurmi Kshatriyatva Darpan* [Reflections on Kurmi-Kshatriya Valor] (Lucknow: Kashi Ram Varma, 1907), cover and ii.

38. See M. S. A. Rao, "Yadava Movement," part 2, 150.

39. See John Richards, "The Indian Empire and Peasant Production of Opium in the Nineteenth Century," *Modern Asian Studies* 15 (February 1981): 59–82.

40. Swami Abhayananda Saraswati, *Kurmi Kshatriya Itihas,* 3–4. According to Saraswati, local meetings had been held in Danapur (the site of an important British garrison just west of Patna) in 1870, and Sonpur (the site of an important annual cattle festival just north of Patna) in 1890. Verma, *Changing Role of Caste Associations,* 13, mentions intermittent Uttar Pradesh meetings in Lucknow, Pilibhit, Barabanki, and Etawah.

41. See Verma, *Changing Role of Caste Associations,* 14–15 and 41. Verma cites Ganesh Swami Sadhu, *Kurmi Bansabali* [Kurmi Genealogy], but gives no bibliographic information.

42. Chaudhari, *Kurmi Kshatriyatva Darpan,* 7. The full bibliographic citation is Eustace J. Kitts, *A Compendium of the Castes and Tribes Found in India: Compiled from the 1881 Census Reports for the Various Provinces, excluding Burmah and Native States of the Empire* (Bombay: Education Society Press, 1885). Most authors of jati reform pamphlets relied in part on British surveys, gazetteers, and antiquarian compendia for historical and ethnographic detail in their efforts to revitalize their communities and, indeed, accorded those European texts nearly the same degree of authoritative respect as they would a textual source in Sanskrit.

43. In this context, Kurmi-kshatriyas claimed links with the Maratha Shivaji. See Rosalind O'Hanlon, *Caste, Conflict, and Ideology: Mahatma Jotirao Phule and Low-Caste Protest in Nineteenth-Century Western India* (Cambridge: Cambridge University Press, 1985), on one important proponent of social reform in Maharashtra. Cf. also D. F. Pocock, *Kanbi and Patidar: A Study of the Patidar Community of Gujarat* (Oxford: Oxford University Press, 1972). Notwithstanding the links with Kunbis claimed by Kurmi kshatriyas, the ideological content of Phule's writing and that of kshatriya reform in north India was markedly different.

44. Chaudhari, *Kurmi Kshatriyatva Darpan,* 8–11. The author argues that the true name of Ramchandra's *Suryavamsh* (solar lineage) was *Kurmvamsh* (Kurm lineage) and that the Kurmi descendants of Kush and Lav were in Gujarat described as *Kushvamshi Kurmis* and *Lavvamshi Kurmis,* respectively,

whereas in Awadh they referred to themselves indiscriminately as *Kurmvamshi Kurmis.* Chaudhari further describes an ancient sage named Kurm whose descendants merged with the *Chandravamsh* (lunar lineage) of Krishna. According to Chaudhari Dipnarayan Sinha, *Kurmi Kshatriya Nirnay* [Rulings of Kurmi Kshatriyas] (Chunar: n.p., 1937–38), 81–83, this particular legend was also cited in support of Kurmi kshatriya identity by Radharcharan Goswami, who is described as the chairman of *pandits* (scholars) of Banaras and Vrindavan: "'In the beginning a king named Prannath was born into the lineage of a sage named Kurmm. . . .' From this 64th verse of the 33rd section of the *Sahyadrikhand* of the *Skanda Purana,* the Kurmvamsh is counted among kshatriyas." Chaudhari, *Kurmi Kshatriyatva Darpan,* 11, also includes as Kurmi progenitors Raja Kuru and Raja Yadu, whose early descendants (the Kauravs and Yadavs, respectively) figure prominently in the Mahabharata; he details (11–12) several other miscellaneous lineages specific to western India.

45. Between 1810 and 1813 Buchanan made frequent reference to the genealogical ties to the "kshatriya tribe" of Krishna and Radha claimed by Goalas. Buchanan, *Bhagalpur, 1810–1811,* 234; *Bihar and Patna, 1811–1812,* 1:338; *Shahabad, 1812–1813,* 204; and Buchanan in Martin, *Eastern India,* 2:467–68.

46. See, for instance, Yadav, *Ahir Itihas ki Jhalak;* and *Yadavesh* (a quarterly newsletter of the Yadav kshatriya jati), first published from Banaras in 1935–36.

47. Yadav, *Ahir Itihas ki Jhalak,* 2–3, 16.

48. Kedarnath-ji Rohan, "Yadavon ka Itihas" [The History of the Yadavs], *Yadavesh* 1, no. 2 (1935–36): 3. It is possible that the Yadav focus on Krishna as a progenitor of a kshatriya lineage contributed to the martial reinvigoration of the Krishna myth, which, it has been argued, evolved into a nonpolitical tale of religious erotism-cum-pastoralism as a result of Muslim political dominance in north India; see David Haberman, *Acting as a Way of Salvation: A Study of Raganuga Bhakti Sadhana* (New York: Oxford University Press, 1988), 43–50; see also Lutgendorf, *The Life of a Text,* 310.

49. For example, Rohan, "Yadavan ka Itihas," 3–4; and Yadav, *Ahir Itihas ki Jhalak,* 7–16.

50. As evidenced by the title of a tract by one Gangaprasad, *Kushvaha Kshatriya, urf Koiri, Kachhi, Murao, Kachhvaha (Vivaran)* [The Kushvaha Kshatris, also known as Koiri, Kachhi, Murao, and Kachhvaha (An Account)] (Banaras: Adarsh Press, 1921).

51. W. W. Hunter, *Statistical Account of Bengal,* vol. 12: *Gaya and Shahabad Districts* (1875–77; reprint, Delhi: D.K. Publishing House, 1973), 195; Risley, *The Tribes and Castes of Bengal,* 1:501. For the following sentence, see Risley, 1:503.

52. Buchanan, *Purnea, 1809–1810,* 228; *Bhagalpur, 1810–1811,* 253; *Bihar and Patna, 1811–1812,* 1:354; *Shahabad, 1812–1813,* 198; and Buchanan in Martin, *Eastern India,* 2:469.

53. Gangaprasad, *Kushvaha Kshatriya,* 2–3, 23; see also 21–24 for the portions cited below.

54. See the discussion regarding "memorials" received by E. A. Gait's highly skeptical ethnography staff, GOI, *Census of India, 1901,* vol. 6, part 1, 378–84.

55. Nirgun Sinha ("Khali"), *Varnashram Vichar-Dhara* [Varnashram Ideology] (Maner, Patna: Nirgun Singh "Khali", 1938–39), 74–75. The author cites

(84–85) a speech by Dr. Munje, chairman of the Hindu Mahasabha, on the need for military training for kshatriyas, calling to mind Vinayak Damodar Savarkar's famous slogan, "Hinduize all politics and militarize Hindudom!"

56. Ibid., 71. For a brief synopsis of the life of Nirgun Sinha ("Khali") see Shivpujan Sahay, *Hindi Sahitya aur Bihar*, 3:206–7.

57. Cited in Lalji Lal, *Tantuvay Anveshan arthat Tanti Jati ka Itihas* [A Study of the Tantuvay, or the History of the Tanti (weavers) Jati] (Sandalpur, Monghyr: Lalji Lal, 1929), 67; and in Nauvat Ray, *Kahar Jati aur Varnavyavastha* [The Kahar Jati and the Varna System] (Firozabad, Agra: Fakirchand, 1920), title page.

58. Ray, *Kahar Jati aur Varnavyavastha*, cover page.

59. "Contribution," *Kurmi Samachar* 1, no. 2 (May 1895): 5–9, and esp. 7–8. This Lucknow publication only survived into its second volume (1896) before fading; see Verma, *Changing Role of Caste Associations*, 36. *Vichar* means "idea" and, since it is not generally employed as a name, suggests that the anonymous author of the dialogue designed that character as an ideologist for Kurmi reform.

60. Ray, *Kahar Jati aur Varnavyavastha*, 7.

61. For a classic description of this intensely popular festival, performed annually all over North India, see Norvin Hein, "The Ram Lila," in Milton Singer, ed., *Traditional India: Structure and Change* (Philadelphia: American Folklore Society, 1959), 73–98; on vijay dashmi, 88.

62. Ray, *Kahar Jati aur Varnavyavastha*, 14–16. According to Hindu mythology, *tretayug* is the second (silver) and *kaliyug* the fourth and last (vice-ridden) age.

63. Karu Ram, *Ramani Nirnay* [Rules of the Ramanis] (Gaya: Magadha Shubhanker Press, 1906), 1. Risley, *The Tribes and Castes of Bengal*, 1:371, speculated that the designation *Ramani Kahar* is a geographic one referring to the headquarters of the jati in Ramanpur near Gaya. However, given the personalized nomenclature described ahead, it seems likely that Kahars began to link the fortuitous term Ramani to the identity of Ramchandra himself. *Ramaraman* means the beloved of Lakshmi, i.e., Vishnu; *Ramaiya* refers to Ramchandra, his avatar.

64. The former listed in Ram, *Ramani Nirnay*, 6–17, the latter listed on 2–5.

65. *Kishan* is colloquial for Krishna; "Chhote Ram Das" means either "little servant of Ram" or the "servant of the child Ram."

66. Among those which conveyed the greatest meaning were Ayodhya Ram, Ramsharan Ram (*Ramsharan* meaning he who takes refuge in Ram), Sahai Ram (Ram's helper), Keval Ram (only Ram), Lachhman Ram (*Lachhman*, colloquial for Lakshman, Ram's devoted younger brother), Tulsi Ram (*tulsi* meaning basil, charged with important Vaishnava ritual connotations), Ganga Bishan Ram (*Bishan*, colloquial for Vishnu), and Narayan Ram (*Narayan* meaning Vishnu).

67. Raghunandan Prasad Sinha Varmma, *Kanyakubja Kshatriyotpatti Bhushan* [The Noble Origins of the Kanyakubja Kshatriyas] (Gaya: R. P. S. Varmma, 1924), 56–57. The term *kanyakubj* implies a geocultural tie to Kannauj, a town on the Ganga east of Etawah in western Uttar Pradesh.

68. Baba Ramchandra, cited in Pandey, "Peasant Revolt and Indian Nationalism," 169. Although Siddiqi, *Agrarian Unrest*, 112 n. 29, cautions us not to make too much of the salutation "Sitaram," his observation that "even Mus-

lim peasants used this greeting in certain parts of Oudh, especially southern Oudh where the legend of Ram and Sita is widely prevalent," speaks volumes for the extent to which Vaishnava rhetoric permeated the region.

69. Nathuni Prasad Yadav, *Jatiya Sandesh* (Darbhanga: Swami Nathu Bhagat Yadav, 1921).

70. The publication in question, *Ahir Itihas ki Jhalak,* was authored by Dilipsinha Yadav and published simultaneously in Lucknow, Allahabad, and Etawah in 1915.

71. Jamuna Prashad Yadav, *Ahiroddhar, arthat Ahir Kul Sudhar* [Ahiroddhar, or the Reform of the Ahir Line] (Jhansi: Jamuna Prashad Yadav Ahir, 1927), 38–39.

72. Janki Ballabh Das, *Devivali Pakhand* [The Heresy of Sacrifice to the Goddess] (Prayag: J. B. Das, 1937), see esp. 19–22, 38–39.

73. Gangaprasad, *Kushvaha Kshatriya,* 27.

74. Baijnath Prasad Yadav, *Ahir-Jati ki Niyamavali* [A List of the Rules of the Ahir Jati] (Varanasi: B. P. Yadav, 1928), 4–40.

75. Sinha, *Kurmi Kshatriya Nirnay,* 77–79.

76. Ibid., 79–83. Unfortunately, I have been able to turn up little more than this brief mention of this event.

77. Ibid., 80.

78. See van der Veer, *Gods on Earth,* 275–76, who lists thirty-seven such caste temples, mostly belonging to jatis formerly regarded as shudra and untouchable in the nineteenth century.

79. "*Shrimate Ramanujaya namah.*" Varmma, *Kanyakubja Kshatriyotpatti Bhushan,* cover and i.

80. Ibid., 2.

81. Ibid., ii.

82. Ibid., 47. Though Varmma describes in detail the miraculous life of the child Krishna, he emphasizes that Krishna's true identity as Vishnu is more important as a religious concept (48–49). Lakshmi, the goddess of wealth, is Vishnu's consort.

83. The application of the tilak on the forehead in a vertical parabola is one of the most visible symbols of being Vaishnava. By contrast, Shaivas employ a marking of three horizontal lines.

84. Varmma, *Kanyakubja Kshatriyotpatti Bhushan,* 57.

85. Ibid., 58–60.

86. Swami Dharnidharacharya, *Shri Awadhvamshi Kshatriya Martandah,* xvii–xviii, 1–140. See Appendix 2 for a discussion of Dharnidharacharya's tract.

87. The brief life narrative that follows is based on ibid., 140–61.

88. See, e.g., ibid., 149–50, citing the *Garg Samhita* (Ashvamedh Khand, section 61, verses 24–25).

89. Ibid., 149.

90. Again Dharnidharacharya cites the *Garg Samhita* (Ashvamedha Khand, section 61, verse 26).

91. *Venkateshwar* is an epithet of Vishnu; Vibhishan *Vibhishan*—a particularly apt title for a Ramanuji setting—is a younger brother of Ravana (and therefore a southerner) in the epic *Ramayana* who emerges as one of the more remark-

able devotees of Ramchandra. This information is taken from an address given on the inside cover page of Dharnidharacharya, *Shri Awadhvamshi Kshatriya Martandah.*

92. Ibid., vi.

93. All this emerges in a letter from one Pandit Shri Dharmanath Sharma of Chapra, ibid., xiii.

94. The reverse side of the title page of *Shri Awadhvamshiya Kshatriya Martandah* gives the addresses of these institutions, in addition to the Awadhavamshiya Kshatriya Sabha office in Chapra.

95. Nevertheless, the complexity of sampraday boundaries makes any strict correlation between religious identity and social ideology difficult in the extreme. Peter van der Veer, *Gods on Earth,* 106, observed, for example, that while brahman as well as shudra Ramanandis chose to align themselves with the Ramanuji view, many brahman monks, "who might secretly have preferred to be Ramanuji, did not disown their Ramanandi affiliation, since that would have incurred considerable disadvantages in North India, where only the Ramanandis are strong."

96. See Ghurye, *Indian Sadhus,* 153–65; Growse, *Mathura: A District Memoir,* 184–240. The Nimbaraki sampraday seems to have undergone ideological transformations not unlike those experienced by Ramanandis in the early twentieth century and that I have described in the previous chapter; see Ghurye, *Indian Sadhus,* 153–55. As with Ramanand, there has been substantial disagreement in this century regarding the identity and dates of Nimbark (he is usually placed in the twelfth century). Writing in the 1870s, F. S. Growse, *Mathura,* 194, claimed that Nimbarkis had "no special literature of their own, either in Sanskrit or Hindi." By contrast, eighty years later Ghurye, *Indian Sadhus,* 153–54, would report that "Nimbarka was a great writer but he always wrote in Sanskrit. It was Sri Bhatta, 31st in the apostolic succession, who wrote in Hindi," and "Harivyasadeva, 32nd in the list, turned his entire attention to promulgating the doctrines and observances of this sect into Hindi." At the very least, the contrast between Growse's and Ghurye's observations suggests some major Nimbarki reinterpretations in the late nineteenth and early twentieth centuries. Perhaps more importantly, in this century there have emerged elements within the sampraday that encourage greater religious liberalism with respect to untouchables; see Ghurye, *Indian Sadhus,* 155.

97. Indeed, an analogous situation is evident as early as 1810–13 in the surveys of Francis Buchanan, who noted that despite their genealogical affinity for Radha and Krishna, Goalas in Bihar and eastern Uttar Pradesh looked for the most part to the demographically powerful Dasnami order for religious guidance. See Buchanan, *Bhagalpur, 1810–1811,* 234; *Bihar and Patna, 1811–1812,* 1:337–38; *Shahabad, 1812–1813,* 204; and Martin, *Eastern India,* 2:467–68. It is significant that the Shaiva orientation of their Dasnami gurus did not normally lead Goalas to abandon their Krishna-centered identity. Only on one occasion did Buchanan note otherwise, in Purnea district (*Purnea, 1809–1810,* 226–27) where Goalas had rejected "the worship of that deified hero [Krishna], and have adopted as guides the Dasnami Sannyasis, who teach them the worship of *Sib* [Shiva]."

98. Buchanan, *Bihar and Patna, 1811–1812,* 1:374: "The Ramanandis in-

deed will instruct their followers in the worship of any god of the side of Vishnu, such as Rama, Krishna, Nrisingha, and Bamana among the Avatars, or Narayan, and Vishnu among his heavenly forms. Although all these are considered as various forms of the same god, yet the mode of worshipping each is different; Vasudeva is considered as the same with Krishna. No separate worship is by this sect offered to the spouses of these gods; but their worship is always conjoined with that of the male, so that Krishna is never worshipped without Radha, nor Rama without Sita."

99. Buchanan, "An Account of the Northern Part of the District of Gorakhpur, 1813." The entire quote is from the topography and antiquities of Khamariya thana: "⁶⁄₁₆ of the Hindus worship Rama, and ³⁄₁₆ prefer Krishna; of these ⁴⁄₁₆ are the followers of the Brahmans, and ⁵⁄₁₆ of the Ramanandis, who even at Ayodhya do not scruple to deliver the form of prayer, by which Krishna is addressed."

100. Jagannath Das, according to Buchanan "the only mahant in these districts who has studied grammar, or can be called a man of learning," maintained "that the proper study of the Mahantas ought to be the Ramayan of Valmiki, the Sri Bhagawat [Purana], and the Bhagawat Gita" (*Bihar and Patna, 1811–1812*, 1:375).

101. Van der Veer, *Gods on Earth*, 276; Freitag, "Introduction" to part 1: "Performance and Patronage," in Freitag, ed.,, *Culture and Power in Banaras*, 26.

102. See Kenneth W. Jones, *Arya Dharm: Hindu Consciousness in Nineteenth-Century Punjab* (Berkeley and Los Angeles: University of California Press, 1976), 204. Swami Dayanand Saraswati (1824–83), a Gujarati brahman, established the Arya Samaj at Bombay in 1875 and at Lahore (in the Punjab) in 1877.

103. Gangaprasad, *Kushvaha Kshatriya*, 3 (italics are added). Similar accounts can be found in Saraswati, *Kurmi Kshatriya Itihas*, 3–11, and 23; Ray, *Kahar Jati aur Varnavyavastha*, 7–13; J. P. Chaudhari, *Kushvaha Kshatriya—(Kuiri, Kachhi, Murao, Kachhvaha) Parichay* [An Introduction to Kushvaha Kshatriyas—(Koiri, Kacchi, Murav, Kachhvaha] (Banaras: Chaudhari and Sons, 1926), 1–5; Varmma, *Kanyakubja Kshatriyotpatti Bhushan*, 1–7; and Dilipsinha Yadav, *Ahir Itihas ki Jhalak*, 1–2.

104. Saraswati, *Kurmi Kshatriya Itihas*, 23, 27–28. Saraswati devotes 17–23 to an etymological/grammatical exposition of the word "Kurmi" and concludes that it is equivalent to *bhupati*, or noble; upon further examination he identifies the term *kurmah* with Indra and *kurm* with Brahma. (A similar argument is put forth by Chaudhari Dipnarayan Sinha, *Kurmi Kshatriya Nirnay*, 4–6.) Asking why members of the reputed Indra jati would begin referring to themselves with the word "Kurmi," Saraswati notes (28) that "the scholars of this jati thought long and hard and decided to begin to refer to themselves by this Vedic term, a term denoting a kshatriya varna."

105. For instance, Gangaprasad, *Kushvaha Kshatriya*, 3–4, 7.

106. See Jones, *Arya Dharm*, 202–5.

107. J. Chaudhari, author of *Kushvaha Kshatriya—(Kuiri, Kachhi, Murav, Kachhvaha) Parichay*. Dayanand Anglo-Vedic schools sprang up throughout much of north India in the late nineteenth and early twentieth centuries as a result of the efforts of the politically oriented Arya Samaji of the Punjab, Lala

Lajpat Rai. The schools combined Western learning with the study of Sanskrit and the Vedas.

108. Rao, "Yadava Movement," part 1, 134. Rao interprets the widespread practice of investiture with the sacred thread, however, as evidence that the Arya Samaj had gained significant inroads among Yadav kshatriyas in eastern Uttar Pradesh and Bihar in the 1910s and 1920s. I argue that such an assessment may be premature.

109. Yadav, *Ahir Itihas ki Jhalak*, 15.

110. Varmma, *Kanyakubja Kshatriyotpatti Bhushan*, 20–21.

111. See Lutgendorf's discussion of the "eternal religion" in *The Life of a Text*, 360–70. Jwalaprasad Mishra, incidentally, also directed his attentions to questions of jati and varna status. See his *Jatibhaskar* [Illuminations on Jati] (Bombay: Khemraj Shri Krishnadas, 1917), a conservative work which comprises extracts from Sankrit texts on the strict divisions and social duties of Hindu society.

112. Lutgendorf, *The Life of a Text*, 367.

113. Chaudhari, *Kurmi Kshatriyatva Darpan*, 17.

114. Saraswati, *Kurmi Kshatriya Itihas*, 110.

115. J. P. Chaudhari, *Kushvaha Kshatriya Parichay*, 44, 45.

116. Sinha, *Kurmi Kshatriya Nirnay*, 80.

117. Varmma, *Kanyakubj Kshatriyotpatti Bhushan*, 16–173, 31.

118. Lal, *Tantuvay Anveshan arthat Tanti Jati ka Itihas*, 39–40.

119. Ray, *Kahar Jati aur Varnavyavastha*, 17.

120. Ibid., 17–18. Ray made no comment whatsoever regarding the question of palanquin-bearing, the occupation often attributed to Kahars.

121. Ibid., 1–3.

122. Hagen, "Indigenous Society," 93. Hagen's argument relies on Buchanan's description of the political economy of Bihar in the early nineteenth century.

123. Nevill, *Ballia: A Gazetteer,* vol. 30 of the District Gazetteers of the United Provinces of Agra and Oudh (Allahabad: Government Press, 1907), 106.

124. See the historiographical discussion in K. N. Panikkar, "Historical Overview," in Sarvepalli Gopal, ed., *Anatomy of a Confrontation: The Babri Masjid-Ramjanmabhumi Issue* (New Delhi: Viking, 1991), esp. 28–33; and Pandey, *The Construction of Communalism.*

Chapter 4

1. Kunwar Chheda Sinha, *Kshatriya aur Kritram Kshatriya*, published simultaneously in English as *Kshatriyas and Would-Be Kshatriyas,* translated by Kunwar Rupa Sinha (Agra: Rajput Anglo-Oriental Press, 1907), 1. Similarly oriented tracts included Pandit Kashinath, *Varnavivek Chandrika* [Moonlight of Varna Wisdom] (Bombay: Shri Venkateshwar Press, 1898); and Jvalaprasad Mishra, *Jati Nirnay* [Jati Rulings] (Bombay: Lakshmi Venkateshwar Press, 1901). Thirty years later, Chaudhari Dipnarayan Sinha of Chunar south of Banaras com-

posed a one-hundred-page argument responding to the attacks and cultural slights contained in these works in his *Kurmi Kshatriya Nirnaya* (1937).

2. Sinha, *Kshatriya aur Kritram Kshatriya,* 1–13. Sinha, not surprisingly, cited the opinions and speculations of British civil servants and ethnographers in India.

3. Imtiaz Ahmad, "Caste Mobility Movements in North India," *Indian Economic and Social History Review* 7, no. 2 (1971): 168.

4. Gyan Pandey, "Rallying Round the Cow: Sectarian Strife in the Bhojpuri Region, c. 1888–1917," in Ranajit Guha, ed., *Subaltern Studies: Writings on South Asian History and Society,* vol. 2 (Delhi: Oxford University Press, 1983), 74–75. Pandey cites Nirmal Sengupta, "Caste as an Agrarian Phenomenon in Twentieth Century Bihar," in Arvind Das and V. Nilakant, eds., *Agrarian Relations in India* (New Delhi: Manohar, 1979), 85–89. See also Nita Kumar, *The Artisans of Banaras: Popular Culture and Identity, 1880–1986* (Princeton: Princeton University Press, 1988), 202, who describes the formation of caste associations as "originally a response to the 1901 Census classifications."

5. L. S. S. O'Malley, in GOI, *Census of India, 1911,* vol. 5: *Bihar and Orissa,* part 1 (page number not given), cited in Ahmad, "Caste Mobility Movements," 169, n. 11. O'Malley served many years as a district officer in Bihar and became something of a local expert on Bihari culture. He subsequently authored many of the Bengal District Gazetteer Reports relating to Bihar which were published in the first decade of the twentieth century.

6. Thus Kumar, *Artisans of Banaras,* 202, describing Banaras: "the Census classification of castes greatly agitated the Kayasthas, Khattris, Kurmis, and Jats."

7. Cf. Lucy Carroll, "Colonial Perceptions of Indian Society and the Emergence of Caste Associations," *Journal of Asian Studies* 37, no. 2 (1978): 233–250. For a sprinkling of the correspondences received by E. A. Gait's "ethnography" staff, see *Census of India, 1901,* vol. 6, part 1, 378–84. This was not a phenomenon restricted to the Gangetic north: the extensive correspondences and circulars regarding the changing dimensions of reform among *Shanar* (toddy-tappers) redefining themselves as Nadar kshatriya in South India are recounted in Robert L. Hardgrave Jr., *The Nadars of Tamilnad: The Political Culture of a Community in Change* (Berkeley and Los Angeles: University of California Press, 1969), 133–36.

8. See Nandy, *The Intimate Enemy,* xv (on psychocultural survival), and 4–11.

9. Ahmad, "Caste Mobility Movements in North India," 168.

10. I employ the term Goala in this section, inasmuch as this movement stood apart from the Goala/Gopa/Ahir articulation of Yadav-kshatriya identity.

11. John R. McLane, *Indian Nationalism and the Early Congress,* 272.

12. Anand A. Yang, "Sacred Symbol and Sacred Space in Rural India: Community Mobilization in the Anti-Cow Killing Riot of 1893," *Comparative Studies in Society and History* 22, no. 4 (October 1980), esp. 590–96.

13. McLane, *Indian Nationalism and the Early Congress,* 273 (for the quote immediately following, 296).

14. See Peter G. Robb, "Officials and Non-officials as Leaders in Popular Agitations: Shahabad 1917 and Other Conspiracies," in B. N. Pandey, ed., *Leadership in South Asia* (New Delhi: Vikas, 1977), esp. 198–203.

15. Pandey, "Rallying Round the Cow," 88, 60–61, 104. The term "ahir"

was common to eastern Uttar Pradesh. See also 89–90 for the "convergence of interest" between Goalas and dvij zamindars over the issue of cow protection.

16. The following descriptions emerge from Government of Bengal, Judicial Department, Police Proceedings (held in the Bihar State Archives, Patna), June 1893, nos. 53–62, "Riots in the Gaya District," 5–7.

17. Pandey, "Rallying Round the Cow," 106. Pandey cites Sandria Freitag, "Religious Rites and Riots: From Community Identity to Communalism in North India, 1870–1940" (Ph.D. diss., University of California, Berkeley, 1980). Freitag cites Oriental and India Office Collection, L/P & J/6/365, File 84 of 1894, Hoey's "Note on the Cow-Protection Agitation in Gorakhpur District," 2, 4.

18. GOI, Home Department, Public Proceedings (held in the National Archives of India, New Delhi), December 1893, no. 212, "Note on the Cow-protection agitation on [sic] the Gorakhpur District," 2. (This is probably a slightly earlier version of Hoey's note, held in the Oriental and India Office Collection, cited by Freitag and Pandey.)

19. Government of Bihar and Orissa, Political Department, Special Section, file no. 171 of 1925, "Subject: Serious riot between Babhans and Goalas at Monghyr. (2) Lakhochak riot." See Hetukar Jha, "Lower-Caste Peasants and Upper-Caste Zamindars in Bihar (1921–1925): An Analysis of Sanskritization and Contradiction between the Two Groups," *Indian Economic and Social History Review* 14, no. 4 (1977): 550–54, for extended extracts from this file, comprising the following: "Reports on the Riot at Kiul by D.I.G., Bihar and Orissa"; "No. 1077, Dated 11th June, 1925, from J. D. Sifton, C.S. to Government of Bihar and Orissa, to the Secretary to the Government of India, Home Department"; and "No. 108 Con. from S. A. Khan, Dist. Officer, Bhagalpur, to the Commissioner of Bhagalpur Division. 7 July, 1925, 'Re: The Goala Movement, its Causes and Character.'" I refer hereafter to the entire report—whether reproduced by Jha or cited directly by me—as Political Special File no. 171 of 1921.

20. Government of Bihar and Orissa, Political Department, Special Section, file no. 79 of 1921, "Goala Movement in Patna City and Other Districts of Bihar."

21. "No. 1077, Dated 11th June, 1925 from J. D. Sifton, C.S. to Government of Bihar and Orissa, to the Secretary to the Government of India, Home Department," cited in Jha, "Lower-Caste Peasants and Upper-Caste Zamindars," 553.

22. Cited in "Letter from Y. A. Godbole, Esq. I.C.S., D.O. of Purnea, to the Commissioner of the Bhagalpur Division, 15 July, 1925," in Political Special File no. 171 of 1925, 105–6. Mukherji refers here to *shraddh*, or funerary purification, during family bereavement. According to Hindu law, shudras were obliged to undergo thirty days of ritual seclusion after a death in the family, whereas the twice-born only had to undergo seclusion for a period of thirteen days.

23. Ibid., 106. The name Swayambara Das indicates a Vaishnava monastic affiliation; the educational employment immediately brings to mind the experience of another, better-known Vaishnava, the Ramanandi Sitaramsharan Bhagvan Prasad.

24. Ibid., 107. Barbers, known as *hajjams*, were required to shave the head of the male bereaved on the day of shraddh. Mukherji, incidentally, noted that

"the movement still requires watching, especially in the Dhamdaha area."
Christopher V. Hill, "History in Motion: The Social Ecology of Purnia District,
1770–1960" (Ph.D. diss., University of Virginia, 1987), has pointed out that
the severe conflict over land control in this region was underscored by extreme
caste polarity.

25. "Letter from Y. A. Godbole, Esq. . . . 15 July, 1925," 106–7.

26. H. M. Elliot, *Memoirs of the History, Folklore, and Distribution of the
Races of the North Western Provinces of India,* 1:156. See also Pandey, *Construction of Communalism,* 85.

27. Baijnath Prasad Yadav, *Ahir-Jati ki Niyamavali,* 37; 6, 11, 33–34; 30–31.

28. Saraswati, *Kurmi Kshatriya Itihas,* 147–55.

29. See the remarks of M. N. Srinivas, *Caste in Modern India,* 46–50, and
"The Changing Position of Indian Women," *Man,* n.s., 12 (1977): 221–38;
and, apropos to Srinivas, see Rama Joshi and Joanna Liddle, *Daughters of Independence: Gender, Caste, and Class in India* (London: Zed, 1986), 60.

30. See, for instance, Shivnath Prasad Yadav, "Akhil Bharat Yadav Mahasabha
ka Itihas" [The History of the All-India Yadav Mahasabha], *Yadavesh* 1, no. 2
(1935–36): 19–20. K. K. Verma, *Changing Role of Caste Associations,* 22, notes
that the women's wing of the Kurmi movement—the "Kurmi kshatriya Mahila
Parishad [council]"—was inaugurated in March 1927 on the occasion of the
fifteenth session of the mahasabha in Lakhimpur in Uttar Pradesh by the wife
of a prominent local zamindar.

31. Ray, *Kahar Jati aur Varnavyavastha,* 19. The sati as the ideal, sacrificial
woman is a complex subject that cannot be dealt with adequately here. See the
discussion of the sati ethic in present-day Rajasthan in Lindsey Harlan, *Religion
and Rajput Women: The Ethic of Protection in Contemporary Narratives* (Berkeley and Los Angeles: University of California Press, 1992), 112–82.

32. *Vir Jaymal,* 3d ed. (Banaras: G. Gupta, 1917); "Jaymala" translates literally as victory garland and is also the garland a bride drapes around the neck
of her groom during the marriage ceremony. *Vir Patni,* 2d ed. (Banaras: Banarsi Prasad Varma, 1912). *Kile ki Rani* 2d ed. (Banaras: Durga Prasad Khatri,
1915). Notwithstanding Reynolds's active participation in nineteenth-century
revolutionary circles in Europe, his fiction has generally been regarded as low-
quality sensational romance.

33. No. 108 Conf. from S. A. Khan, Esq., I.C.S., District Officer of Bhagalpur, to the Commissioner of the Bhagalpur Division, 7 July, 1925, "The Goala
Movement, its Causes and Character," Political Special File no. 171 of 1925,
94. (This extract is reproduced incorrectly in Jha, "Lower-Caste Peasants and
Upper-Caste Zamindars," 554, where the word "begari" is replaced with the
word "benign." While there are many terms that can translate "begari," benign
is not one of them.)

34. "Extract from D.I.G.'s weekly report date the 5th August 1921," 1; "Extract from the Confidential Diary of the Superintendent of Police, Patna, for
week ending the 26th February 1921"; "Copy of Patna Special Report Case
No. 7 of 1921" (Report no. 1, dated the 1st March, 1921; Report no. 2, dated
the 17th March, 1921; Report no. 3, dated the 15th July, 1921), 3–7; all contained in Government of Bihar and Orissa, Political Deparment, Special Sec-

tion, File No. 79 of 1921, "Goala Movement in Patna City and Other Districts of Bihar." Shri Ballab Das was probably, by virtue of his title, a Vaishnava monk, and probably a Nimbarki or Radhaballabhi; *vallabha,* of which "ballab" is a corruption, means beloved and, in the Vaishnava context often refers to the phrase Radha-vallabha, or the beloved of Radha, i.e., Krishna. The association with Krishna here is appropriate given the Krishna-oriented identity of Yadavs. "Gope" or "Gopa" is a variation of Goala and "Jotiya" is the Bengali pronunciation of jati, which would indicate that the official in charge of preparing the report covering this meeting was Bengali. *Bakr-Id* is a Muslim festival, also known as *Bari-Id,* commemorating the readiness of Abraham to sacrifice his son Ishmail.

35. Jha, "Lower-Caste Peasants and Upper-Caste Zamindars," 550. The Samastipur incident involved "Babhans who disliked the idea of the Goalas claiming to be their equal [and] assaulted a Goala girl and left her naked. She lodged a complaint before the S.D.O. at Samastipur who dismissed it without enquiry." Political Special File no. 171 of 1925, cited by Jha, 551.

36. See, for instance "Reports on the Riot at Kiul by D.I.G., Bihar and Orissa," reproduced in Jha, "Lower-Caste Peasants and Upper-Caste Zamindars," 552.

37. "Confidential," no. 269 c, from J. A. Hubback, Esq. I.C.S., Commissioner of the Bhagalpur Division, to the Chief Secretary to the Government of Bihar and Orissa, Political Department, Dated Bhagalpur, 18th July, 1925, "Subject—The underlying causes of the Goala movement," in Political Special File no. 171 of 1925, 92.

38. Gangaprasad, *Kushvaha Kshatriya, urf Koiri, Kachhi, Murav, Kachhvaha,* 2. The phrase "thus a shudra is born" appears in the text in Sanskrit as *janmana jayte shudrah,* and refers most likely to the myth of the primeval man, *Purusha,* whose head became the brahman, torso the kshatriya, loins the vaishya, and feet the shudra. Professor Tessa Bartholomeusz, now of the Department of Religious Studies at Florida State University, kindly aided in the translation.

39. Ray, *Kahar Jati aur Varnavyavastha,* 54.

40. No. 108 Conf., from S. A. Khan, Esq., I.C.S., D.O. of Bhagalpur, to the Commissioner of the Bhagalpur Division, dated 7th July 1925, in Political Special File no. 171 of 1925, 94.

41. Ibid. This leaflet and an extremely sketchy translation are provided in Political Special File no. 171 of 1925, 96–101, from which I take all my citations. A full translation can be found in Appendix 2. Sukirti Sahay, a graduate student in the Department of Sociology at the University of Virginia, and from Gaya District in Bihar, kindly aided in the sharpening of the revised translation.

42. In other words, "there are so many of you." A popular proverb holds that while noble beasts such as the lion and the tiger produce only a few offspring, lowly animals like the monkey produce veritable hordes of children. In this sense Bahuran was taunting Yadavs with insinuations of profligate intemperance.

43. See the section entitled, "The Ancient Present: *Aryavarta,* Dignity, and Labor," in chapter 3, above.

44. Suzanne H. Rudolph and Lloyd I. Rudolph, *Gandhi: The Traditional Roots of Charisma,* 2d ed. (1967; Chicago: The University of Chicago Press, 1983), viii.

45. This description of Sahajanand Saraswati's life is based on portions of his autobiography, *Mera Jivan Sangharsh,* translated in a typescript draft of Walter Hauser, *The Politics of Peasant Activism in Twentieth-Century India* (Delhi: Oxford University Press, forthcoming), 14–35. I am grateful to the author for allowing me to cite this work.

46. Saraswati, *Mera Jivan Sangharsh,* 160, 174, cited in Hauser, ibid., 20–21. Sahajanad Saraswati's status as a *dandi,* or orthodox, Dasnami sanyasi is significant, given the marginal brahman status of the Bhumihar and Jujhautiya Brahman communities in Bihar and eastern Uttar Pradesh, inasmuch as dandis are said to initiate only pure brahmans. He stands therefore as a parallel to Dharnidharacharya, noted in the previous chapters, whose status as a Ramanuji could in and of itself be marshaled as evidence of the high status of the jati community that he was, ostensibly, leaving behind to become a monk.

47. To this end, Sahajanand composed "a massive 1200-page manual of Hindu ritual, under the title *Karmakalap* (Kashi: Swami Sahajanand Saraswati, 1926), a book which very quickly went into a second and subsequently into multiple editions." Naturally, this book was used for the instruction of students at the ashram. See Hauser, *The Politics of Peasant Activism,* 23–24.

48. Hauser, *The Politics of Peasant Activism,* 17.

49. Swami Sahajanand Saraswati, *Gita Hriday* (Allahabad: Kitab Mahal, 1948).

50. Swami Sahajanand Saraswati, *Mera Jivan Sangharsh,* new edition (New Delhi: People's Publishing House, 1985), 173. Sahajanand describes Sitaram Das as a *paramhansa,* a term applicable to both Vaishnava and Shaiva sadhus, referring specifically to someone of particularly progressive views. See Ghurye, *Indian Sadhus,* 72. However, both the name "Sitaram" and the suffix "Das" suggest very strongly his Ramanandi identity.

51. Hauser, *The Politics of Peasant Activism,* 24.

52. Saraswati, *Mera Jivan Sangharsh,* 176. See also Hauser, *The Politics of Peasant Activism,* 27–28.

53. Hauser, *The Politics of Peasant Activism,* 28.

54. Saraswati, *Mera Jivan Sangharsh,* 172. On the other hand, the Swami was forced to contend throughout his political career with the constant criticism that he was nothing but a jati politician gone awry (182).

55. Walter Hauser, "The Bihar Provincial Kisan Sabha, 1929–1949: A Study of an Indian Peasant Movement" (Ph.D. diss., University of Chicago, 1961), 77.

56. Ibid., 77–78.

57. The name "Triveni Sangh" is particularly appropriate: "Sangh" means confederation; "triveni" means "triple braid" and is usually employed to refer to the confluence of the Ganga, Yamuna, and the mythical Saraswati rivers at Prayag (Allahabad), the most auspicious of the four sites for the kumbh mela. The appellation "Triveni Sangh" is usually taken to refer—in its "three-braided" sense—to Kushvaha, Yadav, and Kurmi kshatriyas, the dominant components of the organization. To my mind, the term also refers to the sacred confluence near Prayag and suggests broader mobilizing solidarities, particularly with respect to Vaishnava ideology and the kumbh mela.

58. Verma, *Changing Role of Caste Associations,* 90; Kalyan Mukherjee and Rajendra Singh Yadav, *Bhojpur: Naxalism in the Plains of Bihar* (New Delhi: Rad-

hakrishna Prakashan, 1980), 27. In this remarkable and politically commited account, Mukherjee (a journalist) and Yadav (a political activist) credit Sheopujan Prasad Singh, a Kurmi-kshatriya leader, with originating the name for the Triveni Sangh. My description of the emergence of the Triveni Sangh and its relations with Congress and the Kisan Sabha, unless otherwise noted, is based on this work, 27–32.

59. Mukherji and Yadav, *Bhojpur*, 28.

60. Ibid., 28, n. 31. The authors do not explain the nature of this humiliation.

61. Mukherji and Yadav, 29, credit Tapsi Mahto with the epithet, who had in fact employed a stronger term of abuse, *sala*, meaning "brother-in-law." To refer to someone who is not a brother-in-law as "sala" constitutes a severe affront, inasmuch as it implies that the person doing the insulting has had sexual relations with the other's sister.

62. Ibid., 30. Mukherjee and Yadav recorded this candid reminiscence of 1937 by Ramraj Singh during an interview on 2 December 1980, in Arrah, the headquarters of Shahabad District. A "lathi" is a long, heavy bamboo truncheon, often made more lethal with iron attachments.

63. This logic benefits from Walter Hauser's analysis of political alliances and jati affiliations in Bihar prior to and following Independence, in an unpublished essay entitled "Dynamics of Social Ranking and Political Power among Emerging Caste Groups in Bihar," presented at the "Caste and Politics in Bihar" panel at the nineteenth annual meeting of the Association for Asian Studies, Chicago, March 20–22, 1967. I am grateful to Professor Hauser for allowing me to read and cite this essay.

64. Mukherjee and Yadav, *Bhojpur*, 32.

65. Karpoori Thakur belonged to the *Hajjam* jati, known as masseuses and barbers.

66. See Harry W. Blair, "Rising Kulaks and Backward Classes in Bihar: Social Change in the Late 1970s," *Economic and Political Weekly*, January 12, 1980, 64–74. Karpoori Thakur, chief minister of Bihar from 1977 to 1979, relentlessly pursued a policy that would have reserved 20 percent of all state-level bureaucratic appointments for "backwards," with heavy overrepresentation for Kurmi, Yadav, and Kushvaha kshatriyas. The backward classes movement is discussed in the following chapter; see the section entitled "Forward and Backward."

67. See Mukherjee and Yadav, *Bhojpur; Report from the Flaming Field of Bihar: A CPI (ML) Document* (Calcutta: Prabodh Bhattacharya, 1986); and Christopher V. Hill, "Militant Agrarian Unrest in North India: Perspective and Ideology," review of *India Waits* by Jan Myrdal and *Report from the Flaming Field of Bihar, Peasant Studies* 15, no. 4 (Summer 1988): 297–305.

Conclusions

1. See for example the advertisements on the back cover of *Yadavesh* 1, no. 2 (1935–36).

2. Christopher R. King, *One Language, Two Scripts: The Hindi Movement in Nineteenth-Century North India* (Delhi: Oxford University Press, 1994), 37–48.

3. See Rao, "Yadava Movement," 149–54.

4. The information here on Kurmi-kshatriya organizations is from K. K. Verma, *Changing Role of Caste Associations,* 13–35. On the 1971 meeting, see 30–32.

5. In fact the notion of legislative safeguards for "the Depressed Classes" were evident as early as 1921, the year of the Montague-Chelmsford Reforms. See Lelah Dushkin, "Scheduled Caste Politics," in J. Michael Mahar, ed., *The Untouchables in Contemporary India* (Tucson: University of Arizona Press, 1972), 166–76, esp. 170.

6. See Durga Das Basu, *Introduction to the Constitution of India* (New Delhi: Prentice-Hall, 1982), 20 (on Nehru's resolution) and 87–88 (on the Constitution itself).

7. On this constitutional history and the legal quagmire see Marc Galanter, "Who Are the Other Backward Classes? An Introduction to a Constitutional Puzzle," *Economic and Political Weekly* 13, nos. 43 and 44 (28 October 1978): 1812–28; a pointed and detailed summary of the post-1947 history can be found in K. C. Yadav, *India's Unequal Citizens: A Study of Other Backward Classes* (New Delhi: Manohar, 1994).

8. GOI, Backward Classes Commission, *Report* (New Delhi: Manager of Publications, 1956), 2.

9. Yadav, *India's Unequal Citizens,* 67–73, for a summary of the Mandal Commission report.

10. For a glimpse of the new rhetoric, see Yadav, *India's Unequal Citizens.*

11. See Anand Patwardhan's video documentary, *Ram ke Nam* [In the Name of God], where a candid rank and file "Hindu right" reaction to Advani's jailing is captured.

12. Hence Ranajit Guha: the "central problematic" of Indian historiography should be to understand the "*historic failure of the nation to come to its own,* a failure due to the inadequacy of the bourgeoisie as well as of the working class to lead it into a decisive victory over colonialism and a bourgeois-democratic revolution"; "On Some Aspects of the Historiography of Colonial India," in *Subaltern Studies,* 1:7 (italics in original).

13. Cf. Christopher A. Bayly, "Rallying round the Subaltern," review of *Subaltern Studies,* vols. 1–4, in *Journal of Peasant Studies* 16, no. 1 (October 1988): 113: "'consciousness', cut free from its teleological, positivist and economic groundings, appears for the right in the guise of religion, paternalist values and nationalism, rather than as subaltern struggle."

14. Hence Partha Chatterjee:

Perhaps we have allowed ourselves to be taken in too easily by the general presence of an abstract negativity in the autonomous domain of subaltern beliefs and practices and have missed those marks, faint as they are, of an immanent process of criticism and learning, of selective appropriation, of making sense of and using on one's own terms the elements of a more powerful cultural order. We must, after all, remind ourselves that subaltern consciousness is not merely structure, characterized solely by negativity; it is also history, shaped and developed through a changing process of interaction between the dominant and the subordinate. Surely it would be wholly contrary to our project to go about as though only the dominant culture has a life in history and subaltern consciousness [is?] eternally frozen in its structure of negation.

"Caste and Subaltern Consciousness," in Ranajit Guha, ed., *Subaltern Studies*(Delhi: Oxford University Press, 1992), 6:206–7. These doubts find elaboration, and bear abundant fruit, in P. Chatterjee, *The Nation and Its Fragments: Colonial and Postcolonial Histories* (Delhi: Oxford University Press, 1994), and particularly chapter 8, "The Nation and Its Peasants."

15. This of course brings to mind James Scott, *Weapons of the Weak: Everyday Forms of Peasant Resistance* (New Haven: Yale University Press, 1985), though I am reluctant to characterize peasants and monks as necessarily weak, let alone the ideologies they espoused as weapons of resistance.

16. Attributed to Bharat Bharati, cited in Lal, *Tantuvay Anveshan*, 67; and in Ray, *Kahar Jati aur Varnavyavastha*, title page. See chapter 3, above, for discussion.

17. Ramavatar Yadav, "Yatindr-stav" [Hymn to the Great Renouncer], in *Ramanandank*, 1.

18. "Confidential, No. 269 c, from J. A. Hubback, Esq. I.C.S., Commissioner of the Bhagalpur Division, to the Chief Secretary to the Government of Bihar and Orissa, Political Department, Dated Bhagalpur, 18th July, 1925, "Subject—The underlying causes of the Goala movement," in Political Special File no. 171 of 1925, 92.

Appendix 1

1. Marika Vicziany, "Imperialism, Botany and Statistics in early Nineteenth-Century India: The Surveys of Francis Buchanan (1762–1829)," *Modern Asian Studies* 20, no. 4 (October 1986): 630–32.

2. Ibid., 626, 638–42, 659–60. Buchanan's first aim was to acquire the directorship of the Botanical Garden of Calcutta. But, according to Vicziany, Buchanan's career suffered as a result of his close association with the declining star of Lord Wellesley, whose aggressive political policy caused him to be recalled to London in 1805 by the disgruntled Court of Directors of the English East India Company. After some intense lobbying, Buchanan was finally named as the heir to the directorship of the Botanical Garden of Calcutta in 1807. He never assumed that position, however, because the previous director, the long-ailing William Roxburgh, only left the post in 1813, by which time Buchanan had decided to leave India.

3. Ibid., especially 626, 659–60. The problem, Vicziany argues, stems from a modern misunderstanding of what was meant by the term "statistics" in Buchanan's day. See her comments in this regard on 648–50.

4. See A. K. Bagchi, "Deindustrialisation in Gangetic Bihar, 1807–1901," in Barun De, ed., *Essays in Honour of Professor Susobhan Chandra Sarkar* (New Delhi: People's Publishing House, 1976), 499–522; as well as Marika Vicziany, "The Deindustrialisation of India in the Nineteenth Century: A Methodological Critique of Amiya Kumar Bagchi," and Bagchi's response in the same issue of *Indian Economic and Social History Review*, 16, no. 2 (1979): 105–46.

5. Vicziany, "Imperialism, Botany and Statistics," 660. Buchanan's statisti-

cal tables for Bihar are held in the Oriental and India Office Collection in the British Library, London, under the catalogue number Mss.Eur.G.18–24.

6. Vicziany, "Imperialism, Botany and Statistics," 645.

7. Ibid., 643.

8. There is some discrepancy regarding the dates of the Gorakhpur account. Vicziany, "Imperialism, Botany and Statistics," 643, states that Buchanan travelled to Gorakhpur in 1813–14, but the account itself is dated 1812. See Francis Buchanan (Hamilton), "An Account of the Northern Part of the District of Gorakhpur, 1812," Mss.Eur.D.91–92, Oriental and India Office Collection. According to C. E. A. W. Oldham, in the introduction to his edition of *Journal of Francis Buchanan kept during the Survey of the District of Shahabad in 1812–1813* (Patna: Government Printing, Bihar and Orissa, 1926), i–ii, Buchanan was definitely in Shahabad "during the cold weather months [October to April] of 1812–1813" and in Gorakhpur "in the season 1813–1814." The date of 1812 given for the Gorakhpur account must have been, then, the error of the copyist.

9. The Bihar portions of the "Buchanan-Hamilton Manuscripts" are catalogued under Mss.Eur.D.562. "An Account of the Northern Part of the District of Gorakhpur, 1812," is held under Mss.Eur.D.91–92.

10. Subtitled: *Comprising the Districts of Behar, Shahabad, Bhagalpoor, Goruckpoor, Dinajpoor, Purniya, Rungpoor, and Assam, in relation to their geology, mineralogy, botany, agriculture, commerce, manufactures, fine arts, population, religion, education, statistics, etc.,* 3 vols., (London: Wm. H. Allen, 1838). This work contains tables not published in later editions of the Buchanan accounts (see below) and is referred to in the present work as *Eastern India*.

11. See, for instance, George R. Kaye and Edward H. Johnston, *A Catalogue of Manuscripts in European Languages,* vol. 2, part 2, *Minor Collections and Miscellaneous Manuscripts,* section 1 (London: India Office, 1937), 580–590. See also V. H. Jackson's introduction to *Journal of Francis Buchanan (afterwards Hamilton) kept during the Survey of the Districts of Patna and Gaya in 1811–1812* (Patna: Government Printing, Bihar and Orissa, 1925). Jackson notes that "Montgomery Martin's methods as editor of 'Eastern India', the three-volume abridgement of the Reports published in 1838, have been justly condemned by everyone who has examined the original manuscripts. In deciding what portions of the Reports should be omitted, he followed no consistent plan, but merely, as Sir W. W. Hunter observed, left out 'the parts which he did not understand or which did not interest him.' Matters of topographical and antiquarian interest are the principal feature of the Journals, and in these respects the Reports, and particularly the Report on the districts of Patna and Gaya, have greatly suffered at his hands" (v–vi). Oldham, Introduction to *Journal of Francis Buchanan,* iii–iv, expressed astonishment "that the officials of the India House [formerly in Whitehall, London] should have permitted these volumes to be printed without Buchanan Hamilton's name appearing anywhere on the title-page. . . . I can only add that when I first studied portions of the original manuscripts at the India Office in 1903, I was amazed at the facts disclosed, and impressed with the importance of having the portions scored through (by Mar-

tin's pencil presumably) published." The outcry by students of the manuscripts, such as the influential Oldham and Jackson, led eventually to their publication in Patna.

12. Dr. Francis Hamilton, *Genealogies of the Hindus, Extracted from Their Sacred Writings* (Edinburgh: W. Aitken, 1819). Buchanan added his mother's maiden name, Hamilton, to his own after inheriting her estate.

13. See Appendix 2.

14. Thapar's concern here is not with the fabrications per se but with the representation of the past implicit in them. Romila Thapar, "'Thus It Was': The Early Indian Historical Tradition," Wesleyan University Public Affairs Center Thursday Lecture Series, 19 November 1992.

Appendix 2

1. Allahabad: n.p., 1930; 2d ed., Chapra: Awadhvamshi Kshatriya Sabha, 1936. The first thirty pages of the second edition (which I have used here), up to and including the table of contents, are continually repaginated, so that one section consists of six pages, the following of a new three pages, and so on. To simplify I have ignored the repaginations of the original and have employed lower-case roman numerals in direct sequence to refer to this portion of the text.

2. Dharnidharacharya, *Shri awadhvamshiya kshatriya martandah*, xxvii–xxix. Of the *dharmashastra*, Dharnidharacharya noted here that foremost among the dharmashastric literature is *Manu-smriti*. *Itihas* translates as "thus it was"; hence, works that fall under that rubric (Dharnidharacharya began his list with the *Mahabharata*, included the *Ramayan*, and ended with the *Bhaktmal*) represent a distinct way of conceiving the past. See Romila Thapar, "Society and Historical Consciousness," 353–383.

3. The first volume of this two-volume set was published in 1829, the second in 1832. Since then *Annals and Antiquities of Rajast'han* has seen numerous reprintings; I cite from the edition made available by Routledge and Kegan Paul (London), 1957–60.

4. Dharnidharacharya, *Shri Awadhvamshiya Kshatriya Martandah,* 38. Note that parenthetical comments are in the text itself, whereas bracketed remarks are my own. Italics are mine.

5. To compare with the original, see Tod, *Annals,* 1:20, 75.

6. See, for instance, Kunwar Chheda Sinha, *Kshatriya aur Kritram Kshatriya*. This view is discussed in chapter 4.

7. The copyright page of the 1957–60 edition upon which I rely shows four previous imprints: 1829–32 (the original publication), 1914, 1923, and 1950.

8. Chaube's translation is cited by Dharnidharacharya himself, *Shri Awadhvamshiya Kshatriya Martandah,* 37–38. I am grateful to Dr. Indira Chowdhury Sengupta, Department of English, Jadavpur University, Calcutta, and to Dr. Varsha Joshi, Associate Fellow, Women's Studies Unit, Institute of Development Studies, Jaipur, for bringing the earlier translations to my attention.

9. *Sir William Jones: A Study in Eighteenth-Century British Attitudes to India* (Cambridge: Cambridge University Press, 1968).

10. Tod, *Annals,* 1:75 n, 17, 18. It should be noted that for the nineteenth-century European scholar, the simian connection seemed much more than incidental. See Winthrop Jordan, *The White Man's Burden: Historical Origins of Racism in the United States* (New York: Oxford University Press, 1974), 15–18 and 198–201.

11. Max Müller, *India: What Can It Teach Us?* (London, 1919), 32. The quote is on p. 20 of the more recent edition of Müller published by Munshiram Manoharlal (New Delhi, 1991).

12. Tod, *Annals,* 1:17. However, Tod notes in his introduction (esp. xv–xviii) the utility of bardic poetry and temple inscriptions in compiling Indian history.

13. See Romila Thapar, "Society and Historical Consciousness," for the historiographical potential of the "*itihasa-purana*" tradition.

Appendix 3

1. No. 108 Conf., from S. A. Khan to the Commissioner of the Bhagalpur Division, 7 July 1925, in Political Special File no. 171 of 1925, 94.

2. *Gopa Charitam* is translated as "The Story of the Gopas." This Bihari leaflet and an extremely sketchy translation are provided in Political Special File No. 171 of 1925, 96–101. Sukirti Sahay, a graduate student in the Department of Sociology at the University of Virginia, kindly aided in the translation.

3. A circular dance performed in association with the worship of Krishna and the milkmaids of Vrindaban.

4. The area around Mathura.

5. The idealized, innocent cowherds of Krishna's Vrindaban.

6. Swami Dayanand Saraswati, founder of the Arya Samaj.

7. The author ends every line with the exhortation, "Oh, Gopa jatiyo," which gives the verse a sense of rhythm.

8. This could mean the region of the Goalas, or the village of Golok.

9. The numbers, which represent the sequence of the verse, appear in the original.

10. Raja Kans, fearful of predictions of Krishna's birth, sought to have the infant god killed.

11. The archery instructor from the *Mahabharata.*

12. Earth.

13. Milkmaids.

14. Other names for Krishna.

15. Singing.

16. Having lured the listener in, the author now turns to the thorny question of twice-born status.

17. The third of the four ages according to Hindu mythology, marking the transition from good to the age of vice (*Kaliyuga*).

18. Goala women.

19. High born.
20. This is meant to be severely ironical.
21. A black stone said to represent Vishnu.
22. This is meant to represent long-term bribery.
23. Other designations of Krishna.
24. This is meant to be ironic.

Bibliography

Published Sources

HINDI AND URDU

Many of the publications listed here from the pre-1947 period can be found in the extensive vernacular tracts collections of the Oriental and India Office Collection of the British Library (formerly the India Office Library and Records, and the British Library Department of Oriental Manuscripts and Printed Books), London. More recent publications are available in a number of major research libraries in the U.S., courtesy of the Library of Congress acquisitions program.

Bhagvan Prasad, Sitaramsharan. *Shri Bhaktamal: Tika, Tilak, aur Namavali Sahit* [The Bhaktamal: Text, Commentary, and List of Names]. 2d ed. 2 vols. Kashi [Banaras]: Chandraprabha Press, 1903–9.

———. *Shri Bhaktamal*. Lucknow: Tejkumar Press, 1962.

Bhagavadacharya (formerly Bhagavaddas). *ShriJankikripabhashyasya* [The Discourses of Shri Janaki, or Sita]. Ahmedabad: Swami Shri Ramcharitracharya Vyakaranacharya, 1958.

———. "Shri Ramanandacharya aur Shri Vaishnava Dharma" [Ramanand and Vaishnava Belief]. In Das, ed., *Ramanand-Granth-Mala ka Shri Ramanandank*, 9–14.

———. *ShriRamanandabhashyam* [The Discourses of Shriramanand]. Ayodhya: Swami Shribhagavadacharya-Smaraksadan, [1963?].

———. *Shriramanandadigvijayah* [The World-Conquest of Shri Ramanand]. Ahmedabad: Adhyapika Shrichandandevi, 1967. First edition issued with preface as *Shrimadramanand-digvijayah* (Abu: Shri Ramashabhadas Vaishnaven, 1927).

Brajendraprasad. *Shri Rupkala Vak Sudha* [The Essence of Shri Rupkala's Sayings]. New Delhi: Dr. Saryu Prasad (author's son), 1970.

Chaturvedi, Parshuram. *Uttari Bharat ki Sant-Parampara* [The North Indian Sant Tradition]. 3d ed. Allahabad: Leader Press, 1972.

Chaudhari, Devi Prasad Sinha. *Kurmi Kshatriyatva Darpan* [Reflections on Kurmi-Kshatriya Valor]. Lucknow: Kashi Ram Varma, 1907.

Chaudhari, Dipnarayan Sinha. *Kurmi Kshatriya Nirnay* [Rulings of Kurmi Kshatriyas]. Chunar: n.p., 1937–38.

Chaudhari, J. P. (Pandit). *Kushvaha Kshatriya—(Kuiri, Kachhi, Murao, Kachhvaha) Parichay* [An Introduction to Kushvaha Kshatriyas—(Koiri, Kacchi, Murav, Kachhvaha)]. Banaras: Chaudhari and Sons, 1926.

Das, Avadh Kishor ("Shri Vaishnava"). "*Yogank* aur Shri Ramanandacharya" [*Yogank* and Shri Ramanandacharya]. In Das, ed., *Ramanand-Granth-Mala ka Shri Ramanandank*, 75–76.

———, ed. *Ramanand-Granth-Mala ka Shri Ramanandank* [Special Issue of the Ramanand-Book-Series dedicated to Ramanand] 1, no. 5–6. Ayodhya: Shri Ramanand-Granthmala Prakashan Samiti, 1935–36.

Das, Janki Ballabh. *Devivali Pakhand* [The Heresy of Sacrifice to the Goddess]. Prayag: J. B. Das, 1937.

Das, Saryu. *Shri Vaishnava Dharm Divakar Bhashatika Sahit* [Illuminations (lit., the sun) and Commentary on Vaishnava Religion]. Ayodhya, 1920.

Das, Shyamsundar. "Ramavat Sampraday." *Nagaripracharani Patrika*, n.s., 4, no. 3 (1924): 327–43.

Dharnidharacharya (Swami). *Shri Awadhvamshi Kshatriya Martandah* [Honorable Awadh-lineage Kshatriyas of the Sun]. Allahabad: n.p., 1930; 2d ed., Chapra: Awadhvamshi Kshatriya Sabha, 1936. .

Gangaprasad (see also Gangaprasad Gupta). *Kushvaha Kshatriya, urf Koiri, Kachhi, Murao, Kachhvaha (Vivaran)* [The Kushvaha Kshatris, also known as Koiri, Kachhi, Murao, and Kachhvaha (An Account)]. Banaras: Adarsh Press, 1921.

Gupta, Gangaprasad. *Kile ki Rani* [Queen of the Fort]. Second edition. Banaras: Durga Prasad Khatri, 1915.

———. *Vir Jaymal* [Valiant Defence]. Third edition. Banaras: G. Gupta, 1917.

———. *Vir Patni* [Brave Wife]. Second edition. Banaras: Banarsi Prasad Varma, 1912.

Hariacharya, Swami, ed. *Shrisampraday Manthan* [The Stirrings of the Shrisampraday]. Varanasi: Swami Hariacharya Prakashan, 1991.

Hussain, Saiyyid Muhammad Tassaduq. *Kitab-i Sadhu* [The Book of Sadhus]. Sadhaura, Umballa District: n.p., 1913.

Jayramdas, Swami. "Shrisampraday ke Sajag Prahari Anantshrivibhushit JagadguruRamanandacharya Shriswami Bhagavadacharya ji Maharaj" [The Vigilant Protector of the Shri Sampraday, the Forever-shri-adorned (i.e., infinite shri) JagadguruRamanandacharya Shriswami Bhagavadacharya Ji Maharaj]. In Hariacharya, ed., *Shrisampraday Manthan*, part 2, 120–124.

Kashinath (Pandit). *Varnvivek Chandrika* [Moonlight of Varna Wisdom]. Bombay: Shri Venkateshwar Press, 1898.

Kurmi Samachar [Kurmi Newspaper]. Volumes one and two (1895–1895).

Lal, Lalji. *Tantuvay Anveshan arthat Tanti Jati ka Itihas* [A Study of the

Tantuvay, or the History of the Tanti (weavers) Jati]. Sandalpur, Monghyr: Lalji Lal, 1929.

Lal, Shrikrishna. "Swami Ramanand ka Jivan Charitra" [A Biography of Swami Ramanand]. In *Ramanand ki Hindi Rachnaen* [The Hindi Work of Ramanand], edited by Pitambar Datt Barthwal, 33–50. Kashi: Nagari Pracharani Sabha, 1955.

Mathuradas, Sitaramiya. "Hinduon ka Gaurav arthat Shri Shri Ramanandacharya" [The Saviour of the Hindus, or Shri Shri Ramanandacharya]. In Das, ed.,*Ramanand-Granth-Mala ka Shri Ramanandank*, 5–7.

Mishra, Jvalaprasad. *Jatibhaskar* [Illuminations on Jati]. Bombay: Khemraj Shri Krishnadas, 1917.

———. *Jati Nirnay* [Jati Rulings]. Bombay: Lakshmi Venkateshwar Press, 1901.

Prapann, Vijay Raghav. "Acharya-Parampara ke Apratiya Purush: Swami Bhagavadacharya" [The Skeptic of the Acharya Parampara: Swami Bhagavadacharya]. *ShriMath Smarika* [A Memorial of the ShriMath], 251–258. Varanasi: Shri Math, Panchganga Ghat, 1989.

———. "Ramanand Sampraday men Ujjain Kumbh—Ek Adhyayan" [The Ramanandi Sampraday at the Ujjain Kumbh—an Investigation]. In *Amrit Kalash* [The Nectar Jar], 13–17. Varanasi: Shri Math, Panchganga Ghat, 1992.

Ram, Karu. *Ramani Nirnay* [Rules of the Ramanis]. Gaya: Magadha Shubhanker Press, 1906.

Rameshwaranandacharya, Swami. *Vedarthchandrika* [Illuminations on the Vedas]. Porbandar, Gujarat: ShriRamanandacharyaPith, 1987.

Ray, Nauvat. *Kahar Jati aur Varnavyavastha* [The Kahar Jati and the Varna System]. Firozabad, Agra: Fakirchand, 1920.

Rohan, Kedarnath-ji. "Yadavon ka Itihas" [The History of the Yadavas]. *Yadavesh* 1, no. 2 (1935–36): 3–11.

Sahay, Shivanandan. *Shri Sitaramsharan Bhagvan Prasad-ji ki Sachitra Jivani* [An Illustrated Biography of Shri Sitaramsharan Bhagvan Prasad]. Patna: Khadgavilas Press, 1908.

Sahay, Shivpujan. *Hindi Sahitya aur Bihar* [Hindi literature and Bihar]. Four volumes. Patna: Bihar Rashtrabhasha Parishad, 1960–1984.

Saraswati, Abhayananda (Swami). *Kurmi Kshatriya Itihas* [The History of the Kurmi Kshatriyas]. Banaras: Shivaramsinha, 1927.

Saraswati, Sahajanand (Swami). *Gita Hriday* [The Heart of the Gita]. Allahabad: Kitab Mahal, 1948.

———. *Mera Jivan Sangharsh* [My Life Struggle]. New edition. New Delhi: People's Publishing House, 1985; first edition, Bihta (Patna): Shri Sitaram Ashram, 1952.

Sharma, Kailash Chandra. *Bhaktamal aur Hindi Kavya mem Uski Parampara* [The Bhaktamal and its Tradition in Hindi Poetry]. Rohtak: Manthan Publications, 1983.

Sharma, Sachchidanand. *Udasi Sampraday aur Kavi Sant Rena* [The Udasi Sampraday and the Poet-Saint Rena]. Dehradun: Sahitya Sadan, 1967.

"Shri Ramanand Sampraday ke Vartman-Vidvan" [Contemporary Scholars of the Ramanandi Sampraday]. In Das, ed., *Ramanand-Granth-Mala ka Shri Ramanandank*, 61–63.

Sinha, Bhagwati Prasad. *Ram Bhakti men Rasika Sampraday* [The Rasika Sampraday in Ram Worship]. Balrampur: Avadh Sahitya Mandir, 1957.

Sinha, Chaudhari Dipnarayan. *Kurmi Kshatriya Nirnay* [Rulings of Kurmi Kshatriyas]. Chunar: n.p., 1937–38.

Sinha, Kunwar Chheda. *Kshatriya aur Kritram Kshatriya*. Agra: Rajput Anglo-Oriental Press, 1907. Published simultaneously in English as *Kshatriyas and Would-Be Kshatriyas,* translated by Kunwar Rupa Sinha.

Sinha, Nirgun ("Khali"). *Varnashram Vichar-Dhara* [Varnashram Ideology]. Maner, Patna: Nirgun Singh "Khali," 1938–39.

Sitaram (Lala). *Ayodhya ka Itihas* [History of Ayodhya]. Prayag (Allahabad): Hindustani Academy, 1932.

Swami Bhagavadacharya Shatabdi Smriti Granth [A Book Commemorating a Century of Swami Bhagavadacharya]. Ahmedabad: Shrichandanbahin "Sanskrit bhushana," 1971.

Upadhyay, Baldev. *Vaishnava Sampradayom ka Sahitya aur Siddhant* [The Literature and Philosophy of Vaishnava Sampraday (plural)]. Varanasi: Chaukhamba Amarbharati Prakashan, 1978.

Varmma, Raghunandan Prasad Sinha. *Kanyakubja Kshatriyotpatti Bhushan* [The Noble Origins of the Kanyakubja Kshatriyas]. Gaya: R.P.S. Varmma, 1924.

Yadav, Baijnath Prasad. *Ahir-Jati ki Niyamavali* [A List of the Rules of the Ahir Jati]. Varanasi: B. P. Yadav, 1928.

Yadav, Dilip Sinha. *Ahir Itihas ki Jhalak* [A Glimpse into the History of the Ahirs]. Lucknow, Allahabad, and Etawah: Krishna Press, 1914–1915.

Yadav, Jamuna Prashad. *Ahiroddhar, arthat Ahir Kul Sudhar* [Ahiroddhar, or the Reform of the Ahir Line]. Jhansi: Jamuna Prashad Yadav Ahir, 1927.

Yadav, Nathuni Prasad. *Jatiya Sandesh* [Jati Message]. Darbhanga: Swami Nathu Bhagat Yadav, 1921.

Yadav, Ramavatar. "Yatindra-stav" [Hymn to a Great Sadhu]. In Das, ed., *Ramanand-Granth-Mala ka Shri Ramanandank*, 1.

Yadav, Shivnath Prasad. "Akhil Bharat Yadav Mahasabha ka Itihas" [The History of the All-India Yadav Mahasabha]. *Yadavesh* 1, no. 2 (1935–36): 17–20.

Yadavesh [a quarterly newsletter of the yadav-kshatriya jati]. First published from Banaras in 1935–1936.

ENGLISH

Ahmad, Imtiaz. "Caste Mobility Movements in North India." *Indian Economic and Social History Review* 7, no. 2 (1971): 164–91.

Amin, Shahid. "Gandhi as Mahatma: Gorakhpur District, Eastern UP, 1921–2." In *Subaltern Studies: Writings on South Asian History and Society*, edited by Ranajit Guha, 3:1–61. Delhi: Oxford University Press, 1984.

Appadurai, A. "Is Homo Hierarchicus?" Review article of E. Valentine

Daniel, *Fluid Signs: Being a Person the Tamil Way* (Berkeley and Los Angeles: University of California Press, 1984); R. S. Khare, *The Untouchable as Himself: Ideology, Identity and Pragmatism among the Lucknow Chamars* (Cambridge: Cambridge University Press, 1984); and Ashis Nandy, *The Intimate Enemy: Loss and Recovery of Self Under Colonialism* (Delhi: Oxford University Press, 1983). *American Ethnologist* 13, no. 4 (November 1986): 745–61.

———. *Worship and Conflict under Colonial Rule: A South Indian Case.* Cambridge: Cambridge University Press, 1981.

Bagchi, Amiya Kumar. "Deindustrialisation in Gangetic Bihar, 1807–1901." In *Essays in Honour of Professor Susobhan Chandra Sarkar*, edited by Barun De, 499–522. New Delhi: People's Publishing House, 1976.

———. "Response to Marika Vicziany." *Indian Economic and Social History Review* 16, no. 2 (1979): 144–46.

Bahura, Gopal Narayan, and Chandramani Singh. *Catalogue of Historical Documents in the Kapad Dwara [royal warehouse], Jaipur.* Amber-Jaipur: Jaigarh Public Charitable Trust, 1988.

Bak, János M., and Gerhard Beneke, eds. *Religion and Rural Revolt.* Manchester: Manchester University Press, 1984.

Bakker, Hans. *Ayodhya.* Groningen: Egbert Forsten, 1986.

Barnett, Richard. "Images of India from Alexander to Attenborough." Jefferson Society lecture, University of Virginia, 16 September 1983.

———. *North India between Empires: Awadh, the Mughals, and the British, 1720–1801.* Berkeley and Los Angeles: University of California Press, 1980.

Basu, Durga Das. *Introduction to the Constitution of India.* New Delhi: Prentice-Hall, 1982.

Bayly, Christopher A. *Indian Society and the Making of the British Empire.* Cambridge: Cambridge University Press, 1988.

———. *The Local Roots of Indian Politics: Allahabad, 1880–1920.* Oxford: Clarendon Press, 1975.

———. "Rallying Round the Subaltern." Review article of *Subaltern Studies: Writings on South Asian History and Society*, vols. 1–4. edited by Ranajit Guha (Delhi: Oxford University Press, 1982–1985). *Journal of Peasant Studies* 16, no. 1 (October 1988): 110–20.

———. *Rulers, Townsmen and Bazaars: North Indian Society in the Age of British Expansion, 1770–1870.* Cambridge: Cambridge University Press, 1983.

Beneke, Gerhard, and János M. Bak, eds. *Religion and Rural Revolt.* Manchester: Manchester University Press, 1984.

Bengal District Gazetteers. By L. S. S. O'Malley. Calcutta: Bengal Secretariat Book Depot. Bhagalpur (1911), Champaran (1907), Darbhanga (1907), Gaya (1906), Monghyr (1909), Muzaffarpur (1907), Patna (1907), Purnea (1911), Saran (1908), and Shahabad (1906).

Bhandarkar, R. G. *Vaishnavism, Saivism, and Minor Religious Systems.* Strassburg: J. K. Trubner, 1913; reprint, New Delhi: Asian Educational Services, 1983, 1987.

Bhattacharya, Jogendra Nath. *Hindu Castes and Sects: An Exposition of the*

Origin of the Hindu Caste System and the Bearing of the Sects toward Each Other and toward Other Religious Systems. Calcutta: Thacker, Spink, 1896.

Blair, Harry W. "Rising Kulaks and Backward Classes in Bihar: Social Change in the Late 1970s." *Economic and Political Weekly* 15, no. 2 (12 January 1980) 64–74.

Blumhardt, J. F. *Catalogue of the Hindi, Panjabi and Hindustani Manuscripts in the Library of the British Museum.* London: British Museum, 1899.

———. *Catalogue of the Library of the India Office Library.* Vol. 2, part 3: *Hindi, Panjabi, Pashtu, and Sindhi Books.* London: India Office Library, 1902.

Broughton, Thomas D. *Letters Written in a Maratha Camp in 1809.* London: J. Murray, 1813.

Brown, Peter. "The Rise and Function of the Holy Man in Late Antiquity." In *Society and the Holy in Late Antiquity.* Berkeley and Los Angeles: University of California Press, 1982.

Buchanan (later Hamilton), Francis. *An Account of the District of Bhagalpur in 1810–1811.* Patna: Bihar and Orissa Research Society, 1939; no reprint edition has been issued.

———. *An Account of the Districts of Bihar and Patna in 1811–1812.* 2 vols. Patna: Bihar and Orissa Research Society, 1934; reprint, New Delhi: Usha Jain, 1986.

———. *An Account of the District of Purnea in 1809–1810.* Patna: Bihar and Orissa Research Society, 1928; reprint, New Delhi: Usha Jain, 1986.

———. *An Account of the District of Shahabad in 1812–1813.* Patna: Bihar and Orissa Research Society, 1934; reprint, New Delhi: Usha Jain, 1986.

———. *Genealogies of the Hindus, Extracted from their Sacred Writings.* Edinburgh: W. Aitken, 1819.

———. *Journal of Francis Buchanan (afterwards Hamilton) kept during the Survey of the Districts of Patna and Gaya in 1811–1812.* Edited with notes and introduction by V. H. Jackson. Patna: Government Printing, Bihar and Orissa, 1925.

———. *Journal of Francis Buchanan kept during the Survey of the District of Shahabad in 1812–1813.* Edited with notes and an introduction by C. E. A. W. Oldham. Patna: Government Printing, Bihar and Orissa, 1926.

Burghart, Richard. "The Founding of the Ramanandi Sect." *Ethnohistory* 25, no. 2 (Spring 1978): 121–39.

———. "The History of Janakpurdham: A Study of Asceticism and the Hindu Polity." Ph.D. diss., School of Oriental and African Studies, University of London, 1978.

———. "Renunciation in the Religious Traditions of South Asia." *Man*, n.s., 18, no. 4 (December 1983): 635–53.

Carroll, Lucy. "Caste, Community and Caste(s) Association: A Note on the Organization of the Kayastha Conference and the Definition of a Kayastha Community." *Contributions to Asian Studies* 10 (1977): 3–24.

———. "Colonial Perceptions of Indian Society and the Emergence of Caste Associations." *Journal of Asian Studies* 37, no. 2 (1978): 233–50.

————. "The Temperance Movement in India: Politics and Social Reform."
   Modern Asian Studies 10, no. 3 (1976): 417–47.
Casey, Edward S. *Remembering: A Phenomenological Study*. Bloomington:
   Indiana University Press, 1987.
Chartier, Roger. *The Cultural Uses of Print in Early Modern France*. Trans-
   lated by Lydia G. Cochrane. Princeton: Princeton University Press, 1987.
Chatterjee, Partha. "Caste and Subaltern Consciousness." In *Subaltern
   Studies: Writings on South Asian History and Society*, edited by Ranajit
   Guha, 6:169–209. Delhi: Oxford University Press, 1992.
————. *The Nation and Its Fragments: Colonial and Postcolonial Histories*.
   Delhi: Oxford University Press, 1994
Chatterjee, Suranjan. "New Reflections on the Sannyasi, Fakir and Peasants'
   War." *Economic and Political Weekly* 19, no. 4 (28 January 1984):
   PE2–PE13.
Chattopadhyay, Bankim Chandra. *Anandamatha*. Originally published in
   1882 in *Bangadarshan*, Bankim's literary monthly. Translated into English
   as *The Abbey of Bliss* by Nares Chandra Sen-Gupta (Calcutta: P. M. Neogi,
   1906); 1941 translation by Basanta Koomar Roy (New Delhi: Orient
   Paperbacks, 1992).
Cohn, Bernard S. *An Anthropologist among the Historians and Other Essays*.
   Delhi: Oxford University Press, 1990.
————. "The Census, Social Structure and Objectification in South Asia." In
   An Anthropologist among the Historians and Other Essays. Delhi: Oxford
   University Press, 1990.
————. "The Role of the Gosains in the Economy of Eighteenth and
   Nineteenth-Century Upper India." *Indian Economic and Social History
   Review* 1, no. 4 (1964): 175–82.
Crooke, William. *The Popular Religion and Folklore of Northern India*. 2 vols.
   2d ed., revised and illustrated. London: A. Constable, 1896. Fourth
   reprint, New Delhi: Munshiram Manoharlal, 1978. (Originally published
   in 1894 as *An Introduction to the Popular Religion and Folklore of North-
   ern India*.)
Dasgupta, Atis K. *The Fakir and Sannyasi Uprisings*. Calcutta: K. P. Bagchi,
   1992.
De, Sushil Kumar. *Vaishnava Faith and Movement in Bengal*. 1942; 2d ed.,
   Calcutta: K. L. Mukhopadhyaya, 1961.
Dirks, Nicholas B. "Castes of Mind." *Representations* 37 (Winter 1992):
   56–78.
Dumont, Louis. *Homo Hierarchicus: The Caste System and its Implications*.
   Translated by Mark Sainsbury, Louis Dumont, and Basia Gulati. Chicago:
   University of Chicago Press, 1980.
Duncan, Jonathan. "An Account of Two Fakeers, with their Portraits."
   Asiatic Researches 5 (1808).
Dushkin, Lelah. "Scheduled Caste Politics." In *The Untouchables in Contem-
   porary India*, edited by J. Michael Mahar, 165–226. Tucson: University of
   Arizona Press, 1972.

Eaton, Richard. "Approaches to the Study of Conversion to Islam in India."
In *Approaches to Islam: Religious Studies*, edited by R. C. Martin. 107–23.
Tucson: University of Arizona Press, 1985.

———. *The Rise of Islam and the Bengal Frontier, 1204–1760*. Berkeley and
Los Angeles: University of California Press, 1993

Elliot, Henry Miers. *Memoirs of the History, Folklore, and Distribution of the
Races of the North Western Provinces of India*. Two volumes. London:
Trubner, 1869; reprint ed., under the title, *Encyclopaedia of Caste,
Customs, Rites and Superstitions of the Races of Northern India*, Delhi:
Sumit, 1985. Compiled in 1844 as a supplement to Horace Hayman
Wilson, *Glossary of Judicial and Revenue Terms and of Useful Words
Occuring in Official Documents Relating to the Administration of British
India*. London: Wm. H. Allen & Co., 1855; reprint ed., Delhi: Munshi-
ram Manoharlal, 1968.

Embree, Ainslee T., ed. *1857 in India: Mutiny or War of Independence?*
Boston: D. C. Heath, 1963.

Farquhar, J. N. "The Fighting Ascetics of India." *Bulletin of the John Rylands
Library* 9 (1925): 431–52.

———. "The Historical Position of Ramanand." *Journal of the Royal Asiatic
Society*, April 1920, 185–92; July 1922, 373–80.

———. "The Organization of the Sannyasis of the Vedanta." *Journal of the
Royal Asiatic Society*, July 1925, 479–86.

Fox, Richard G. *Lions of the Punjab: Culture in the Making*. Berkeley and Los
Angeles: University of California Press, 1985.

Freitag, Sandria B. *Collective Action and Community: Public Arenas and the
Emergence of Communalism in North India*. Berkeley and Los Angeles:
University of California Press, 1989.

———. Introduction to part 1: "Performance and Patronage." In Freitag,
ed., *Culture and Power in Banaras: Community, Performance, and
Environment, 1800–1980*, 25–33.

———, ed. *Culture and Power in Banaras: Community, Performance, and
Environment, 1800–1980*. Berkeley and Los Angeles: University of
California Press, 1989.

Galanter, Marc. "The Abolition of Disabilities—Untouchability and the
Law." In *The Untouchables in Contemporary India*, edited by J. Michael
Mahar, 227–314. Tucson: University of Arizona Press, 1972.

———. "Who Are the Other Backward Classes? An Introduction to a
Constitutional Puzzle." *Economic and Political Weekly* 13, nos. 43 and 44
(28 October 1978) 1812–28.

Ghosh, Jamini Mohan. *Sanyasi and Fakir Raiders in Bengal*. Calcutta: Bengal
Secretariat Book Depot, 1930.

Ghurye, G. S. *Indian Sadhus*. 1953; 2d rev. ed. Bombay: Popular Prakashan,
1964.

Giri, Sadananda (Swami). *Society and Sannyasin (A History of the Dasnami
Sannyasins)*. Rishikesh: Swami Sadananda Giri, 1976.

Gold, Daniel. *The Lord as Guru: Hindi Sants in the Northern Indian Tradition*. New York: Oxford University Press, 1987.

Gopal, Sarvepalli, ed. *Anatomy of a Confrontation: The Babri Masjid-Ramjanmabhumi Issue*. New Delhi: Viking, 1991.

Gordon, Stewart. "Scarf and Sword: Thugs, Marauders, and State-Formation in Eighteenth-Century Malwa." *Indian Economic and Social History Review* 6, no. 4 (1969): 403–29.

Government of India. Backward Classes Commission. *Report*. New Delhi: Manager of Publications, 1956.

Government of India. *Census of India, 1891*. Vol. 5: *The Lower Provinces of Bengal and their Feudatories*. Calcutta: Bengal Secretariat Press, 1893.

———. *Census of India, 1901*. Vol. 1: *India*. Calcutta: Office of the Superintendent of Government Printing, 1903. (This volume contains H. H. Risley, "Ethnographic Appendices.")

———. *Census of India, 1901*. Vol. 6: *The Lower Provinces of Bengal and their Feudatories*. Part 1: "Report," by E. A. Gait. Calcutta: Bengal Secretariat Press, 1902.

———. *Census of India, 1901*. Vol. 6-A: *The Lower Provinces of Bengal and their Feudatories*. Part 2: "Imperial Tables." Calcutta: Bengal Secretariat Press, 1902.

———. *Census of India, 1901*. Vol. 6-B: *The Lower Provinces of Bengal and their Feudatories*. Part 3: "Provincial Tables." Calcutta: Bengal Secretariat Press, 1902.

———. *Census of India, 1901*. Vol. 16-A: *North-West Provinces and Oudh*. Part 2: "Imperial Tables." Allahabad: Superintendent, Government Press, 1902.

———. *Census of India, 1911*. Vol. 5: *Bihar and Orissa*. Part 1: "Report" by E. A. Gait. Calcutta: Bengal Secretariat Book Depot, 1913. (This volume contains remarks by L. S. S. O'Malley.)

———. *Census of India, 1911*. Vol. 5: *Bihar and Orissa*. Part 3: "Imperial Tables." Calcutta: Bengal Secretariat Book Depot, 1913.

———. *Census of India, 1911*. Vol. 15: *United Provinces of Agra and Oudh*. Part 1: "Report." Allahabad: Government Press, 1912.

———. *Census of India, 1911*. Vol. 15: *United Provinces of Agra and Oudh*, part 1: "Report." Allahabad: Government Press, 1912.

———. *Census of India, 1931*. Vol. 1: *India*. Part 4: "Social and Linguistic Maps." Simla: Government of India, 1933.

———. *Report on the Census of Bengal, 1872*. Calcutta: Bengal Secretariat Press, 1872.

Grierson, George A. *Bihar Peasant Life, being a Discursive Catalogue of the Surrounding of the People of that Province*. 1885; reprint, Delhi: Cosmo Publications, 1975.

———. "Gleanings from the Bhakta-Mala." *Journal of the Royal Asiatic Society*, 1909, 607–44.

———"Ramanandis, Ramawats." In *Encyclopedia of Religion and Ethics*, edited by James Hastings. New York: Charles Scribner and Sons, 1921.

Growse, F. S. *Mathura: A District Memoir*. 1880; 2d ed., revised and enlarged, Allahabad: Northwest Provinces and Oudh Government Press, 1883.

Guha, Ranajit. *Elementary Aspects of Peasant Insurgency in Colonial India.*
Delhi: Oxford University Press, 1983.

———. "On Some Aspects of the Historiography of Colonial India."
Introduction to *Subaltern Studies: Writings on South Asian History and
Society*, edited by Ranajit Guha, 1:1–8. Delhi: Oxford University Press,
1982.

Gupta, R. D. "The *Bhaktirasabodhini* of Priya Dasa," *Le Muséon* 81, no. 3–4
(1968): 547–62.

———. "Priya Dasa, Author of the *Bhaktirasabodhini.*" *Bulletin of the School
of Oriental and African Studies* 32, no. 1 (1969): 57–70.

Haberman, David L. *Acting as a Way of Salvation: A Study of Raganuga
Bhakti Sadhana.* New York: Oxford University Press, 1988.

Hagen, James R. "Indigenous Society, the Political Economy, and Colonial
Education in Patna District: A History of Social Change from 1811 to
1951 in Gangetic North India." Ph.D. dissertation, University of Virginia,
1981.

———, and Anand A Yang. "Local Sources for the Study of Rural India: The
'Village Notes' of Bihar." *Indian Economic and Social History Review* 13,
no. 1 (January-March 1976): 75–84.

Hardgrave, Robert L., Jr. *The Nadars of Tamilnad: The Political Culture of a
Community in Change.* Berkeley and Los Angeles: University of California
Press, 1969.

Harlan, Lindsey. *Religion and Rajput Women: The Ethic of Protection in
Contemporary Narratives.* Berkeley and Los Angeles: University of
California Press, 1992.

Hauser, Walter. "The Bihar Provincial Kisan Sabha, 1929–1949: A Study of
an Indian Peasant Movement." Ph.D. dissertation, University of Chicago,
1961.

———. "Dynamics of Social Ranking and Political Power among Emerging
Caste Groups in Bihar." Paper presented at a panel on "Caste and Politics
in Bihar," annual meeting of the Association for Asian Studies, Chicago.
March 20–22, 1967.

———. *The Politics of Peasant Activism in Twentieth-Century India.* Delhi:
Oxford University Press, forthcoming.

———. "Swami Sahajanand and the Politics of Social Reform." Paper
presented at the annual meeting of the Association for Asian Studies,
Washington, D.C. 4 April 1992.

———, ed. *Sahajanand on Agricultural Labor and the Rural Poor.* New
Delhi: Manohar, 1994.

Hawley, John Stratton. "The Sant in Sur Das." In Schomer and McLeod,
eds., *The Sants: Studies in a Devotional Tradition of India*, 191–211.

———, and Mark Juergensmeyer, eds. and trans. *Songs of the Saints of India*
New York: Oxford University Press, 1988.

Hein, Norvin. "The Ram Lila." In *Traditional India: Structure and Change*,
edited by Milton Singer, 73–98. Philadelphia: American Folklore Society,
1959.

Hess, Linda, and Shukdev Singh, ed. and trans. *The Bijak of Kabir.* First

Indian edition. Delhi: Motilal Banarsidass, 1986.

———, and Richard Schechner. "The Ramlila of Ramnagar." *Drama Review* 21, no. 3 (1977): 51–82.

Hill, Christopher V. "History in Motion: The Social Ecology of Purnia District, 1770–1960." Ph.D. diss., University of Virginia, 1987.

———. "Militant Agrarian Unrest in North India: Perspective and Ideology." Review of *India Waits* by Jan Myrdal (Madras: Sangam Books, 1980) and *Report from the Flaming Fields of Bihar* (Calcutta: Prabodh Bhattacharya, 1986). *Peasant Studies* 15, no. 4 (Summer 1988): 297–305.

Hunter, W. W. *Statistical Account of Bengal*. Vol. 12: *Gaya and Shahabad Districts*. 1875–77; reprint, Delhi: D.K. Publishing House, 1973.

Inden, Ronald. *Imagining India*. Oxford: Basil Blackwell, 1990.

Jha, Hetukar. "Lower-Caste Peasants and Upper-Caste Zamindars in Bihar (1921–1925): An Analysis of Sanskritization and Contradiction between the Two Groups." *Indian Economic and Social History Review* 14, no. 4 (1977): 523–49.

Jones, Kenneth W. *Arya Dharm: Hindu Consciousness in Nineteenth-Century Punjab*. Berkeley and Los Angeles: University of California Press, 1976.

———. *Socio-Religious Reform Movements in British India*. Cambridge: Cambridge University Press, 1989.

Jordan, Winthrop. *The White Man's Burden: Historical Origins of Racism in the United States*. New York: Oxford University Press, 1974.

Joshi, Rama, and Joanna Liddle. *Daughters of Independence: Gender, Caste, and Class in India*. London: Zed, 1986.

Kapur, Rajiv A. *Sikh Separatism: The Politics of Faith*. London: Allen and Unwin, 1986.

Kaye, George R., and Edward H. Johnston. *A Catalogue of Manuscripts in European Languages*. Volume 2, part 2: *Minor Collections and Miscellaneous Manuscripts*. Section 1. London: India Office, 1937.

Khare, R. S. "The One and the Many: Varna and Jati as a Symbolic Classification." In *American Studies in the Anthropology of India*, edited by Sylvia Vatuk, 35–61. New Delhi: Manohar, 1978.

———. *The Untouchable as Himself: Ideology, Identity, and Pragmatism among the Lucknow Chamars*. Cambridge: Cambridge University Press, 1984.

King, Christopher R. *One Language, Two Scripts: The Hindi Movement in Nineteenth-Century North India*. Delhi: Oxford University Press, 1994.

Kitts, Eustace J. *A Compendium of the Castes and Tribes found in India: Compiled from the 1881 Census Reports for the Various Provinces, excluding Burmah and Native States of the Empire*. Bombay: Education Society Press, 1885.

Kolff, Dirk H. A. *Naukar, Rajput and Sepoy: The Ethnohistory of the Military Labour Market in Hindustan, 1450–1850*. Cambridge: Cambridge University Press, 1990.

———. "Sanyasi Trader-Soldiers." *Indian Economic and Social History Review* 8 (1971): 213–20.

Kopf, David. "Hermeneutics versus History." *Journal of Asian Studies* 39,

no. 3 (May 1980): 495–506. This essay is part of a review symposium on
Edward Said, *Orientalism* (New York: Pantheon Books, 1978).

Kumar, Kapil. "The Ramacharitamanas as a Radical Text: Baba Ram Chandra
in Oudh, 1920–1950." In *Social Transformation and Creative Imagination*, edited by Sudhir Chandra, 311–33. New Delhi: Allied, 1984.

Kumar, Nita. *The Artisans of Banaras: Popular Culture and Identity,
1880–1986*. Princeton: Princeton University Press, 1988.

The Laws of Manu. Introduction and notes by Wendy Doniger. Translated by
Doniger and Brian K. Smith. New York: Penguin, 1991.

Leach, Edmund. "Caste, Class and Slavery: The Taxonomic Problem." In
Caste and Race: Comparative Approaches, edited by Anthony de Reuck
and Julie Knight, 5–16. Boston: Little, Brown, 1967.

Leonard, Karen. *The Social History of an Indian Caste: The Kayasths of
Hyderabad*. Berkeley and Los Angeles: University of California Press,
1978.

Lewis, Bernard. *History—Remembered, Recovered, Invented*. Princeton:
Princeton University Press, 1975.

Lorenzen, David. "Traditions of Non-Caste Hinduism: The Kabir Panth."
Contributions to Indian Sociology, n.s., 21, no. 2 (1987): 263–83.

———. "Warrior Ascetics in Indian History." *Journal of the American
Oriental Society* 98, no. 1 (1978): 61–75.

Ludden, David. *Peasant History in South India*. Princeton: Princeton
University Press, 1985.

Lutgendorf, Philip. *The Life of a Text: Performing the "Ramcaritmanas" of
Tulsidas*. Berkeley and Los Angeles: University of California Press, 1991.

———. "Ram's Story in Shiva's City: Public Arenas and Private Patronage."
In Freitag, ed., *Culture and Power in Banaras: Community, Performance,
and Environment, 1800–1980*, 34–61.

Magagna, Victor V. *Communities of Grain: Rural Rebellion in Comparative
Perspective*. Ithaca: Cornell University Press, 1991.

Martin, Robert Montgomery. *The History, Antiquities, Topography, and
Statistics of Eastern India: Comprising the Districts of Behar, Shahabad,
Bhagalpoor, Goruckpoor, Dinajpoor, Purniya, Rungpoor, and Assam, in
relation to their geology, mineralogy, botany, agriculture, commerce, manufactures, fine arts, population, religion, education, statistics, etc.* Vol. 1:
Behar and Shahabad. Vol. 2: *Bhagulpoor, Goruckpoor, and Dinajepoor.* Vol.
3: *Puraniya, Rongopoor and Assam.* London: Wm. H. Allen, 1838.

McLane, John. *Indian Nationalism and the Early Congress*. Princeton:
Princeton University Press, 1977.

McLeod, William H. *The Evolution of the Sikh Community: Five Essays*. Delhi:
Oxford University Press, 1975.

———. *The Sikhs: History, Religion, and Society*. New York: Columbia
University Press, 1989.

———, ed. and trans. *Textual Sources for the Study of Sikhism*. Manchester:
Manchester University Press, 1984.

Mintz, Sidney. "A Note on the Definition of Peasants." *Journal of Peasant
Studies* 1, no. 1 (1973): 91–106.

Mukherjee, Kalyan, and Rajendra Singh Yadav. *Bhojpur: Naxalism in the Plains of Bihar*. New Delhi: Radhakrishna Prakashan, 1980.

Mukherjee, S. N. *Sir William Jones: A Study in Eighteenth-Century British Attitudes to India*. Cambridge: Cambridge University Press, 1968.

Müller, Max. *India: What Can It Teach Us?* 1919; reprint, New Delhi: Munshiram Manoharlal, 1991.

Nandy, Ashis. *The Intimate Enemy: Loss and Recovery of Self under Colonialism*. New Delhi: Oxford University Press, 1983.

Nehru, Jawaharlal. *The Discovery of India*. New York: John Day, 1946.

Nevill, H. R. *District Gazetteers of the United Provinces and Oudh*. Vol. 30: *Ballia*. Allahabad: Government Press, 1907.

O'Hanlon, Rosalind. *Caste, Conflict, and Ideology: Mahatma Jotirao Phule and Low-Caste Protest in Nineteenth-Century Western India*. Cambridge: Cambridge University Press, 1985.

Omvedt, Gail. *Cultural Revolt in a Colonial Society: The Non-Brahman Movement in Western India, 1873 to 1930*. Bombay: Scientific Socialist Education Trust, 1976.

Orr, W. G. "Armed Religious Ascetics in Northern India." *The Bulletin of the John Rylands Library* 25 (1940): 81–100.

Pandey, Gyanendra. *The Construction of Communalism in Colonial North India*. Delhi: Oxford University Press, 1990.

———. "Peasant Revolt and Indian Nationalism: The Peasant Movement in Awadh, 1919–1922." In *Subaltern Studies: Writings on South Asian History and Society*, edited by Ranajit Guha, 1:143–97. Delhi: Oxford University Press, 1982.

———. "Rallying Round the Cow: Sectarian Strife in the Bhojpuri Region, c. 1888–1917." In *Subaltern Studies: Writings on South Asian History and Society*, edited by Ranajit Guha, 2:60–129. Delhi: Oxford University Press, 1983.

Panikkar, K. N. "Historical Overview." In *Anatomy of a Confrontation: The Babri Masjid-Ramjanmabhumi Issue*, edited by Sarvepalli Gopal, 22–37. New Delhi: Penguin, 1991.

Parkash, Ved. *The Sikhs in Bihar*. Patna: Janaki Prakashan, 1981.

Pinney, Christopher. "Colonial Anthropology in the 'Laboratory of Mankind.'" In *An Illustrated History of Modern India, 1600–1947*, edited by C. A. Bayly, 252–63. London: National Portrait Gallery, 1990.

Pocock, D. F. *Kanbi and Patidar: A Study of the Patidar Community of Gujarat*. Oxford: Oxford University Press, 1972.

Rao, M. S. A. "Yadava Movement." Parts 1 and 2. In *Social Movements and Social Transformation*, 123–203. New Delhi: Manohar, 1987.

Rao, V. Narayana, D. Shulman, and S. Subrahmanyam. *Symbols of Substance: Court and State in Nayaka Period Tamilnadu*. Delhi: Oxford University Press, 1992.

Raychaudhuri, Tapan. *Europe Reconsidered: Perceptions of the West in Nineteenth-Century Bengal*. Delhi: Oxford University Press, 1988.

Report from the Flaming Field of Bihar: A CPI (ML) Document. Introduction by Vinod Mishra. Calcutta: Prabodh Bhattacharya, 1986.

Richards, John. "The Indian Empire and Peasant Production of Opium in the Nineteenth Century." *Modern Asian Studies* 15 (February 1981): 59–82.

Risley, Herbert Hope. *The People of India.* Calcutta: Thacker, Spink, 1915.

———. *The Tribes and Castes of Bengal.* 2 vols. Calcutta: Bengal Secretariat Press, 1891; reprint, Calcutta: Firma Mukhopadhyay, 1981.

Robb, Peter G. "Officials and Non-officials as Leaders in Popular Agitations: Shahabad 1917 and Other Conspiracies." In *Leadership in South Asia,* edited by B. N. Pandey, 179–210. New Delhi: Vikas, 1977.

Rose, H. A. "Udasis." In *Encyclopedia of Religion and Ethics,* edited by James Hastings. New York: Charles Scribner and Sons, 1921.

Roy, A. K. *History of the Jaipur City.* New Delhi: Manohar, 1978.

Rudolph, Suzanne H., and Lloyd I. Rudolph. *Gandhi: The Traditional Roots of Charisma.* 1967; 2d ed., Chicago: University of Chicago Press, 1983.

Said, Edward. *Orientalism.* New York: Pantheon, 1978.

Sarkar, Sumit. "The Conditions and Nature of Subaltern Militancy: Bengal from Swadeshi to Non-Co-operation, c. 1905–22." In *Subaltern Studies: Writings on South Asian History and Society,* edited by Ranajit Guha, 3:271–320. Delhi: Oxford University Press, 1984.

Sarkar, Sushobhan C. "A Note on Puran Giri Gosain." *Bengal Past & Present* 43 (April–June 1932): 83–87.

Sastri, K. A. Nilakanta. *A History of South India from Prehistoric Times to the Fall of Vijayanagar.* 3d ed. Madras: Oxford University Press, 1966.

Schomer, Karine. "The Sant Tradition in Perspective." Introduction to Schomer and McLeod, eds., *The Sants: Studies in a Devotional Tradition of India,* 1–17.

———, and W. H. McLeod, eds. *The Sants: Studies in a Devotional Tradition of India.* Delhi: Motilal Banarsidas, 1987.

Scott, James. *The Moral Economy of the Peasant: Rebellion and Subsistence in Southeast Asia.* New Haven: Yale University Press, 1976.

———. *Weapons of the Weak: Everyday Forms of Peasant Resistance.* New Haven: Yale University Press, 1985.

Shanin, Teodor. "Peasantry: Delineation of a Sociological Concept and a Field of Study." *European Journal of Sociology* 12 (1971): 289–300.

Shastri, R. M. "A Comprehensive Study into the Origins and Status of the Kayasthas." *Man in India* 2 (1931): 116–59.

Siddiqi, Majid. *Agrarian Unrest in Northern India.* New Delhi: Vikas, 1978.

Singh, Chandramani, and Gopal Narayan Bahura. *Catalogue of Historical Documents in the Kapad Dwara [royal warehouse], Jaipur.* Amber-Jaipur: Jaigarh Public Charitable Trust, 1988.

Singh, Kushwant. *A History of the Sikhs.* 2 vols. Princeton: Princeton University Press, 1963.

Sinha, Surajit, and Baidyanath Saraswati. *Ascetics of Kashi: An Anthropological Exploration.* Varanasi: N. K. Bose Memorial Foundation, 1978.

Sleeman, William Henry (Colonel). *A Report on the System of Megpunnaism or, The Murder of Indigent Parents for their Young Children (who are sold as Slaves) as it prevails in the Delhi Territories, and the Native States of Rajpootana, Ulwar, and Bhurtpore.* Calcutta: Serampore, 1839.

Srinivas, M. N. *Caste in Modern India and Other Essays.* Bombay: Asia Publishing House, 1962.

———. "The Changing Position of Indian Women." *Man,* n.s., 12 (1977): 221–38.

———. "Mobility in the Caste System." In *Structure and Change in Indian Society,* edited by Milton Singer and Bernard Cohn, 189–200. Chicago: Aldine Publishing Co., 1968.

———. *Religion and Society among the Coorgs of South India.* Oxford: Oxford University Press, 1952.

Stahl, J. F. "Sanskrit and Sanskritization." *Journal of Asian Studies* 22, no. 3 (May 1963): 261–75.

Stein, Burton. "Social Mobility and Medieval South Indian Sects." In *Social Mobility in the Caste System in India,* edited by J. Silverberg, 78–94. The Hague: Mouton, 1968.

Tambiah, S. J. "From Varna to Caste through Mixed Unions." In *The Character of Kinship,* edited by Jack Goody, 191–229. Cambridge: Cambridge University Press, 1973.

Thapar, Romila. "Genealogy as a Source of Social History," *Indian Historical Review* 2, no. 2 (January 1976): 259–81.

———. "The Image of the Barbarian in Early India," *Comparative Studies in Society and History* 13, no. 4 (1971): 408–36; reprinted in his *Ancient Indian Social History.* 2d ed. 1978; New Delhi: Orient Longman, 1984, 152–92.

———. "Interpretations of Ancient Indian History." *History and Theory* 7, no. 3 (1968): 318–35.

———. "Origin Myths and the Early Indian Historical Tradition." In his *Ancient Indian Social History: Some Interpretations,* 294–325. 2d ed. New Delhi: Orient Longman, 1984.

———. "Religion, Communalism, and the Interpretation of Indian History." Public lecture, Wesleyan University, 18 November 1992.

———. "Renunciation: The Making of a Counter-Culture?" In his *Ancient Indian Social History: Some Interpretations,* 63–104. 2d ed. New Delhi: Orient Longman, 1984.

———. "Society and Historical Consciousness: The *Itihasa-Purana* Tradition." In *Situating Indian History for Sarvepalli Gopal,* edited by S. Bhattacharya and R. Thapar, 353–83. Delhi: Oxford University Press, 1986.

———."'Thus It Was': The Early Indian Historical Tradition." Wesleyan University, Public Affairs Center Thursday Lecture Series, 19 November 1992.

Thiel-Horstmann, Monika. "Warrior Ascetics in Eighteenth-Century Rajasthan and the Religious Policy of Jai Singh II." Unpublished essay, no date.

Thorner, Daniel. "Peasantry." *International Encyclopedia of the Social Sciences,* edited by David Sills. New York: Macmillan, 1968.

Tod, James (Lt.-Colonel). *Annals and Antiquities of Rajas'than, the Central and Western Rajpoot States of India.* 2 vols. London: Smith, Elder and Co., 1829–32; reprint, London: Routledge and Kegan Paul, 1957–60.

Upadhyaya, K. N. *Guru Ravidas: Life and Teachings*. Dera Baba Jaimal Singh, Punjab: Radha Soami Satsang Beas, 1982.

van der Veer, Peter. *Gods on Earth: The Management of Religious Experience and Identity in a North Indian Pilgrimage Centre*. London: Athlone, 1988.

———. *Religious Nationalism: Hindus and Muslims in India*. Berkeley and Los Angeles: University of California Press, 1994.

———. Review of *The Lord as Guru: Hindi Sants in the Northern Indian Tradition* by Daniel Gold (New York: Oxford University Press, 1987). *The Journal of Asian Studies* 47, no. 3 (August 1988): 678–79.

———. "Taming the Ascetic: Devotionalism in a Hindu Monastic Order." *Man*, n.s., 22, no. 4 (December 1987): 680–95.

Vaudeville, Charlotte. *Kabir*. Volume 1. Oxford: Oxford University Press, 1974.

———. "*Sant mat:* Santism as the Universal Path to Sanctity." In Schomer and McLeod, eds., *The Sants: Studies in a Devotional Tradition of India*, 21–40.

Verma, K. K. *Changing Role of Caste Associations*. New Delhi: National Publishing House, 1979.

Vicziany, Marika. "The Deindustrialisation of India in the Nineteenth Century: A Methodological Critique of Amiya Kumar Bagchi." *Indian Economic and Social History Review* 16, no. 2 (1979): 105–43.

———. "Imperialism, Botany and Statistics in Early Nineteenth-Century India: The Surveys of Francis Buchanan (1762–1829)." *Modern Asian Studies* 20, no. 4 (October 1986): 625–60.

von Stietencron, Heinrich. "Hinduism: On the Proper Use of a Deceptive Term." In *Hinduism Reconsidered*, edited by Gunther D. Sontheimer and Hermann Kulke, 11–27. New Delhi: Manohar, 1989.

Wilson, Horace Hayman. *A Glossary of Judicial and Revenue Terms and of Useful Words Occuring in Official Documents Relating to the Administration of the Government of British India*. London: Wm. H. Allen, 1855; reprint, Delhi: Munshiram Manoharlal, 1968.

———. *Sketch of the Religious Sects of the Hindus*. Calcutta: Bishop's College Press, 1846; reprint, New Delhi: Cosmo, 1977. (First published in the 1828 and 1831 issues of *Asiatic Researches*.)

Wurgaft, Lewis. *The Imperial Imagination: Magic and Myth in Kipling's India*. Middletown: Wesleyan University Press, 1983.

Yadav, K. C. *India's Unequal Citizens: A Study of Other Backward Classes*. New Delhi: Manohar, 1994.

Yang, Anand A. *The Limited Raj: Agrarian Relations in Colonial India, Saran District, 1793–1920*. Berkeley and Los Angeles: University of California Press, 1989.

———. "Sacred Symbol and Sacred Space in Rural India: Community Mobilization in the Anti-Cow Killing Riot of 1893." *Comparative Studies in Society and History* 22, no. 4 (October 1980): 576–96.

Yule, Henry (Colonel), and A. C. Burnell. *Hobson-Jobson: A Glossary of Colloquial Anglo-Indian Words and Phrases, and of Kindred Terms,*

Etymological, Historical, Geographical and Discursive. London, 1903.
Zysk, Kenneth G. *Asceticism and Healing in Ancient India: Medicine in the Buddhist Monastery.* New York: Oxford University Press, 1991.

Unpublished Official Documents
(see footnotes in text for references to select portions)

National Archives of India, New Delhi.
    Government of India. Home Department, Public Proceedings.
    Government of India. Foreign Department, Secret Proceedings.
Bihar State Archives, Patna (Bihar).
    Government of Bengal. Judicial Department, Police Proceedings.
    Government of Bihar and Orissa. Political Department, Special Proceedings.
Arrah (Shahabad), Gaya, and Patna Collectorate Record Rooms (Bihar).
    Village Notes. 1909–14.

Manuscripts

ORIENTAL AND INDIA OFFICE COLLECTION,
BRITISH LIBRARY, LONDON

Buchanan-Hamilton Papers. Mss.Eur.D.562. The Gorakhpur Account is catalogued separately, as Mss.Eur.D.91–92. Statistical tables for Bihar are held under Mss.Eur.G.18–24.
Grierson Papers. Mss.Eur.E.223.
Luard Papers. Mss.Eur.E.139
Risley Papers. Mss.Eur.E.295.

Index

233